New Lenses on Intellectual Disabilities

This book gathers together recent international research in intellectual disability (ID), examining the diverse modes of existence that characterise living with intellectual disabilities in the 21st century.

Ranging from people with no speech and little mobility who need 24-hour care, to people who marry or hold down jobs, this book moves beyond the typical person with ID imagined by public policy: healthy, with mild ID and a supportive family, and living in a welcoming community. The book is divided into three sections. The first, 'A richer picture of people and relationships', expands our understanding of different people and lifestyles associated with ID. The second section, 'Where current policies fall short', finds that Supported Living provides just as 'mediocre' a form of care as group homes, and concludes that services for people with challenging behaviour are unrelated to need. The contributors' research identifies no effective employment support strategies, as well as technological and legal changes that prevent organisations from employing people with ID. With nearly a quarter of this population in poor health, the contributors reflect on whether 'social model' approaches should be allowed to trump medical considerations. The third section, 'New thinking about well-being', reveals that being old, poor, and living alone increases health risk, and that medication administration is significantly more complex for people with ID.

Moving beyond 20th century certainties surrounding intellectual disability, this book will be of interest to those studying contemporary issues facing those living with ID, as well as those studying public health policy more widely.

The chapters in this book were originally published in issues of the *Journal of Intellectual & Developmental Disability.*

Jennifer Clegg is Adjunct Professor at La Trobe University, Australia, and Honorary Associate Professor at the University of Nottingham, UK. She was an academic Consultant Clinical Psychologist in intellectual disability with Nottinghamshire Healthcare NHS Trust until 2015. She continues to edit, write, examine, and teach about non-behavioural approaches to complex needs; her publications include longitudinal research into the transition out of school, conceptual history, and the ethics of practice. She is currently examining the impact of neoliberalism on those living with intellectual disabilities. She is the co-Chair of the International Association for the Scientific Study of Intellectual and Developmental Disabilities' Special Interest Research Group on Ethics.

New Lenses on Intellectual Disabilities

Edited by
Jennifer Clegg

Routledge
Taylor & Francis Group
LONDON AND NEW YORK

First published 2020
by Routledge
2 Park Square, Milton Park, Abingdon, Oxon, OX14 4RN

and by Routledge
52 Vanderbilt Avenue, New York, NY 10017

Routledge is an imprint of the Taylor & Francis Group, an informa business

British Library Cataloguing in Publication Data
A catalogue record for this book is available from the British Library

ISBN 13: 978-0-367-33502-1

Typeset in Minion Pro
by RefineCatch Limited, Bungay, Suffolk

Publisher's Note
The publisher accepts responsibility for any inconsistencies that may have arisen during the conversion of this book from journal articles to book chapters, namely the inclusion of journal terminology.

Contents

Citation Information

The chapters in this book were originally published in the *Journal of Intellectual & Developmental Disability*. When citing this material, please use the original page numbering for each article, as follows:

Editorial
New lenses
Jennifer Clegg
Journal of Intellectual & Developmental Disability, volume 43, issue 3 (September 2018), p. 251

Chapter 1
Intellectual disability and attachment theory among adults: An early systematic review
Georgina Mullen
Journal of Intellectual & Developmental Disability, volume 43, issue 3 (September 2018), pp. 252–263

Chapter 2
Staff perspectives on paperwork in group homes for people with intellectual disability
Claire Quilliam, Christine Bigby and Jacinta Douglas
Journal of Intellectual & Developmental Disability, volume 43, issue 3 (September 2018), pp. 264–273

Chapter 3
Spirituality and social networks of people with intellectual and developmental disability
Precious N. Sango and Rachel Forrester-Jones
Journal of Intellectual & Developmental Disability, volume 43, issue 3 (September 2018), pp. 274–284

Chapter 4
Reasons for marriage of educated Bedouin women to Bedouin men with intellectual disability from the point of view of the women
Iris Manor-Binyamini
Journal of Intellectual & Developmental Disability, volume 43, issue 3 (September 2018), pp. 285–294

Chapter 5
Kathleen M. Brian and James W. Trent Jr. (eds), Phallacies: historical intersections of disability and masculinity
John Cromby
Journal of Intellectual & Developmental Disability, volume 43, issue 4 (December 2018), pp. 515–516

Chapter 6
Comparing costs and outcomes of supported living with group homes in Australia
Christine Bigby, Emma Bould and Julie Beadle-Brown
Journal of Intellectual & Developmental Disability, volume 43, issue 3 (September 2018), pp. 295–307

Chapter 7
Service receipt of adults with rare genetic syndromes who engage in challenging behaviour
N. Awan, C. Oliver, L. Wilde, K. Eden and J. Waite
Journal of Intellectual & Developmental Disability, volume 43, issue 3 (September 2018), pp. 308–316

Chapter 8

What constitutes effective support in obtaining and maintaining employment for individuals with intellectual disability? A scoping review
Cindy Cheng, Jodi Oakman, Christine Bigby, Ellie Fossey, Jillian Cavanagh, Hannah Meacham and Timothy Bartram
Journal of Intellectual & Developmental Disability, volume 43, issue 3 (September 2018), pp. 317–327

Chapter 9

Emerging trends affecting future employment opportunities for people with intellectual disability: The case of a large retail organisation
Katherine Moore, Paula McDonald and Jennifer Bartlett
Journal of Intellectual & Developmental Disability, volume 43, issue 3 (September 2018), pp. 328–338

Chapter 10

Factors that affect the perceived health of adults with intellectual disability: A Western Australian study
Errol Cocks, Allyson Thomson, Stian Thoresen, Richard Parsons and Lorna Rosenwax
Journal of Intellectual & Developmental Disability, volume 43, issue 3 (September 2018), pp. 339–350

Chapter 11

Complexity of medication regimens of people with intellectual and developmental disabilities
Steven R. Erickson, Drita Nicaj and Sasha Barron
Journal of Intellectual & Developmental Disability, volume 43, issue 3 (September 2018), pp. 351–361

Chapter 12

Does intellectual disability research consider the potential impact of geographic location?
Stuart Wark
Journal of Intellectual & Developmental Disability, volume 43, issue 3 (September 2018), pp. 362–369

Chapter 13

Dialogue between workers and family members is related to their attitudes towards self-determination of individuals with intellectual disability
Vicente Martínez-Tur, Yolanda Estreder, Carolina Moliner, Esther Gracia, Luminiţa Pătraş and Ana Zornoza
Journal of Intellectual & Developmental Disability, volume 43, issue 3 (September 2018), pp. 370–379

Notes on Contributors

N. Awan has been affiliated with the Cerebra Centre for Neurodevelopmental Disorders in the School of Psychology at the University of Birmingham, UK.

Sasha Barron is a Clinical Pharmacist at Detroit Medical Center Children's Hospital of Michigan, USA.

Jennifer Bartlett is an Associate Professor in the School of Advertising, Marketing and Public Relations at Queensland University of Technology, Australia.

Timothy Bartram is Professor of Management at RMIT University, Australia.

Julie Beadle-Brown is Professor of Disability at the Living with Disability Research Centre at La Trobe University, Australia, and Professor of Intellectual and Developmental Disabilities at the Tizard Centre at the University of Kent, UK.

Christine Bigby is a Professor and Director of the Living with Disability Research Centre in the School of Allied Health in the College of Science, Health and Engineering at La Trobe University, Australia.

Emma Bould is a Senior Research Fellow at the Living with Disability Research Centre at La Trobe University, Australia.

Jillian Cavanagh is a Senior Lecturer in Business at RMIT University, Australia.

Cindy Cheng is a Postdoctoral Research Fellow at the Living with Disability Research Centre in the School of Allied Health in the College of Science, Health and Engineering at La Trobe University, Australia.

Jennifer Clegg is Adjunct Professor at La Trobe University, Australia, and Honorary Associate Professor at the University of Nottingham, UK.

Errol Cocks is Professor Emeritus in the School of Occupational Therapy and Social Work at Curtin University, Australia.

John Cromby is Professor of Psychology at the University of Leicester, UK.

Jacinta Douglas is Professor of Acquired Disability Studies and Speech Pathology at the Living with Disability Research Centre, and the Summer Foundation Research Chair at La Trobe University, Australia.

K. Eden is a Doctoral Researcher at the Cerebra Centre for Neurodevelopmental Disorders in the School of Psychology at the University of Birmingham, UK.

Steven R. Erickson is Associate Professor of Social and Administrative Sciences and Clinical Pharmacy at the University of Michigan College of Pharmacy, USA.

Yolanda Estreder is a PDI Associate at the Research Institute on Human Resources Psychology, Organizational Development and Quality of Working Life (IDOCAL) at the University of Valencia, Spain.

Rachel Forrester-Jones is a Professor in the Department of Social and Policy Sciences at the University of Bath, UK, and Honorary Professor at the Tizard Centre at the University of Kent, UK.

Ellie Fossey is a Professor in the Department of Occupational Therapy in the School of Primary Health Care at Monash University, Australia.

Esther Gracia is an Associate Professor and member of the Research Institute on Human Resources Psychology, Organizational Development and Quality of Working Life (IDOCAL) at the University of Valencia, Spain.

Paula McDonald is a Professor in the School of Management at Queensland University of Technology, Australia.

Iris Manor-Binyamini is a Lecturer and Senior Faculty Member in the Department of Special Education at the University of Haifa, Israel.

Vicente Martínez-Tur is Professor of Organizational Psychology and member of the Research Institute on Human Resources Psychology, Organizational Development and Quality of Working Life (IDOCAL) at the University of Valencia, Spain.

Hannah Meacham is a Lecturer in the Department of Management at La Trobe University, Australia.

Carolina Moliner is Associate Professor of Work and Organizational Psychology and a member of the Research Institute on Human Resources Psychology, Organizational Development and Quality of Working Life (IDOCAL) at the University of Valencia, Spain.

Katherine Moore is a Lecturer in the School of Management at Queensland University of Technology, Australia.

Georgina Mullen is a Graduate Student in the School of Psychology at University College Dublin, Ireland.

Drita Nicaj is a Pharmacy Resident at St Joseph Mercy Oakland Hospital, USA.

Jodi Oakman is an Associate Professor and Head of the Centre for Ergonomics and Human Factors in the School of Psychology and Public Health in the College of Science, Health and Engineering at La Trobe University, Australia.

C. Oliver is Professor of Neurodevelopmental Disorders and Director of the Cerebra Centre for Neurodevelopmental Disorders in the School of Psychology at the University of Birmingham, UK.

Richard Parsons is a Senior Lecturer in Statistics in the School of Occupational Therapy and Social Work at Curtin University, Australia.

Luminiţa Pătraş is a Postdoctoral Research Fellow at the Research Institute on Human Resources Psychology, Organizational Development and Quality of Working Life (IDOCAL) at the University of Valencia, Spain.

Claire Quilliam is a Shepparton PhD Candidate with the Living with Disability Research Centre at La Trobe University, Australia.

Lorna Rosenwax is an Adjunct Professor in the School of Occupational Therapy and Social Work at Curtin University, Australia.

Precious N. Sango is a Lecturer in Applied Social Studies at the University of Bedfordshire, UK.

Allyson Thomson is a Research Associate in the School of Occupational Therapy and Social Work at Curtin University, Australia.

Stian Thoresen is a Senior Research Fellow in the School of Occupational Therapy and Social Work at Curtin University, Australia.

J. Waite is a Lecturer in Psychology in the School of Life and Health Sciences at Aston University, UK, and a Research Fellow at the Cerebra Centre for Neurodevelopmental Disorders in the School of Psychology at the University of Birmingham, UK.

Stuart Wark is the Year 2 Clinical Academic Co-ordinator in the School of Rural Medicine at the University of New England, Australia.

L. Wilde is a Research Fellow at the Cerebra Centre for Neurodevelopmental Disorders in the School of Psychology at the University of Birmingham, UK.

Ana Zornoza is Associate Professor of Work and Organizational Psychology and a member of the Research Institute on Human Resources Psychology, Organizational Development and Quality of Working Life (IDOCAL) at the University of Valencia, Spain.

Acknowledgements

Journals such as the *Journal of Intellectual & Developmental Disability* (*JIDD*) continue the incredible tradition of academics working for nothing simply to help researchers avoid error and write more clearly. When they are lucky, their reward is being present at the birth of something new. So thanks to the 89 international academics whose always thoughtful and often detailed reviews shaped our papers last year, and to the 15 Associate Editors whose wide-ranging expertise pushes its standards ever higher:

Christine Bigby – La Trobe University, Australia
Douglas Boer – University of Canberra, Australia
Roy Brown – University of Calgary, Canada
W. Ted Brown – University of Sydney, Australia
Paula Dhiman – University of Oxford, UK
Carl Dunst – Orelena Hawks Puckett Institute, USA
Phil Foreman – University of Newcastle, Australia
Edward Hall – University of Dundee, UK
Richard Hastings – University of Warwick, UK
Chris Hatton – Lancaster University, UK
Yona Lunsky – University of Toronto, Canada
Marcus Redley – University of Cambridge, UK
Carlo Schuengel – Vrije Universiteit Amsterdam, The Netherlands
Jeff Sigafoos – Victoria University of Wellington, New Zealand
Julian Trollor – UNSW Sydney, Australia

Thanks also to Wendy Southward, *JIDD*'s Assistant Editor, for the integrity and professionalism she brings to her many and various roles.

New lenses

1. A richer picture of people and relationships

Attachment is a growing field of endeavour, despite struggling for air in a policy environment dominated by individualism. Mullen summarises research and the development of measures. Rather than treating care staff as lacking free will and in need of "training," Quilliam et al. examine staff perspectives on paperwork. They reveal gaps and ways that it hinders them from supporting residents well, concluding that organisations should consult staff to design paperwork with goodness of fit to practice. Sango and Forrester-Jones explore religious and spiritual communities, which have maintained a presence in intellectual disability despite their lack of congruence with contemporary secular policies. People supported in faith-based residential services had significantly larger networks than those living in non-faith-based services: faith communities can be a conduit to companionship. Finally, Manor-Binyamini explores intra-cultural diversity: educated Bedouin women who marry men with intellectual disability.

2. Where current policies fall short

Bigby et al. compared supported living with group homes: despite claims about the greater potential of supported living, quality of life was "mediocre" for people residing in both. There were particular shortcomings in physical health, personal development, and interpersonal relationships. Awan et al. examined services for adults with rare genetic syndromes who engage in challenging behaviour. There was no association between the degree of challenging behaviour and service receipt. This echoes previous research, while highlighting the added sophistication demanded by complex conditions that require the integration of behavioural and physiological interventions. The remaining two papers question whether employment should remain the only answer to *what makes a meaningful adult life*? Cheng et al.'s scoping review found it impossible to identify effective support strategies, suggesting a focus on organisational interventions that achieve a better fit between employees and the organisation. Moore et al. did this by investigating a large retail organisation that had tailored jobs previously. Yet centralised recruitment processes, technological changes, and productivity and efficiency demands meant they had ceased to employ people with intellectual disability.

3. New thinking about wellbeing

Even though the social model appears to be in the ascendancy, the vast majority of people with intellectual disabilities experience physical or mental health problems, or both. Cocks et al.'s cross-sectional survey of adults with intellectual disability found 22% in poor health: being old, poor, and living alone increased the risk. Erickson et al. explain the implications of people with intellectual disability having significantly more complex medication regimens: not only more medications, but also more frequent and constrained administration (time of day, avoiding food or other drugs, through routes other than the mouth). Wark urged attention to location since researchers rarely specify place, despite reduced access to health services in rural settings. Finally, Martínez-Tur et al. analyse services that do not manage to overcome differences in perspective between service staff and parents. While 30% of organisations achieved high mutual communication between workers and family members, severe disability made differences about self-determination more likely.

4. Conclusions

These papers raise new topics for consideration, and highlight complexity and diversity. They should provoke new conceptualisations that move beyond twentieth-century dichotomies (social–medical, urban–rural), and neoliberal focus on employment, to develop twenty-first-century concepts that allow for multiplicity and diverse modes of existence, across people and the lifespan.

Jennifer Clegg

Intellectual disability and attachment theory among adults: An early systematic review

Georgina Mullen

ABSTRACT

Background: The aim of this systematic review was to identify and critically appraise empirical research regarding attachment theory among adults with an intellectual disability.

Method: A systematic search was carried out in Psycinfo and CINHAL databases. Only five studies met selection criteria.

Results: Three main findings were identified: (1) there is a scarcity of empirical research regarding attachment concepts among adults with ID, related to a lack of established measures among this population; (2) there is some evidence that insecure attachment among adults with ID is associated with adverse early life experiences and current mental health difficulties; and (3) there is conflicting evidence that attachment behaviours may present as challenging to supporters.

Conclusions: Further research seeking valid and reliable measures is needed with greater numbers of participants with diverse levels of ID.

Almost half (47%) of adults with an intellectual disability (ID) also experience mental health difficulties (Lehotkay, 2009; Lin et al., 2014). Roughly a quarter of the general population experience mental health difficulties (World Health Organisation [WHO], 2001). One potential interpretation of this disparity is that there are gaps in understanding the needs for well-being among those with ID. Arguments within the disability rights movement have suggested that the social marginalisation of individuals with disabilities along with reduced access to societal structures may contribute to reduced well-being (Oliver, 2013). The social model of disability offers a framework through which to understand disability as arising due to a mismatch between a societal structures and attitudes, and an individual's functioning. This framework has developed in response to the previous largely medical model of disability which aimed to use medical approaches to adjust factors within the individual in order to reduce disability (Martinez-Perez & Del Cura, 2016). In line with the social model of disability, researchers have emphasised the importance of creating inclusive research "with" participants rather than "on" participants (Walmsley & Johnson, 2003). In the area of ID this can present researchers with challenges due to differences in language and other cognitive functions between participant and researcher. Perhaps this is a contributing factor to the relatively smaller body of research regarding psychology and mental health among those with ID. It could be argued that researchers have focused on the development of cognitive functioning and neglected other aspects of psychology including intra- and inter-personality functioning among those with ID. One such area of psychological research that is considered a core theory in understanding human development in terms of intra-personal and interpersonal functioning, and mental health and ill health is attachment theory.

Attachment theory

Attachment theory developed from John Bowlby's (1969/1982) observations of children who were separated from their caregivers, and Mary Ainsworth's observations of infant–mother interactions (Ainsworth & Wittig, 1969). Bowlby (1969/1982) proposed that all humans are born with an innate psychobiological attachment system that motivates infants to seek proximity to or availability of a caregiver, in order to increase their likelihood of survival. Bowlby (1969/1982) suggested that individuals create internal working templates based on their experiences of being cared for, that then act as predictive models of future interactions, guiding present and future behaviour. From their observations, Ainsworth and Wittig (1969) suggested that infants used their mothers as a secure base which allowed them to explore their environment, but that this tendency varied along with quality of interaction. Ainsworth, Blehar, Waters, and Wall (1978) further explored these observations through the Strange Situation Procedure (SSP) during which infants were separated from their mother and their responses were coded and grouped to develop three suggested attachment classifications: secure, insecure-ambivalent and insecure-avoidant. Ainsworth et al. (1978) noted that children whose mothers were more sensitively responsive were more likely to be categorised as secure, suggesting that maternal or primary caregiver sensitivity is an important factor in developing secure attachment patterns. Later Main and Solomon (1990) suggested a third insecure classification of disorganised. A brief description of these categories is presented in Table 1. Classification on the SSP can be stable over time, or may change, with negative life events suggested to contribute to a change from secure to insecure classification (Waters, Merrick, Treboux, Crowell, & Albersheim, 2000). Despite its fundamental role in developing the empirical knowledge base regarding infant–caregiver attachment, there are limitations to the SSP. For example, Rutter (1995) has questioned whether a relatively brief observation could be a sufficient reflection of the entire attachment relationship, while Fraley and Spieker (2003) found statistical support for understanding attachment patterns as dimensional, rather than categorical. Ziv and Hotam (2015) make the argument that while the SSP may be a useful measure of one aspect of a wider phenomenon of attachment theory, it is unlikely that any single measurement protocol will comprehensively reflect a complex multifaceted psychological theory.

In 1985, George, Kaplan and Main developed the Adult Attachment Interview (AAI) based on the SSP classifications. The AAI is a semi-structured interview which asks respondents to describe their early attachment relationships. Transcripts are coded based on the way in which respondents speak about and remember early attachment relationships, with a particular emphasis on coherence of discourse. From this coding participants can be classified as secure, preoccupied (similar to the ambivalent classification on the SSP), avoidant, or unresolved, or disorganised. Hamilton (2000) found associations between classifications made for individuals on the SSP as children and classifications made when they completed the AAI as adults. Fonagy, Steele, and Steele (1991) found that parental classifications on the AAI also corresponded with their children's classifications on the SSP, suggesting transgenerational transmission of attachment patterns. George and West (1999) later developed the Adult Attachment Projective Picture System (AAP) which asked adults to tell a story in response to attachment related picture stimuli. Though the AAP was considered to measure a similar construct to the AAI (state of mind regarding early attachment memories), there have been mixed findings regarding agreement of classification on the AAP and AAI (Jones-Mason, Allen, Hamilton, & Weiss, 2015).

Alongside this stream of attachment research largely within the developmental psychology tradition, researchers largely within the social psychology tradition also explored adult attachment, but with a focus on romantic and other relatively current relationships. This stream of research generally used self-report measures (Hazan & Shaver, 1987). They began with asking people to consider which category of attachment pattern based on the SSP classifications (secure, avoidant, and ambivalent) was most similar to their romantic relationship history. Later Bartholomew and Horowitz (1991) proposed that attachment patterns could be understood through examining individuals' internal working representations of other and self, and through this model they added a fourth attachment classification of fearful avoidant. Fraley and Waller (1998) were concerned with whether attachment patterns best suited a categorical or a dimensional approach. They suggested that their data better fit a dimensional model rather than the four categories, and thus a number of researchers began conceptualising and measuring adult attachment as represented by two dimensions of avoidance and anxiety (Fraley, Hudson, Heffernan, & Segal, 2015; Fraley, Waller, & Brennan, 2000). The two dimensions of attachment are considered to map on to the four categories proposed by Bartholomew and Horowitz's

Table 1. Attachment styles as elicited by the strange situation (Ainsworth et al., 1978; Main & Solomon, 1990).

Attachment style	Infant's behaviours	Associated parenting style
Secure	Child plays freely when the parent is present, is upset when the parent leaves, but pleased when they return.	Attachment figure generally available to the child and meets emotional needs enough of the time.
Insecure-avoidant	Child avoids or ignores the caregiver when they return. Shows little emotion and exploration. Considered a mask for distress (later supported by heart rate studies [Sroufe & Waters, 1977]).	Attachment figure may disapprove of closeness and expressions of need or vulnerability.
Insecure-ambivalent	Child shows high levels of distress and is difficult to sooth on the caregiver's return, showing signs of resentment or helplessness.	Attachment figure is likely inconsistently responsive to child's attachment behaviours.
Disorganised or disorientated	Child shows unexpected behaviours such as freezing, rocking, and both approaching and avoiding the caregiver.	The attachment figure may act as a source of both comfort and considerable stress, for example in cases of caregiver abuse and neglect.

(1991), both of which are depicted in Figure 1. More recently Fraley et al. (2015) have continued to report support for a dimensional rather than categorical measurement of attachment patterns measured by self-report in adulthood, allowing for greater sensitivity towards individual differences. Roisman, Fraley, and Belsky (2007) and Fraley and Roisman (2014) also suggest that there is some evidence that (secure versus dismissing) attachment patterns as measured by the AAI are better understood dimensionally rather than categorically. Despite this, some have argued that continuing to use categorical classifications may be useful in clinical practice as it can facilitate rapid diagnosis and decision making (Ravitz, Maunder, Hunter, Sthankiya, & Lancee, 2010).

It has been recognised that the self-report and interview approaches to assessment likely do not measure the same constructs within attachment theory (Crowell & Treboux, 1995). While the AAI is considered to measure potentially unconscious states of mind regarding early attachment relationships, self-report questionnaires measure conscious self-appraisal of feeling, thought and behaviour in adult relationships (Crowell & Treboux, 1995; Roisman, Holland, et al., 2007).

Attachment insecurity is considered a major contributor to mental ill health (Mikulincer & Shaver, 2012). A number of correlational and longitudinal studies suggest a connection between insecurity and vulnerability to mental health problems, while there is some evidence that heightening attachment security reduces the intensity of mental ill health symptoms (Mikulincer & Shaver, 2012). Theory has proposed that secure early attachments can facilitate an infant to learn how to understand their own and others' minds, and to regulate emotion, cognition, and behaviour in a way that allows for resilience in the face of adverse experiences (Fonagy & Target, 1996). It has also been argued that social connectedness is a core aspect of human well-being, and thus disruption to important relationships and social connectedness likely contributes to ill health (Coan, 2008; House, Landis, & Umberson, 1988; Siegal, 2012).

Within the psychiatric tradition, the *Diagnostic and statistical manual* – Fifth Edition (American Psychiatric Association [APA], 2013) and the *International classification of diseases* – Tenth Edition (World Health Organisation [WHO], 1993 recognise two conditions of interpersonal relating in children which appear to reflect disorganised attachment patterns of either extreme indiscriminate affection and care-seeking from strangers, or extreme avoidance or unresponsiveness to care when offered. These are labelled reactive attachment disorder (RAD) and disinhibited attachment disorder (DAD) and are most likely to occur among infants in the context of significant abuse and/or neglect (APA, 2013; WHO, 1993). Similar to concerns regarding attachment patterns within social and developmental psychology traditions, researchers have question whether the current categorical criteria for RAD and DAD best reflect the experiences of infants who demonstrate highly disturbed attachment patterns (Borris & Zeanah, 1999).

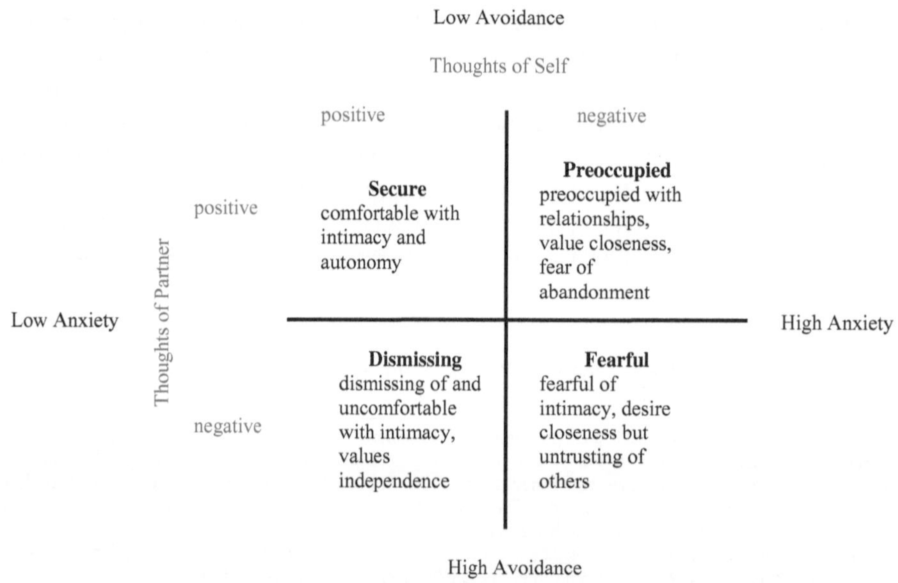

Figure 1. Adult attachment styles according to the two dimensions of avoidance and anxiety (Fraley & Waller, 1998), and the corresponding internal working models of self and others (Bartholomew & Horowitz, 1991).

Attachment theory and intellectual disability

There are a number of reasons why attachment theory may be particularly relevant to those with ID. Firstly developments within the social model of disability and social neuroscience have highlighted the importance of social inclusion and connectedness for those with ID, and attachment patterns can be an important factor in developing and maintaining relationships. Secondly, those with ID have been found to have higher levels of mental health difficulties than the general population (Lin et al., 2014; WHO, 2001). Given the relevance of attachment patterns and states of mind and emotion regulation in mental health among those without ID (Bakermans-Kranenburg & van IJzendoorn, 2009; Mikulincer & Shaver, 2012), understanding attachment concepts among those with ID may be important for clinical practice and in promotion of well-being. Schuengel, Clasien de Schipper, Sterkenburg, and Kef (2013) reviewed ID and attachment research and its relevance to mental health, challenging behaviour, and attachment-based assessment and intervention. There is some suggestion that children with ID are less likely to show secure attachment to caregivers and more likely to show disorganised or atypical attachment styles (Schuengel& Janssen, 2006). It is hypothesised that this may contribute to difficulties in regulating emotion which may put those with ID at greater risk of developing mental health difficulties (Schuengel & Janssen, 2006). Schuengel, de Schipper, Sterkenburg, and Kef (2012) point out that attachment relationships for children with ID may be of particular importance given the varied needs that can arise for them, yet they may be less likely to experience secure, organised attachment relationships. Attachment behaviours can be observed and measured by the Secure Base Safe Haven Observation list for children (SBSHO; de Schipper & Schuengel, 2010), and the Manchester Attachment Scale-Third Party Observational Scale for adults (MAST; Penketh, Hare, Flood, & Walker, 2014).

Review rationale and aim

There is emerging evidence that attachment theory applied to those with ID may be a useful in informing clinical practice and supporting well-being among those with ID. Schuengel et al.'s (2012) review identified that there is more research and application among children and suggest further work should be done with adults with ID. Thus the present systematic review aims to review empirical research regarding attachment theory among adults with ID.

Method

The methodology for this systematic review followed the Preferred Reporting Items for Systematic Reviews and Meta-Analyses (PRISMA; Moher, Liberati, Tetzlaff, & Altman, 2009) guidelines. The review involved five stages, (1) identifying the research question, (2) setting eligibility criteria and selecting relevant studies, (3) study selection, (4) charting the data, and (5) collating, summarising, and reporting results.

Search strategy and eligibility criteria

A systematic search was carried out in Psycinfo and CINHAL databases on 08/11/2016. Search terms included (attachment) AND ("intellectual disability" or "general learning disability" or "mental retardation"). See Figure 2 for a flow diagram of the study selection process.

The following eligibility criteria guided study selection, which was independently applied by two reviewers, with full agreement.

- English language, peer reviewed quantitative or qualitative empirical research
- Involving adults with a diagnosis of ID
- Using some attempt to systematically measure attachment

Data extraction and summary

A form was developed to extract study characteristics including, authors, publication year, study design, participant characteristics, measure of attachment, additional constructs measures, relevant finding(s), and limitations. This information was then presented in Table 2 and 3, with an accompanying narrative. Data were extracted by a second independent reviewer for 40% of the included articles. There were no discrepancies between the two reviewers regarding article screening or data extraction.

Results

Only five studies met the inclusion criteria. One included a series of case studies (Study [S] 5), the other four ranged from 43 to 60 participants. Reported mean ages were 23, 48.5, and 32.7. S3 did not report age. Between 19% and 54% ($M = 42.26\%$) of participants were female. Four studies stated or measured level of ID (S1, S2, S4, and S5). S1 stated level of ID, S2 used a psychometric measure of adaptive functioning, S4 used a psychometric

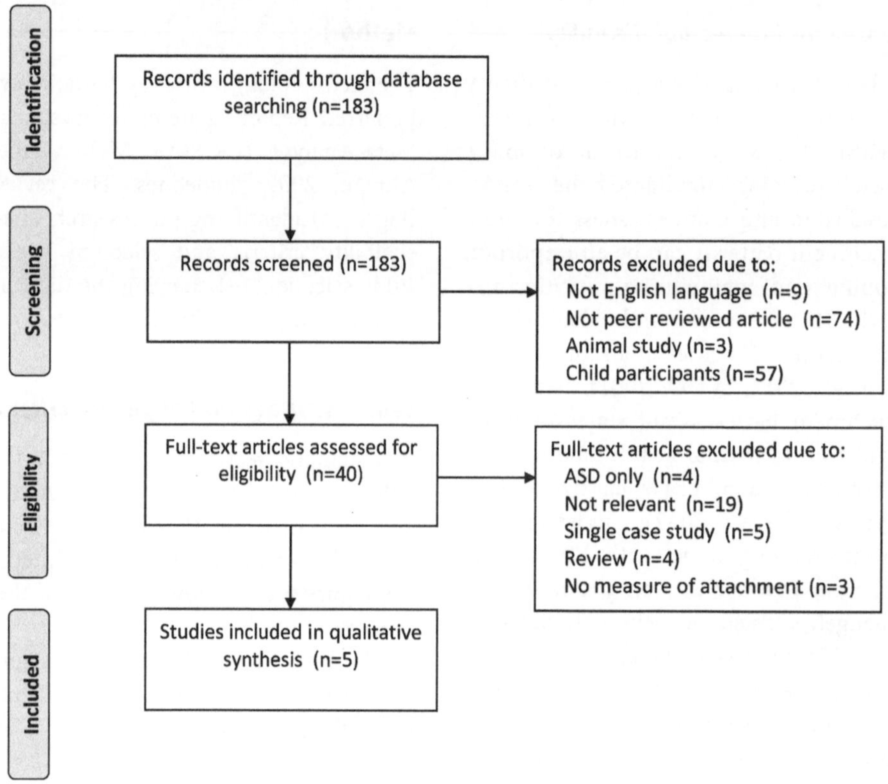

Figure 2. Flow diagram of study selection process.

measure of cognitive and adaptive functioning, and S5 used a psychometric measure of cognitive functioning. S3 did not specify level of ID; however, participants were required to be able to read relatively simple vignettes. Two studies included participants with severe and profound ID (S1, S2), while three included participants that appeared to be closer to the mild or moderate range (S3, S4, and S5). Three studies (S2, S4, and S5) combined participants' self-report with input from another respondent or the researcher. S1 and S3 used respondent reports of individual's behaviour. Most designs were cross-sectional using relatively small convenience samples. One study included a longitudinal design as it was assessing reliability of a psychometric measure (S4).

Attachment was measured in a variety of ways. S1 asked supporters to report on "attachment behaviours" with a focus on over-investment in relationships. S2 measured RAD symptoms using the Relationship Problems Questionnaire (RPQ). S3 asked participants to read and choose a description of attachment style (based on Hazan and Shaver [1987] descriptions) in adult friendships, that seemed most like them. S4 asked respondents to complete an observational measure developed from clinicians' descriptions of secure attachment among those with ID. S5 asked participants to tell a story based on eight ambiguous line drawings which refer to attachment themes of loss, separation, death, threat, solitude, and illness in order to identify attachment states of mind. All measures used had very limited validity and reliability. However, S4 and S5, respectively, demonstrated greatest efforts to seek reliability and validity for the MAST and the AAP for use among those with ID.

All studies included additional measures regarding behaviour, mental health or psychological functioning. S1, S3, and S4 also included some measure of "challenging behaviour." S2 included a measure of other impairments, health concerns and early adverse experiences. S3 included a measure of mental health difficulties. S4 included measures of carer–client relationship and styles of coping. S5 included additional diagnoses.

Overall findings from the five studies suggest that those who support people with ID do report a number of behaviours that may be related to insecure attachment styles (S1, S2, S3, and S4). In two studies over-investment in the caregiver was perceived as a challenging behaviour (S1 and S3). In S1 this was considered attachment behaviour; however, in S3 insecure attachment style was not associated with such challenging behaviour. In S2 greater RAD symptomology was associated with childhood adverse events, and in S3 insecure attachment was associated with mental health difficulties.

Table 2. Characteristics and limitations of included studies.

Study no	Author, Year	Participant characteristics: *N*	Age	Gender % Female	Study characteristics: Participants and respondents	Study design & analysis	Attachment measure	Additional constructs measured	Limitations
1	Clegg and Sheard (2002)	43 (50.6% participation rate)	*M* = 23 *R* = 20–26	53.7	Participants: school leavers with severe ID. Respondents: Primary caregiver and one placement staff member per participant	Retrospective investigation of a database of cross-sectional survey data provided by primary caregiver and placement staff member. Chi square analysis to demonstrate likelihood of presence or absence of problem behaviours or over-investment behaviours	Twenty-four questions regarding challenging or attachment behaviour over the past three months. Questions asked if the individual avoids problems, how they relate to others, how they affect others, how they engage with the physical environment, and how they use or react to their body. For example "Does this person overinvest in one or a few relationships which become a source of jealousy?"	Challenging behaviour measured by the same survey. Open comments regarding respondents' concerns.	Relatively small sample size. Measure of attachment behaviour very limited, focusing on over-investment behaviour. Not an established measure of attachment or challenging behaviour, with no validity or reliability reported. Diagnostic criteria for ID not reported. No reporting of procedure re-ethics and consent.
2	Minnis et al. (2010)	50 (92.6% participation rate)	*M* = 48.4 SD = 15.3	30	Participants: Adults living in two long stay ID hospitals. Level of ID measured by Vineland Adaptive Behaviour Scale (Sparrow, Balla, & Cicchetti, 1984) Mild ID (*n* = 2; 4%) Moderate ID (*n* = 6; 12%) Severe ID (*n* = 14; 28%) Profound ID (*n* = 28; 56%) Respondents: Participant and one carer interviewed by author, author completed written questionnaires.	Cross-sectional survey completed by interview. Two-tailed Student's *t*-test performed for RAD scores and demographic characteristics, disability, childhood adversity and number of years of institutionalised care. Backwards stepwise linear regression including variables that were significantly associated with higher scores on the RPQ, to determine independent associations with RPQ.	RAD measured by RPQ (Minnis et al., 2007). Authors report the RPQ has been validated in a sample of children of a similar developmental age to participants. Internal consistency (Cronbach's alpha 0.85) reported in a large general population sample.	Visual impairment (*n* = 6; 12%) Hearing impairment (*n* = 2; 4%) Urinary incontinence (*n* = 15; 30%) Bowel incontinence (*n* = 16; 32%) Mobility impairment (*n* = 17; 34%) Epilepsy (*n* = 20; 40%) Years of institutional living (*M* = 7; SD = 6) Childhood adversity (*n* = 25; 50%) -including childhood abuse, neglect, bullying, time away from family, severe poverty, maternal death	Relatively small sample size. Difficulties in measurement reliability and validity of childhood adversity. Reliability and validity of RPQ not reported for this sample or previously in a similar sample.
3	Larson, Alim, and Tsakanikos (2011)	60	NR	48.3	Participants: Adults with ID attending services in South East England. Level of ID was not measured, participants were required to be able to read and respond to the survey independently. Supporter respondents: 39 people who supported participants also completed a survey. All reported knowing the participant fairly well, 41% reported knowing the participant very well.	Two cross-sectional surveys, one completed by participants themselves, and one by a person who supports them. Pearson's chi squared test were used to calculate association between variables.	Participants were asked to select one of three descriptions of attachment styles modified from Hazan and Shaver's (1987) original text. Modifications were made to shorten the sentences, clarify meaning and to refer to friendships rather than romantic relationships. The same vignettes in the third person were included in supporter questionnaires.	Mental health difficulties Challenging behaviour	Relatively small sample size. The study removes the option for participants to reference their attachment style in romantic relationships. Reliability and validity of the measure of attachment and challenging behaviour is unknown. No measure of comprehension of the vignettes was used and thus there is greater risk of random responding. No reporting of procedure re-ethics and consent.
4	Penketh et al. (2014)	57	*M* = 32.7 *R* = 18–63	19.3	Participants: Adults with ID attending UK ID services. Respondents: NHS staff (*n* = 40) of varied disciplines working in community (30%) and forensic teams (70%).	Repeated measures design. Internal reliability of measure and correlations between MAST and other measures to assess validity.	The MAST was developed by Walker (2009). Reliability and validity is investigated in this study. The MAST requires the informant to rate observable attachment behaviour on a four point Likert scale. Example items include: "The individual actively solicits	The ERS – designed for the present study, a three item analogue measure of the perceived quality of the relationships and emotional closeness between staff and client. The ERS was used to assess whether MAST scores are independent of relationship	A relatively small convenience sample was used. Assessment of validity was limited as there is no existing valid and reliable measure of attachment among those with ID. Participants showed relatively low score on the LDCS, suggesting mild levels

(Continued)

Table 2. Continued.

		Participant characteristics			Study characteristics				
Study no	Author, Year	*N*	Age	Gender % Female	Participants and respondents	Study design & analysis	Attachment measure	Additional constructs measured	Limitations
							comforting when distressed," "The individual accepts carers" attention to others', "The individual acts to maintain social interaction." The score is obtained by summing all items, with negatively worded items being reverse scored.	quality. Level of ID and challenging behaviour was measured by the LDCS (Pendaries,1997). Use of the scale to assess level of ID has shown good reliability and validity and fair validity for challenging behaviours (Pendaries,1997). The EZPQ (Zigler, Bennett-Gates, Hodapp, & Henrich, 2002), a measure of was adapted for ID population to assess concurrent validity. The SRAAS (Smith & McCarthy, 1996) was also used to assess concurrent validity. The SRAAS asks participants about how they cope with negative emotions, including to tell someone, to deny feelings, or to express in an uncontrolled way (e.g., throw things, scream, and hurt self).	of ID. Thus, it is not clear if validity and reliability would be similar for those with moderate and severe levels of ID.
5	Gallichan and George (2014)	5	$M = 36.2$| $R = 21–53$	60	Participants: five service users attending outpatient clinical psychology in Plymouth, UK *Full Scale IQ* $M = 60$ $R = 53–72$ Verbal IQ $M = 62.8$ $R = 55–70$ *Performance IQ* $M = 60.8$ $R = 56–66$ *Aetiology of ID* Global developmental delay of unknown origin ($n = 4$) Head injury aged 4 years ($n = 1$)	Five cases using the AAP were presented and discussed regarding feasibility, validity, and reliability of measurement. Analysis by trained judges consists of coding transcripts of participants' stories for attachment state of mind and attachment trauma markers.	The AAP is a 20–30 minute task in which individuals are asked to describe a story in response to eight ambiguous line drawings which include scenes relevant to solitude, separation, death, illness and threat. It has been shown to be a valid and reliable measure of attachment states of mind among adults without ID (George & West,2001). The authors suggest it may be appropriate for those with ID given the relatively low demand on memory, language, and meta-cognition, and that it uses pictures as a stimuli which is often used in communication with individuals with ID.	*Additional diagnoses* Dysthymia or depression ($n = 1$) Complex PTSD or BPD ($n = 1$) None ($n = 2$) ASD ($n = 1$)	A series of case studies limits generalisability. Though face validity was explored no other psychometric assessments were used to explore convergent validity, for example, ways of coping with distress. Inter-rater reliability was explored, but test re-test was not.

Notes: AAP: Adult Attachment Projective Picture System; ASD: autism spectrum disorder; BPD: borderline personality disorder; ERS: Emotional Rating Scale; EZPQ: Edward Zigler-Yale Personality Questionnaire; ID: intellectual disability; LDCS: Learning Disability Casemix Scale; MAST: Manchester Attachment Scale-Third Party Observational Measure; PTSD: post-traumatic stress disorder; RAD: reactive attachment disorder; SRAAS: self-report assessment of attachment security

Table 3. Overview of key findings of included studies.

Study no.	Authors; Year	Key Findings
1	Clegg and Sheard (2002)	• Placement staff rated 16 students (34%), and carers rated seven students (15%), as over-investing in relationships. • No effect for gender, communication skill or presence or absence of sibling was identified on over-investing behaviour. • Those not living in the family home were more likely to be reported by carers to engage in over-investment behaviours. • Students who did not over-invest were significantly less likely to show other challenging behaviours. • The data lends minimal support to the contention that some challenging behaviour may be related to insecure attachment styles and highlights the level of variation seen when asking respondents to comment on others' behaviours. • Authors report that open comments also described attachment issues and provide three quotes to illustrate.
2	Minnis et al. (2010)	• Some adults with ID do display reactive attachment disorder (RAD) symptoms and these were not associated with ability level. • RAD symptoms (RPQ scores) were significantly lower in older participants and higher in adults who had experienced childhood adversity.
3	Larson et al. (2011)	• Over half of participants (58.9%) self-reported a secure attachment style, 16.1% reported insecure-anxious style, and 25% reported insecure-avoidant, similar to patterns among non-ID populations. • Of the total sample, 55% were accompanied by a supporter response. Those who submitted a supporter report were more likely to endorse an insecure attachment style. Of this group, participants self-reported as secure (45.7%), insecure-anxious (31.4%), and insecure-avoidant (22.9%). Supporter's reports did not differ significantly from self-reports. • A trend towards more mental health problems in participants with insecure attachment was reported. Specifically, those with avoidant insecure attachment were more likely than expected to experience depression. The relationship between anxiety and attachment was not significant. • Sixty-four percent of supporters reported challenging behaviour. The most common reported challenging behaviour was "becoming overly fond of support staff, for example, following around, crying when staff leave (28.2%). • Refusing medication was more likely endorsed for those with insecure attachment styles. • No association was observed for other challenging behaviour and attachment style.
4	Penketh et al. (2014)	• The MAST shows adequate reliability (Cronbach's alpha = 0.75) and test re-test reliability over 14–29 days (M = 18 days). • Concurrent validity is suggested as MAST scores were significantly associated with EZQP subscale scores, "Positive-reaction tendency," "Negative-reaction tendency," and "Obedience." A significant positive association was observed between the MAST and the SRAAS. • Greater security scores on the MAST was associated with lower levels of wariness of others, reluctance to interact with strangers, less need for approval from others, and less likely to rely on others for guidance.
5	Gallichan and George (2014)	• Authors were able to administer and code the AAP with participants with ID. • Three changes were made to standard administration of the AAP, all approved by the original AAP author: o certain instructions simplified o increased practice stimuli from one to three neutral pictures, to teach the task o a small amount of positive feedback was provided after the neutral practice pictures, for example, "that's a good story" • Authors agreed on classifications for three blind cases and reached consensus on a fourth. • Analyses demonstrated strong face validity when considering participants' life histories, presenting problem, content and style of information presented during clinical interview, and case notes. The information gathered from the AAP informed formulation and intervention and authors suggest such information would not have been readily available in regular clinical interview, particularly given participants' presenting concerns and verbal ability.

Notes: AAP: Adult Attachment Projective Picture System; EZPQ: Edward Zigler-Yale Personality Questionnaire; ID: intellectual disability; MAST: Manchester Attachment Scale-Third Party Observational Measure; RAD: reactive attachment disorder; RPQ: Relationship Problems Questionnaire; SRAAS: self-report assessment of attachment security

In S4 greater observed secure attachment behaviours on the MAST were associated with less wariness of others, less need for guidance from others, and less need for approval from others, adding to validity of the MAST. In S5 analyses demonstrated face validity when considering participants' life histories, presenting problem, content and style of information presented during clinical interview. Attachment information gathered in S5 was used by the author to inform assessment and intervention.

Discussion

The present systematic review aimed to report on empirical research measuring attachment concepts among adults with ID. Three main findings were identified, and their relevance to theory, practice and research is discussed here. Firstly, there is a scarcity of empirical research regarding attachment concepts among adults with ID. Only five studies met the relatively lax inclusion criteria. This is likely related to the lack of an established measure of attachment among adults with ID. However, the five studies reviewed demonstrate that some measure of attachment is possible and likely relevant to clinical practice and promoting well-being among this group. Two recent studies published some evidence of validity and reliability to support the use of specific attachment measures among this population (the MAST and the AAP) which will likely facilitate future research. The second main finding is that there is early evidence to suggest that insecure, disorganised attachment and RAD symptoms among adults with ID is associated with adverse early life experiences and current mental health difficulties. The third main finding is that there is some conflicting evidence that certain attachment behaviours may present as challenging to staff, particularly "over-investment" in relationships with carers.

Much research has gone into the development of valid and reliable measures of attachment among adults without ID, with the result being self-report measures of attachment patterns in adult relationships, and interview or projective measures that are analysed by trained researchers to identify attachment state of mind. Thus, there are two forms of measurement related to somewhat distinct concepts both of which can be considered "attachment measures" (Roisman, Holland, Fortuna, & Fraley, 2007b; Shaver, Belsky, & Brennan, 2000). This variation in measurement has likely developed because attachment theory is multidimensional, and can be understood as a general regulatory theory relevant to many aspects of human functioning including behaviour, mental representations, memory, cognition, and emotional and physiological activation (Bowlby, 1969/1982; Schore, 2000). The aspect of attachment being studied will differ depending on who you ask (the individual or someone who knows them) and depending on how you ask (e.g., conscious self-report [Zayas, Mischel, Shoda, & Abber, 2011], accessing memory and cognitive styles through activating attachment memories [George, Kaplan, & Main, 1985], or monitoring physiological responses to attachment memories and/or distress [Farina, Speranza, Imperatori, Quintiliani, & Marca, 2015; Gander & Buchheim, 2015]). This complexity combined the complexity of conducting research with a group whose communication and comprehension is different from the majority of researchers' contributes to measurement challenges among adults with ID.

Within the limited available research only studies using the MAST and the AAP sought to ascertain validity and reliability of the measure within their study (Gallichan & George, 2014; Penketh, Hare, Flood, & Walker, 2014). Further evidence of inter-rater reliability and face validity for the AAP among a larger sample of 20 participants with ID has also been found (D. J. Gallichan, personal communication, December 12, 2016). However, it is important to recognise that they likely measure different aspects of attachment. The MAST offers carers' subjective reports of participants' behaviours that are deemed relevant to secure or insecure attachment patterns. The AAP aims to offer an interpretation of participants' states of mind when telling a story in relation to attachment stimuli, and seeks to identify trauma related to attachment experiences, through observing content and process of story-telling. However, it is important to note that Jones-Mason et al. (2015) found some evidence to suggest that the AAP and the AAI may measure different constructs among adults without ID. The RPQ measurement of RAD had previously demonstrated validity and reliability in a general child population, but not within Minnis, Flemming, and Cooper's (2010) sample population. The concept of RAD which reflects significantly disturbed attachment behaviour located consistently within the individual, is considered to be different to a pattern or style of attachment, which occurs in the context of a relationship (Minnis, Marwick, Arthur, & McLaughlin, 2006). While both descriptions of RAD and attachment patterns may have implications for care-giving and receiving, emotional and behavioural regulation, and well-being, these implications may differ by degree or type and further research is needed to clarify similarities and differences between these concepts.

Further research should continue to offer information regarding validity and reliability of measurements of attachment concepts among those with ID, with greater numbers of participants and greater diversity in levels of ID. The reviewed studies generally included more participants with moderate and severe ID than would be representative in the general population, thus further research among those with mild ID may be warranted. Researchers may wish to consider exploring whether the AAI could be used as a valid and reliable measure of attachment among adults with mild ID. The available measures could be used together in future research to offer greater insight into measurement and theoretical concerns regarding attachment styles and states of mind among this group and weather they are best understood as categorical or dimensional. Research using objective physiological measures related to attachment may also be particularly relevant, as has been carried out among adults without ID (Farina et al., 2015; Gander & Buchheim, 2015). This may include electroencephalogram (EEG) or heart rate variability.

The second finding is that there is emerging evidence that insecure attachment and interpersonal trauma by a caregiver is associated with adverse early life experiences and current mental health difficulties among those with ID. This finding is also supported by recent research that has found that a group of mothers with mild intellectual disabilities were more likely to show lower sensitivity to their children when they themselves had experienced maltreatment, and that their low sensitivity was predictive of disorganised attachment patterns in their children (Granqvist, Forslund, Fransson, Springer, & Lindberg, 2014; Lindberg, Fransson, Forslund, Springer, & Granqvist, 2017). This suggestion is in line with findings from research among those without ID (Bakermans-Kranenburg & van IJzendoorn, 2009; Mikulincer & Shaver, 2012). Thus, emphasising the importance of continued research regarding adverse life experiences, the implication for attachment patterns, and the implications for understanding and treating mental health difficulties.

Further well-designed research with larger sample sizes using a valid and reliable measure is also needed to add clarity to the third main finding, that there is limited inconsistent evidence that certain attachment behaviours may present as challenging to care staff. It will be important to also consider carers' attachment in this research as attachment behaviour occurs in a relationship and context (Schuengel, Kef, Damen, & Worm, 2010). Understanding carer's own attachment patterns and states of mind can allow us to understand how care-receivers' behaviours may be perceived by caregivers. Understanding these reciprocal roles can shed light on potential rupture or difficulties that arise within the caring relationship. Thus, considering the relevance of attachment theory for both caregiver and receiver can help to inform service provision (McCluskey, 2005; Schuengel et al., 2010).

The primary articles were not quantified systematically but rather considered qualitatively which is a limitation of the review. Additionally, the very small number of studies included limit the reliability of the review findings considerably, but they highlight the need for future research. Though there have been a number of theoretical reviews regarding the relevance of attachment theory to assessment and intervention work among adults with ID, this review suggests that the need now is to focus on building a body of empirical research with appropriate measures to support or augment theory and practice.

Acknowledgements

Thank you to Claudia Scully for her assistance with inter-rater reliability.

Disclosure statement

No potential conflict of interest was reported by the author.

References

Ainsworth, M. D., Blehar, M., Waters, E., & Wall, S. (1978). *Patterns of attachment: A psychological study of the strange situation*. Hillsdale, NJ: Lawrence Erlbaum.

Ainsworth, M. D., & Wittig, B. A. (1969). Attachment and the exploratory behaviour of one year old in a strange situation. In B. M. Foss (Ed.), *Determinants of infant behaviour* (pp. 113–136). London: Methuen.

American Psychiatric Association (APA). (2013). *Diagnostic and statistical manual of mental disorders* (5th ed.). Washington, DC: Author.

Bakermans-Kranenburg, M. J., & van IJzendoorn, M. H. (2009). The first 10,000 adult attachment interviews: Distributions of adult attachment representations in clinical and non-clinical groups. *Attachment and Human Development*, *11*(3), 223–263.

Bartholomew, K., & Horowitz, L. M. (1991). Attachment styles among young adults: A test of a four-category model. *Journal of Personality and Social Psychology*, *61*, 226–244.

Borris, N. W., & Zeanah, C. H. (1999). Disturbances and disorders of attachment in infancy: An overview. *Infant Mental Health Journal*, *20*, 1–9.

Bowlby, J. (1969/1982). *Attachment and loss: Vol. 1. attachment* (2nd ed.). New York, NY: Basic Books. (Original work published 1969).

Clegg, J., & Sheard, C. (2002). Challenging behavior and insecure attachment. *Journal of Intellectual Disability Research*, *46*(6), 503–506.

Coan, J. A. (2008). Toward a neuroscience of attachment. In J. Cassidy & P. R. Shaver (Eds.), *Handbook of attachment: Theory, research, and clinical applications* (pp. 241–268). New York, NY: Guilford.

Crowell, J. A., & Treboux, D. (1995). A review of adult attachment measures: Implications for theory and research. *Social Development*, *4*, 294–327.

De Schipper, J. C., & & Schuengel, C. (2010). Attachment behaviour towards support staff in young people with intellectual disabilities: Associations with challenging behaviour. *Journal of Intellectual Disability Research*, *54*(27), 584–596.

Farina, B., Speranza, A. M., Imperatori, C., Quintiliani, M. I., & Marca, G. D. (2015). Change in heart rate variability after the adult attachment interview in dissociative patients. *Journal of Trauma and Dissociation*, *16*, 170–180.

Fonagy, P., Steele, M., & Steele, H. (1991). Maternal representations of attachment during pregnancy predict the organization of infant-mother attachment at one year of age. *Child Development*, *62*, 880–893.

Fonagy, P., & Target, M. (1996). Playing with reality: II. The development of psychic reality from a theoretical perspective. *International Journal of Psychoanalysis*, *77*, 459–479.

Fraley, C. R., Hudson, N. W., Heffernan, M. E., & Segal, N. (2015). Are adult attachment styles categorical or dimensional? A taxometric analysis of general and relationship-specific attachment orientations. *Journal of Personality and Scoial Psychology*, *109*(2), 354–368.

Fraley, R. C., & Roisman, G. I. (2014). Categories or dimensions? A taxometric analysis of the adult attachment interview. *Monographs of the Society for Research in Child Development*, *79*(3), 36–50.

Fraley, R. C., & Spieker, S. J. (2003). Are infant attachment patterns continuously or categorically distributed? A taxometric analysis of strange situation behavior. *Developmental Psychology*, *39*, 387–404.

Fraley, R. C., & Waller, N. G. (1998). Adult attachment patterns: A test of the typological model. In J. A. Simpson & W. S. Rholes (Eds.), *Attachment theory and close relationships* (pp. 77–114). New York, NY: Guilford Press.

Fraley, R. C., Waller, N. G., & Brennan, K. A. (2000). An item response theory analysis of self-report measures of adult attachment. *Journal of Personality and Social Psychology*, *78*, 350–365.

Gallichan, D. J., & George, C. (2014). Assessing attachment status in adults with intellectual disabilities: The potential of the adult attachment projective picture system. *Advances in Mental Health and Intellectual Disabilities*, *8*(2), 103–119.

Gander, M., & Buchheim, A. (2015). Attachment classification, psychophysiology and frontal EEG asymmetry across the lifespan: A review. *Frontiers in Human Neuroscience, 9* (79), 1–16.

George, C., Kaplan, N., & Main, M. (1985). *Adult attachment interview* (Unpublished manuscript). University of California, Berkeley.

George, C., & West, M. (1999). *The adult attachment projective picture system.* . New York, NY: Guilford Press.

George, C., & West, M. (2001). The development and preliminary validation of a new measure of adult attachment: The adult attachment projective. *Attachment & Human Development*, *3*(1), 30–61.

Granqvist, P., Forslund, T., Fransson, M., Springer, L., & Lindberg, L. (2014). Mothers with intellectual disability, their experiences of maltreatment, and their children's attachment representations: A small group matched comparison study. *Attachment and Human Development, 16*, 417–436.

Hamilton, C. E. (2000). Continuity and discontinuity of attachment from infancy through adolescence. *Child Development, 71*(3), 690–694.

Hazan, C., & Shaver, P. R. (1987). Romantic love conceptualized as an attachment process. *Journal of Personality and Social Psychology, 52*, 511–524.

House, J. S., Landis, K. R., & Umberson, D. (1988). Social relationships and health. *Science, 241*(4865), 540–545.

Jones-Mason, K., Allen, E., Hamilton, S., & Weiss, S. J. (2015). Comparative validity of the adult attachment interview and the adult attachment projective. *Attachment and Human Development, 17*(5), 429–447.

Larson, F., Alim, N., & Tsakanikos, E. (2011). Attachment style and mental health in adults with intellectual disability: Self-reports and reports by carers. *Advances in Mental Health and Intellectual Disabilities, 5*, 15–23.

Lehotkay, R. (2009). Intellectual disability and psychiatric disorder: More than a dual diagnosis. *Swedish Archive of Neurology and Psychiatry, 160*(3), 105–115.

Lin, E., Balogh, R., Isaacs, B., Ouellette Kuntz, H., Selick, A., Wilton, A. S., ... Lunsky, Y. (2014). Strengths and limitations of health and disability support administrative databases for population based health research in intellectual and developmental disabilities. *Journal of Policy and Practice in Intellectual Disabilities, 11*(4), 235–244.

Lindberg, L., Fransson, M., Forslund, T., Springer, L., & Granqvist, P. (2017). Maternal sensitivity in mothers with mild intellectual disabilities in related to experiences of maltreatment and predictive of child attachment: A matched-comparison study. *Journal of Applied Research in Intellectual Disabilities, 30*, 445–455.

Main, M., & Solomon, J. (1990). Procedures for identifying infants as disorganized/disoriented during the Ainsworth strange situation. In M. T. Greenberg, D. Cicchetti, & E. M. Cummings (Eds.), *Attachment in the preschool years: Theory, research, and intervention* (pp. 121–161). Chicago: University of Chicago Press.

Martinez-Perez, J., & Del Cura, M. (2016). Exploring disability in the past: On perspectives, methodologies and themes in disability history. *Asclepio; Archivo Iberoamericano De Historia De La Medicina Y Antropologia Medica, 68*(2), 145–152.

McCluskey, U. (2005). *To be met as a person: The dynamics of attachment in professional encounters.* London: Karnac.

Mikulincer, M., & Shaver, P. R. (2012). An attachment perspective on psychopathology. *World Psychiatry, 11*, 11–15.

Minnis, H., Flemming, G., & Cooper, S. A. (2010). Reactive attachment disorder symptoms in adults with intellectual disabilities. *Journal of Applied Research in Intellectual Disabilities, 23*, 398–403.

Minnis, H., Marwick, H., Arthur, J., & McLaughlin, A. (2006). Reactive attachment disorder – a theoretical model beyond attachment. *European Child and Adolescent Psychiatry, 15*, 336–342.

Minnis, H., Reekie, J., Young, D., O'Connor, T., Ronald, A., Gray, A., & Plomin, R. (2007). Genetic, environmental and gender influences on attachment disorder behaviours. *The British Journal of Psychiatry, 190*, 490–495.

Moher, D., Liberati, A., Tetzlaff, J., & Altman, D. G., The PRISMA Group. (2009). Preferred reporting items for systematic reviews and meta-analyses: The PRISMA statement. *PLoS Med, 6*, 7.

Oliver, M. (2013). The social model of disability: Thirty years on. *Disability and Society, 28*(7), 1024–1026.

Pendaries, C. (1997). Pilot study on the development of learning disability. *British Journal of Learning Disabilities, 25*(3), 122–126.

Penketh, V., Hare, D. J., Flood, A., & Walker, S. (2014). Attachment in adults with intellectual disabilities: Preliminary investigation of the psychometric properties of the Manchester attachment scale – third party observational measure. *Journal of Applied Research in Intellectual Disabilities, 27*, 458–470.

Ravitz, P., Maunder, R., Hunter, J., Sthankiya, B., & Lancee, W. (2010). Adult attachment measure: A 25 year review. *Journal of Psychosomatic Research, 69*, 419–432.

Roisman, G. I., Fraley, C., & Belsky, J. (2007). A taxometric study of the adult attachment interview. *Developmental Psychology, 43*(3), 675–686.

Roisman, G. I., Holland, A., Fortuna, K., & Fraley, C. R. (2007). The adult attachment interview and self-reports of attachment style: An empirical rapprochement. *Journal of Personality and Social Psychology, 92*(4), 678–697.

Rutter, M. (1995). Clinical implications of attachment concepts: Retrospect and prospect. *Journal of Child Psychology and Psychiatry, and Allied Disciplines, 36*(4), 549–571.

Schore, A. (2000). Attachment and the regulation of the right brain. *Attachment and Human Development, 2*(1), 23–47.

Schuengel, C., Clasien de Schipper, J., Sterkenburg, P. S., & Kef, S. (2013). Attachment, intellectual disabilities and mental health: Research, assessment and intervention. *Journal of Applied Research in Intellectual Disabilities, 26*, 34–46.

Schuengel, C., de Schipper, J. C., Sterkenburg, P. S., & Kef, S. (2012). Attachment, intellectual disability and mental health: Research, assessment and intervention. *Journal of Applied Research in Intellectual Disabilities, 26*(1), 34–46.

Schuengel, C., & Janssen, C. G. C. (2006). People with mental retardation and psychopathology: Stress, affect regulation and attachment. *A Review. International Review of Research in Mental Retardation, 32*, 229–260.

Schuengel, C., Kef, S., Damen, S., & Worm, M. (2010). 'People who need people': Attachment and professional caregiving. *Journal of Intellectual Disability Research*, *54* (1), 38–47.

Shaver, P. R., Belsky, J., & Brennan, K. A. (2000). The adult attachment interview and self-reports of romantic attachment: Associations across domains and methods. *Personal Relationships*, *7*, 25–43.

Siegal, D. J. (2012). *Pocket guide to interpersonal neurobiology: An integrative handbook of the mind*. London: W.W. Norton.

Smith, P., & McCarthy, G. (1996). The development of a semi-structured interview to investigate the attachment related experiences of adults with learning disabilities. *British Journal of Learning Disabilities*, *24*, 154–160.

Sparrow, S. S., Balla, D. A., & Cicchetti, D. V. (1984). *A revision of the Vineland social maturity scale by E.A. Doll*. Circle Pines, Minnesota: American Guidance Services.

Sroufe, L. A., & Waters, E. (1977). Attachment as an organizational construct. *Child Development*, *48*, 1184–1199.

Walker, S. (2009). *Attachment in Adults with Intellectual Disabilities: The Development and Preliminary Validation of a New Criterion Q Sort Scale* (Doctoral dissertation). University of Manchester, Manchester, UK.

Walmsley, J., & Johnson, K. (2003). *Inclusive research with people with learning disabilities: Past, present and future*. London: Jessica Kingsley.

Waters, E., Merrick, S., Treboux, D., Crowell, J., & Albersheim, L. (2000). Attachment security in infancy and adulthood: A twenty-year longitudinal study. *Child Development*, *71*(3), 684–689.

World Health Organisation (WHO). (1993). *The ICD-10 classification of mental and behavioural disorders. Diagnostic criteria for research*. Geneva: Author.

World Health Organisation (WHO). (2001). *The world health report: Mental health: New understanding, new hope*. Geneva: Author.

Zayas, V., Mischel, W., Shoda, Y., & Aber, J. (2011). Roots of adult attachment: Maternal caregiving at 18 months predicts adult peer and partner attachment. *Social Psychological and Personality Science*, *2*(3), 289–297.

Zigler, E., Bennett-Gates, D., Hodapp, R., & Henrich, C. (2002). Assessing personality traits in individuals with mental retardation. *American Journal on Mental Retardation*, *107*, 181–193.

Ziv, Y., & Hotam, Y. (2015). Theory and measure in the psychological field: The case of attachment theory and the strange procedure. *Theory and Psychology*, *25*(3), 274–291.

OPEN ACCESS

Staff perspectives on paperwork in group homes for people with intellectual disability

Claire Quilliam, Christine Bigby and Jacinta Douglas

ABSTRACT

Background: Paperwork can transform organisational aims into action in group homes, but it can also be problematic for staff. The aim of this study was to explore frontline staff perspectives on paperwork in group homes for people with intellectual disability.

Methods: Constructivist grounded theory methodology guided the study. Data were collected from 29 participants through semi-structured interviews, participant observations and journaling. Coding and sorting methods were used to analyse participants' perspectives.

Results: Staff have nuanced paperwork perspectives. They described and evaluated paperwork in terms of its value and fit with resident-focused practice. They identified gaps in paperwork and reimagined its design and use.

Conclusions: Frontline staffs' reflection suggests some paperwork hinders them from supporting residents well. This suggests organisations could consult better with staff to design paperwork that has a goodness of fit to their practice. Further research could explore how staff manage the limiting characteristics of paperwork.

Paperwork is a large part of daily service provision in group homes for people with intellectual disability because it is a technology that can transform organisational intentions including policy into daily service action (Levinson, 2010; Mansell & Beadle-Brown, 2012). We refer to pieces of paperwork as *paper tools* and to the process of using these tools as *paperwork*. Paper tools include written tools such as paper-based medication forms or electronic tools like emails, as well as the systems that help organise paperwork, for example, the resident folders and electronic information systems. Over recent years, the number of paper tools used in group homes appears to have increased markedly as shown by an 80% increase from 1988 to 2009 (Quilliam, Bigby, & Douglas, 2015). This increase in paperwork possibly reflects its growing use for achieving organisational aims beyond transforming policy intentions into practice, for example, to aid employee surveillance (Lyon, 2001) and meet the increasing contemporary focus of minimising risk (Beck, 2001).

The small amount of literature on group home paperwork emphasises a number of problems with frontline staffs' paperwork, particularly practices that are unexpected by the organisation or that negatively impact residents' lives (see Clement & Bigby, 2010; Hamilton, 2014; Nunkoosing & Haydon-Laurelut, 2011; Poppes, Van der Putten, & Vlaskamp, 2014). The potential for incongruence between organisational expectations and the way staff actually use paperwork raises questions about the conventional practice of using group home paperwork to evidence quality of support (McEwan, Bigby, & Douglas, 2014). Given the possible increase in paper tools and emerging problems around their use, there is a need to better understand how staff think about and use paperwork as a service tool in group homes for people with intellectual disability.

The theoretical lens researchers use to explore the way staff use paperwork influences how they perceive these frontline practices and therefore their findings and recommendations. Group home and disability services researchers (e.g., Poppes et al., 2014) typically frame paperwork use that deviates from expected practices as problematic. However, Garfinkel (1967) adopted a functional theoretical lens for his research on paperwork in psychiatric services where he found staffs' use of paperwork previously labelled as problematic or acts of resistance to organisational power were actually incidences of staff demonstrating agency by adapting paperwork to enable them to work more effectively. Accordingly he suggested researchers avoid labelling paperwork practices as problematic without first understanding how they meet the requirements of the stakeholders using them. Building on Garfinkel's suggestion, bureaucracy theorist Lipsky (1980) proposed frontline human services staff consider some paperwork as more important for meeting organisational goals than benefiting service users. Adopting this lens to group home paperwork research changes the focus of enquiry from exploring why staff engage in poor paperwork practices to one that seeks to understand how staff experience or perceive paperwork. Exploring this line of enquiry must be done from the perspective of frontline staff because paperwork is integral to their practice – they refer to it, create it, and share it with other stakeholders (Levinson, 2010).

An understanding of frontline staffs' perspective of paperwork could help disability service organisations adapt paper tools to better fit workplace requirements and daily service practices. The development of more suitable service tools could help staff better transform organisational values and policy approaches into daily practice (Bigby, Knox, Beadle-Brown, & Clement, 2015). In a rare study that canvassed staffs' own perceptions of paperwork, Davis et al. (2015) found that staff considered asthma plans, devised by health professionals for people with intellectual disability living in group homes, did not fit well with their day-to-day practice. This study along with our earlier research (Quilliam, Bigby, & Douglas, 2017) suggests that staff can provide an expert's perspective around paperwork because their workplace experiences provide them with contextual knowledge. Thus, in this study, our aim was to explore frontline staffs' perspectives of paperwork in group homes for people with intellectual disability using the question – how do staff perceive paperwork?

Methods

Methodology and design

A constructivist epistemological approach and constructivist grounded theory methodology (CGT) suited the exploratory nature of the study, recognising that participants and researchers co-construct knowledge from their social positioning and previous experiences (Mills, Bonner, & Francis, 2006). CGT allows researchers to systematically collect and analyse data to guide initial exploration of social processes and identify alternative conceptual constructions, with the aim of constructing theory that explains processes within phenomena (Charmaz, 2014). This study used CGT methods to achieve the former and is part of a larger enquiry exploring the processes underpinning frontline staffs' experiences with paperwork. The study was guided by the criteria Charmaz suggested should be used to evaluate the quality of CGT studies: credibility, originality, resonance, and usefulness.

Participants

La Trobe University human ethics committee granted clearance to recruit participants and collect data. Three non-government disability service organisations in Victoria, Australia were invited through a convenience sampling method to participate in the study; two of these agreed to participate. Data were collected at three group homes – one rural and two metropolitan. We recruited 29 participants including 14 group home residents, all of whom had intellectual disability, 3 casual support workers, 10 part-time support workers, and 2 part-time supervisors. Consent from residents was sought, and next-of-kin permission was obtained for the nine resident participants who were unable to provide informed consent. Although resident participants were not asked to actively participate because the study aimed to explore how staff perceive paperwork, data collection was conducted in their homes and information regarding their activities were included in the field notes. All participant, service and organisation names were replaced with pseudonyms and participants are not listed by their group home to maintain anonymity.

Data collection

Data were generated via individual and group interviews, participant observations, and reflective journal. The first author conducted 17 semi-structured interviews in total – 14 initial individual interviews with 14 staff, 2 follow-up group interviews with 9 staff, and 1 follow-up interview with 1 individual. The individual interviews ranged from 50 minutes to 1.5 hours and were conducted at a time and location that suited participants – either at the group home or another organisational building. The interviews were conducted outside of staffs' work hours to reduce impacts on resident support. In line with the study's exploratory nature, interview guides evolved throughout the collection period and included open-ended questions that aimed to generate discussion around staffs' experiences with, and perspectives on paperwork. Interview questions included: "Could you tell me about the paperwork here [at the group home?]," and "Generally speaking, how do you feel about paperwork here at [the service]?" With participant permission interviews were audio recorded and transcribed. Eleven participants reviewed and agreed that their respective transcript(s) reflected their paperwork perspectives, while others chose not to review their transcripts. The two group interviews, the first involving three participants and the second with six participants, provided an opportunity to share initial findings with participants, gain a sense of resonance and usefulness and further understand emerging theoretical concepts (Charmaz, 2014).

Fifteen staff members participated in 50 hours of unstructured participant observations over 18 sessions, ranging from 1 hour to 3.5 hours in length. Staff interactions with paperwork were captured within everyday service events between 7:00am and 9:00pm, during the week and weekend (see Bigby, Knox, Beadle-Brown, & Bould, 2014). The first author adopted a *minimally participating observer* stance during the sessions to mimic the informal group home nature (see Bryman, 2012), and completed in-depth field notes after each observation session.

Finally, the first author recorded information about the research context and reflections from the collection and analysis process via reflective journal, using three prompts: "General reflections," "What does the data say?" "What does this mean for future data collection/analysis?"

Analysis

Data were analysed via initial, focused and subcategory coding, constant comparison of data, memo writing, and theoretical sorting (Charmaz, 2014). Interview data were hand coded line-by-line and observation data incident-by-incident, by asking data questions such as: "What is this data a study of?" (Glaser, 1978, in Charmaz, 2014, p. 116). Larger chunks of data were coded and analysed through memo writing to arrive at a more conceptual understanding of the data. The codes were sorted into subcategories within an overarching conceptual category to generate meaning around staffs' paperwork perspectives. Table 1 illustrates the overarching conceptual category, subcategories, focused codes, initial codes, and experiential consequences resulting from the grounded theory analysis. Comparison of journal notes, interview, and observation data through frequent discussion between the three authors helped refine the codes and subcategories and ensure that the processes identified in the conceptual category were credible, for instance that strong links between the data and argument existed. The study's originality was established through various conference presentations where the findings were presented to, and challenged by, relevant stakeholders in the field (Charmaz, 2014).

Results

Group home paper tools

Paperwork was one of the many different kinds of tools available to staff; others included opportunities for verbal interaction such as informal discussion, handover and team meetings, supervisor support, and reflective opportunities during shifts. Although staff valued non-paper tools, this study focused on their perspectives about paper tools and paperwork. Staff from one group home collectively described 55 paper tools. These tools took different forms, for instance, paper-based forms and folders, and electronic forms and information systems. They were used in different ways – sometimes read and written on by staff, or only read or only written on. Some tools were used every shift or daily while others were used monthly or rarely. Some tools remained in the group home and were only processed for archiving and others moved beyond the group home site. These latter tools, for example, incident reports, typically had multiple authors and were read or processed by a variety of stakeholders including group home staff, support staff from other services, organisational managers, health practitioners, family members, and service auditors. Participants described the paperwork in their workplace and evaluated individual paper tools (see Table 1). Their perspectives are described in the following sections.

Describing paperwork

Staff talked about having a large volume of paperwork to complete: "There is a lot of paperwork" (Beth, Support worker). They described paper tools as fitting in two categories: *just for us* and *for management.* The just for us tools primarily helped frontline staff provide good support to residents during everyday activities and events. This category included informal tools like shopping lists, reminder notes in the form of sticky notes for oncoming staff, and shift allocation books. Renae, a support worker, described the communication book as a just for us paper tool: "There's the communication book; [it's] just good to have a look at … it's just for us sort of thing. It doesn't go any further than us." For management tools primarily met the needs of stakeholders beyond the group home context, particularly organisational managers. Sometimes staff also described these paper tools as *have to* paperwork, highlighting their lack of choice over the use of them. These tools were typically formal in nature and included monthly reports, policy, and audit documents. Carol, a supervisor and Tess, a support worker, described the monthly report as a have to tool for "higher uppers":

> Carol: With the monthly report … I have to give [it] to my service manager so she's got an overview of what's going on in the house and with the residents –
>
> Tess: [It's] more for higher uppers [managers]. … It's just administration *have-to* work.

Table 1 . Analysis of frontline staffs' process for describing and evaluating paper tools in group homes for people with intellectual disability (Charmaz, 2014).

Conceptual category	Subcategories	Focused codes	Initial codes	Experiential consequences
Being critically reflective	Describing paperwork	Just for us	Finding time for quick paper-based paperwork	Finding tool gaps and reimagining paperwork
		For management	Doing "have to" paperwork	
	Evaluating paper tools	Finding value in paper tools	Communicating Being official	
		Finding limitations in paper tools	Paper tools that captured information irrelevant to daily practice Paper tools that made staff feel uncomfortable Paper tools that took staff too long to complete	
		Identifying goodness of fit	Finding fit tools Finding unfit tools	

The just for us and for management categories were not discrete. Staff often described paper tools as simultaneously meeting the needs of both management and frontline staff. For example, the following excerpts illustrate how Di, a support worker, initially identified the food stickers as a for management tool because staff used these to meet auditing procedural requirements, but they also offered a more resident-focused purpose as a tool that prevented staff from serving expired food to residents:

> Yeah we have to [do the food stickers], because we get audited ... We have to make sure we do it ... It's probably a good idea [to use the food stickers] because sometimes you might have stuff [food] in there [the fridge] that you don't know how long it's been there for. So at least if you have a date on it, you know that it is [okay] ... It's good to know it hasn't been there for five years and we're giving it to the guys to eat.

Staff described the extent of paperwork and broke it down into different categories that demonstrated how it related to day-to-day practice on the frontline. However, they spent more time evaluating individual paper tools used in their day-to-day work.

Evaluating paper tools

Staff drew on their context knowledge to critically reflect on how each paper tool and the tasks it entailed helped or restricted them from completing daily work. They found valuable and limiting characteristics, identified goodness of fit, and as a result, found gaps and reimagined paper tools. Overall, staff held nuanced paperwork perspectives; they found paper tools helpful in some instances and problematic in other instances. Alisha, a support worker, demonstrated this nuanced perspective: "[In] one sense it [the paperwork] is okay because ... paperwork is for giving information ... So it's good to have paperwork. But for us ... when you [staff] are really busy, sometimes it can be too much."

Finding value in paper tools

Staff valued paper tools that helped them complete work they considered important in providing good resident support. They highlighted two characteristics of particular value – those that helped staff with *communicating* and *being official.*

Communicating. Staff communicated via paperwork because they often lacked opportunities to communicate verbally: "So we just write [in the note pad] because you ... don't see the afternoon [staff]" (Sue, Support worker). Some paper tools allowed them to share and receive information with their counterparts and other stakeholders, to capture information as a reminder for a later time, or to flag the whereabouts of important information in other paper tools. These characteristics helped staff to improve their practice by being consistent and working together. Renae explained how certain paper tools allowed them to share information with staff working other times and days, and Greer explained how receiving information through paperwork informed their practice:

> There's also a comments book where you can write comments ... Like a direct message to someone saying "You need to do this on this shift" ... It might be for the next person on or it might be for someone like two days down the track, so that's communicated. (Renae, Support worker)

> By reading notes of what other staff have made then we can help different residents in certain ways, we can change ways of doing things or bring other ideas in to help them. (Greer, Support worker)

Staff also valued paper tools because they facilitated informal communication between them in a similar way that family members living together might communicate. They often threw away informal tools like reminder notes once the message had been communicated with another staff member, as Sue, a support worker, explained: "We just write little notes there [on the note pad], 'Can you get such and such out for tea' ... It's just a bit of communication. … We scribble [them] up and chuck [them] in the bin when we're done."

Being official. Staff valued paper tools with being official characteristics because these allowed them to evidence their practice, highlight foreseeable risks to staff and residents, and to ensure their legal protection. Overall, tools with these characteristics allowed staff to officially document their good work and demonstrate that their practices were in line with organisational procedures. They preferred to evidence practice through paperwork because it brought a formality to communication that verbal tools could not offer: "When you put something in print, it makes it more official" (Tess, Support worker). Support workers Julie, Magentha and Beth illustrated how staff valued paperwork that enabled staff to formally document service events:

> During a team meeting, Julie and Magentha talk about the upcoming local community shows and rate the different shows according to how friendly the shows are for families to attend. All staff agree that the residents should go to one particular show if this is feasible. Beth, who has been taking notes during the meeting, asks the team if she should record this decision in the meeting notes. The team decides on their recommendation to attend the chosen show. Beth scribbles the team's final decision into the meeting notebook. (Field notes)

Staff valued paper tools that evidenced potential risks to their own health, their counterparts', or the residents' health. They believed that by using certain tools to document risks, they could influence the organisation's actions surrounding the risk. Georgia, a support worker, explained how completing incident reports and evidencing ongoing risks could sway the organisation's funding allocation:

> It is actually about giving people who fund [resident support] the information; the justification for the funding. That's in the [incident report] paperwork. If you say [to the managers], "We need extra help because she's becoming completely unmanageable", then the people who are giving you the money are saying, "But there's no evidence of that" … I see paperwork, in that sense, really as very important.

Staff found particular value in *covering yourself*, that is, using the official nature of paperwork to legally protect themselves and prepare for situations where other stakeholders, such as service managers, might use paperwork to scrutinise staffs' practice: "If something does come up you can go back and look at the paperwork … It helps to cover you as a worker and you can sort of say what has happened from your perspective" (Renae, Support worker). Paper tools with the characteristics of being official enabled staff to officially document that they provided good resident support and followed procedures accordingly, as Di, a support worker, noted: "So if anything unforeseen happened, we've got to have that paper trail for them [managers] to go check back on to make sure there's been no neglect. … To see there was nothing that we hadn't done." Overall, staff valued paper tools that enabled them to communicate and evidence practice. However, they also found limitations in paper tools.

Finding limitations of paper tools

Staff found paper tools limiting when they mismatched what they required in a paper tool. They highlighted three paper tool characteristics that prevented them from completing work they considered important in providing good resident support: paper tools that required staff to capture information irrelevant to daily practice, made staff feel uncomfortable, or took too long to complete.

Paper tools that captured information irrelevant to daily practice. Staff felt that some tools required them to capture irrelevant information, duplicate information across a number of different tools or limit their notes to predefined topics. This meant they often wrote the same information under different headings on the same paper tool, as Alisha explained, or they wrote similar information every day which captured unhelpful information, as Sue described:

> We just used to write "Oh yeah he's [the resident has] been good, blah, blah" – just [capture] the [important] things. Now we have specific things [topics to address]. We have a structured way to write … [But] you are … writing the same things again and again. (Alisha, Support worker)

> You have other days where nothing out of the ordinary's happened, same old routine, but you've still got to write up what they [the residents] did. … It can get monotonous, where you've got the same thing happening every single day, every single shift. (Sue, Support worker)

Paperwork that made staff feel uncomfortable. Some paper tools required staff to capture information in ways that they were not comfortable with or would not naturally adopt. Sue, a support worker, explained how using formal language in paper tools made staff feel incompetent, particularly because they were aware other stakeholders observed their paperwork: "You can't just say what's actually happened, like you've got to watch what you write." Staff felt pressured to describe service events using non-descriptive language rather than how they actually occurred, as Josh, a support worker, explained:

> Certain paperwork *is* fucked because you've got to be so careful in the way you word things. ... If I write, "[A resident] was *agitated*," it means he's being disruptive, horrendous, attention seeking, ruining everyone else's night. But you can't really put that. ... And that's really annoying because agitated could be a very personal, private thing ... It's not descriptive in any way, shape, or form.

This meant that some paper tools did not allow staff to share their own interpretations of events as they could with verbal tools, as June, a support worker, explained:

> There's so much more you can express when you're talking. You can't show emotions or anything in writing. So you can kind of go [while talking], "This happened, but I kinda think it's because of this". [But] you can't really write, "Watch out for that person with that person."

Paperwork that took staff too long to complete. During busy service periods, staff squeezed paperwork around resident support, as Alisha, a support worker, noted: "[There are] so many things you have to do at the same time." They did not like wasting time on paperwork and found significant limitations with paper tools that took longer to complete a task than using other non-paper tools such as a phone call or informal discussion might. They found some electronic tools particularly challenging for this reason. Georgia described how staff spent unnecessary time locating the electronic daily file notes and recording information in it, and Wendy explained how information technology complications slowed practice:

> See, there's a complete difference between picking this up [picks up a paper-based booklet] and turning the page. I have found what I want immediately [in the paper-based tool], whereas getting into [electronic tool is like] ... "Oh, so obviously nothing happened [for the resident] on the Thursday. Well, what about Wednesday?" So you have to go out of Thursday [paperwork] and find it [the other file] and go into Wednesday [paperwork]. It's just a longer process, less user friendly. (Georgia, Support worker)

> But because this computer's so slow it's like, the scanning [process] ... To me it's a time waster. It's quicker to write something than to get on the computer. (Wendy, Support worker)

Staff were particularly critical of tools that seemingly served no purpose in daily practice. They believed organisations used tools such as these to demonstrate service quality; however, they felt other tools, particularly observation, would better capture service quality:

> Tess They [organisational managers] want [paperwork]. It's probably a trust factor and they want proof; there's got to be proof ...
> Carol And it's got to be the written word ...
> Tess They can't come in and get the [residents'] parents and feel the feel of the house and see how wonderfully happy their people are ... No. Administration have to have paperwork. (Carol, Supervisor, and Tess, Support worker)

Identifying goodness of fit

Staff arrived at their own stance on the value of each paper tool by setting aside organisational logic and drawing on their knowledge to identify tools that were fit and unfit for facilitating good resident support.

Finding fit tools. When staff saw significant value in a paper tool they embraced it with confidence. The communication book was an example of a paper tool considered fit for facilitating good support. The communication book was an A4 paper-based tool that sat on the computer desk in the staff room. It was considered fit for use because it acted as a central tool which staff could quickly flick through to learn about recent events, gather instructions from other staff for the coming shift, or handwrite reminders for others, as Tess and Alisha illustrated:

> I think the communication book is a good tool ... The communication book directs staff to more information ... The more information you have sometimes, the more informed you are ... It's a benefit for the whole house really, I would say. (Tess, Support worker)

> The communication book is very important ... because [of] the information you get ... If you go through the communication book then [you read]: "[The client] has been to a doctor appointment", "There has been some changes in her" ... "Please refer [to] these notes on this date" ... Even like sometimes there will be a message for the staff, "Okay cook this food, not this one, this has been in the freezer, blah, blah, there are no ingredients for this one [meal], so you can use this one [another meal]". So it's good. (Alisha, Support worker)

Perhaps most importantly, the communication book allowed staff to remain focused on providing good resident support because they were able to use the tool easily within typical group home time pressures, as Alisha, a support worker, demonstrated:

> Alisha walks around the lounge room and dining area, opens the curtains, walks outside via the back door, and quickly returns to the lounge room and hangs a piece of linen on a clothes hanger in the corner of the room. She walks to the office. ... and clicks a few buttons on the computer, sits down at the desk and logs onto the computer. She turns her focus to the communication book which was sitting on the desk, quickly writes a few notes and stores it away along with the other books and folders standing vertically on the desk near the

> computer. ... She walks out the office and towards a resident's room, knocks on the door then opens it, and says "good morning" to the resident. (Field notes)

Finding unfit tools. When staff found significant limitations in a paper tool or paperwork, they typically rejected the tool. For example, staff in one group home found significant limitations with the sign in book – an A3 paper-based book that sat open on a small desk in the office. Managers expected staff to record the arrival and departure of residents, staff and visitors in the book. Staff felt the tool was unfit for facilitating good support because they were expected to capture what they considered irrelevant information and unnecessarily duplicate information listed in other tools. They considered the tool redundant because they supported the residents to leave the house, and shared information about residents' whereabouts through informal discussion. They believed the sign in book was unrelated to their primary task of providing good resident support:

> That [sign in book] has got to be the most useless [holder of] of information on the planet because it's [the information is] already in about five different areas already. So we know when the guys are out ... because it's all on daily reports; everyone says where [the residents] are ... Here [at this group home] you tend to either do a group thing or maybe one person [resident] or two people go out with a staff member. ... So they're [the residents are] always with a staff person, so you know where they are. You haven't got residents going for a walk around the block by themselves. (Tess, Support worker)

Finding tool gaps and reimagining paper tools

It made sense to staff that they should have access to paper tools that helped them do their job well, because well-fitting tools enabled them to support residents well: "We do good work and we need good tools ... We need to do the job properly; we need to be able to have access to things [tools]" (Olivia, Supervisor). Their ability to evaluate the paper tools and identify fit and unfit tools meant they often found gaps in the tools available for completing necessary tasks. For instance, Wendy, a support worker, found a gap in the tools available for organising housework:

> This doona [Wendy points at the quilt on the bed] ... I'm just thinking maybe we need to wash that, so I thought, "Well, Tuesday night I'll come on [shift], I'll strip it and do it". But I have no idea when that was washed last because each staff could be just leaving it to me [to do]. It could be months since that's been done, for all we know. We don't know. That's the kind of thing that is lacking through paperwork.

To address tool gaps, staff reimagined paper tools in ways that removed limitations and increased value. For instance, they suggested certain tools could be redesigned to capture more meaningful information and reduce the collection of duplicated or redundant information. Such changes would allow staff to share and receive pertinent information through paper tools rather than using multiple tools to record information. Sue, a support worker, reimagined the resident file notes to collect pertinent information about changes over time in residents' lives rather than repetitive and unhelpful information:

> The bottom line is, you need somewhere to write, "Nil issues" [in the file notes]. Like, to say that you have written [in the notes] but there's nothing to write [about]. ... If there was a terminology that you could put [in the paperwork] that says, "Same routine, nothing out of the ordinary" ... If you could just press on a button, that would be a lot easier. ... And then if something out of the ordinary did happen, then write it in [to the file notes], then you know that something's different and something's changed [with the resident].

Renae, a support worker, reimagined paper tools having a clear statement of purpose and instructions for use: "Even just have a bit more of an explanation of how to do things [paperwork] at the start [of the tool]? Because I think some of it is sort of left up to the person [staff member] to interpret." Overall, the approach of staff to paperwork could be seen to reflect an active evaluative process with multiple practice consequences.

Discussion

This study aimed to explore frontline staffs' perspectives of paperwork in group homes for people with intellectual disability. Staff held nuanced perspectives of paperwork because they evaluated individual paper tools rather than paperwork generally. This finding was unexpected but nevertheless indicates that frontline staff are more critical in their approach to paperwork than conventionally portrayed in the group home literature. Their critical approach reflects Davis et al.'s (2015) findings and suggests that future research in this area should focus on staffs' perspectives of individual paper tools rather than of paperwork more broadly.

Staff valued some paper tools for similar reasons demonstrated by early group home researchers (Quilliam et al., 2015). Like Mansell, Felce, Jenkins, de Kock, and Toogood (1987) suggestions that paper tools should aid inter-staff discussion, act as a central place for sharing and gaining important resident-related information, and direct resident-focused action, this study found that staff valued just for us paper tools as enabling them to focus on support and meet residents' needs. Our finding that staff valued being official paper tools reflected Felce's (1989) conceptualisation of paperwork as a way of evidencing staff practices. However, they were subtly different, as staff in this study valued these tools for their evidencing ability because they felt surveilled by service managers, as also demonstrated in Quilliam et al. (2017).

Staffs' just for us paperwork category highlights the value they found in paperwork. Ultimately, they considered tools that met their need for inter-staff communication as more relevant to their day-to-day practice. Staff understood the purposes of the paperwork they categorised as for management, such as documenting and surveying service provision with the aim of managing risk (Beck, 2001; Lyon, 2001), although its alignment with organisational needs meant these tools were sometimes irrelevant to their day-to-day practice. This reflects Lipsky's (1980) notion that frontline staff consider some paperwork more useful for managing organisationally focused aims than facilitating service user outcomes. Following Lipsky, staffs' critical perspectives of paper tools – particularly those they categorise as for management, may to some extent hinder organisations from achieving their specific purposes for paperwork, such as transforming policy aims into practice, surveillance, and managing risk. Further research could explore how staff actually use tools considered primarily for management, and in particular, if at times whether they are used in ways that appear consistent with procedure and perhaps offer staff a sense of legal protection, but have no positive impact on practice.

Staff only described a quarter of the paper tools possibly available to them as listed in a Victorian 2009 group home service manual (55 of 220, respectively, Quilliam et al., 2015). However, it is very possible they only mentioned tools demonstrating points of value or limitation, and did not mention rarely used tools, such as policy documents. It might also be possible, as Garfinkel (1967) explained, that they refrained from talking about some paper tools because they did not feel comfortable doing so. Staffs' critical stance that some paper tools restricted them from supporting residents, especially those unnecessarily complicating practice and wasting opportunities to engage with residents, suggests that organisations may benefit from rethinking the use of particular tools. For example, staff described electronic paper tools as particularly limiting, which is concerning given the general shift towards electronic tools in disability services (e.g., Department of Health and Human Services, 2016). Rather than simply introducing electronic paper tools, organisations could engage staff in discussions regarding plans to shift from paper-based to electronic tools to ensure they remain relevant in day-to-day practice. Staff also emphasised limitations with paperwork used to record the transformation of organisational policy and procedure into practice. This finding prompts the question: how can policies and procedures guide staffs' practices without relying on paper tools for confirmation? Laragy, Ramcharan, Fisher, McCraw, and Williams (2013) suggested that organisations should adopt a range of communication tools to engage frontline staff in discussions on service procedures, such as, interactive online platforms, ongoing training, informal supervision which allows opportunities for support worker-led enquiry, and pairing new support workers with counterparts who have developed understanding around service procedures. Our findings support Laragy et al.'s suggestions and we extend these to suggest that a tool such as practice leadership could act as a vehicle for frontline staff to critically and reflectively discuss procedural knowledge and its application to the service context (Beadle-Brown, Bigby, & Bould, 2015).

Finally, staff demonstrated their ability to draw on unique context knowledge accumulated through daily frontline experiences to evaluate paper tools. This finding supports those from a previous study that demonstrates frontline staff hold a unique practice wisdom about the context of their specific workplace and group home practice in general (Quilliam et al., 2017). The present study demonstrates that staff also hold practice wisdom around the specific tools available and those that are most suited for use. In this way group home frontline staff are a stakeholder group with their own particular tool requirements and evaluation methods. This finding reflects both Garfinkel's (1967) and Lipsky's (1980) ideas that frontline staff exercise agency in the way they approach paperwork. Agency is rarely discussed in the literature about frontline staff in group homes (e.g., Poppes et al., 2014). This lack of evidence of agency in staffs' practice is possibly because they are expected to implement rather than critically engage with procedure in practice (Arnott, 2017). Bandura (2006) explained four properties of human agency: intentionality, forethought, self-reactiveness, and self-reflectiveness. The former, intentionality, reflects staffs' ability to identify goodness of fit in paper tools because it refers to the process of forming of intentions and developing plans to achieve these. The latter, self-reflectiveness, echoes staffs' ongoing critical reflection on paper tools in day-to-day practice and how it helps achieve the overall goal of supporting people with intellectual disability to live good lives. Frie's (2011) description of agency as human action within the situated context helps to explain how staffs' nuanced perspectives of paper tools relate to their unique and situated practice insights. Further research is required to explore if and how staff transform their critical thinking about paperwork into their practice.

Limitations

This study is the first to explore frontline staffs' perspectives of paperwork in group homes for people with intellectual disability, although as with all research, there are limitations. The findings illustrate how staff conceptualise paperwork and evaluate paper tools, but offer only partial insight into staffs' experiences because it is part of a broader enquiry exploring paperwork in group homes. In line with Charmaz's suggestion that CGT offers a systemic approach to theorising as "an ongoing activity" (2014, p. 244), the findings arising from this study show the importance exploring staffs' paperwork experiences, and suggest avenues for further research with the aim of generating theory around staffs' experiences for guiding practices in disability service organisations. For instance, the findings suggest that staff perceive tools in ways that make sense to them, from their position in group homes. Further research could explore how staff use contextual knowledge and to what extent their critical perspectives about paperwork impact on their use of it in their everyday practice. The findings from this study, in conjunction with those demonstrating staffs' paperwork practices could, in time, reveal broader processes underpinning staffs' decisions around tool use in practice.

In line with the constructivist lens of the study, the findings are particular to the staff, group homes, and organisations that participated – all of which are located in one Australian state jurisdiction. Further research could explore whether group home staffs' evaluation of paper tools reflect the perspectives of frontline staff in other disability services, for instance day services, and also in other Australian states or countries.

Further research could also use different theoretical lenses to build knowledge around staffs' paperwork experiences. For example, building on these findings that staff felt compelled to complete paperwork in ways that positively benefited the organisation rather than their practice of supporting service users, future research could adopt a Foucauldian lens to explore paper tools as technologies of power that reinforce dominant service discourses. Research using this lens could also explore staffs' reproduction of paperwork as tools for supporting people with intellectual disability to lead full lives (Foucault, 1972). An action research design (see Brydon-Miller, Kral, Maguire, Noffke, & Sabhlok, 2011) could ground the research in the frontline perspective, whereby staff select and analyse paper tools with researchers.

The findings in this study were constructed from the experiences of frontline staff, who – due to their low hierarchical position in their workplace – could be described as a vulnerable group (see Liamputtong, 2007; Quilliam et al., 2017). It was difficult to recruit prospective participants because they feared losing their jobs. Many participants were careful with the information they provided to researchers and others asked researchers to refrain from publishing certain data, for fear of being identified. Initial concerns that the limitations to data collection and dissemination with this vulnerable group could impair the credibility of the study (Charmaz, 2014) were dismissed when the first author's experience as a group home support worker appeared to foster the development of rapport with participants, and thus the collection of novel insights into staffs' perspectives.

Conclusion

This study, which has enhanced understanding about how staff think about paperwork, demonstrates they have nuanced paperwork perspectives grounded in the service context and important insight into the goodness of fit of paper tools. Staffs' critical reflections suggest that some paperwork may actually prevent them from effectively supporting residents to live good lives, rather than transforming well-meaning organisational intentions into service action. These perspectives and insights qualify frontline staff to be listened to by other stakeholders. Organisations could use the paper tool characteristics identified in this study as a conversational starting point with staff to explore the development of paper tools that meet their requirements to facilitate good resident support, for instance, tools that enable communication between peers. Organisations could also consult staff about paper tools preventing them from supporting residents well. Future research could explore how frontline staff use paper tools in group homes or other disability services, and could focus on how they use paper tools they consider as having limiting characteristics.

Acknowledgements

We presented an earlier version of this work orally at the 2016 International Association for the Scientific Study of Intellectual and Developmental Disabilities World Congress. Thank you to the participating organisations and participants for their valuable contributions to the project.

Disclosure statement

No potential conflict of interest was reported by the authors.

ORCID

Claire Quilliam http://orcid.org/0000-0002-7344-0133
Christine Bigby http://orcid.org/0000-0001-7001-8976
Jacinta Douglas http://orcid.org/0000-0003-0940-6624

References

Arnott, G. (2017). *The disability support worker* (2nd ed.). South Melbourne: Cengage Learning Australia.

Bandura, A. (2006). Toward a psychology of human agency. *Perspectives on Psychological Science, 1*(2), 164–180. doi:10.1111/j.1745-6916.2006.00011.x

Beadle-Brown, J., Bigby, C., & Bould, E. (2015). Observing practice leadership in intellectual and developmental disability services. *Journal of Intellectual Disability Research, 59*(12), 1081–1093. doi:10.1111/jir.12208

Beck, U. (2001). Risk society: Towards a new modernity (M. Ritter, Trans.). In A. Giddens (Ed.), *Sociology: Introductory readings* (Rev. ed., pp. 398–401). Cambridge, UK: Polity Press.

Bigby, C., Knox, M., Beadle-Brown, J., & Bould, E. (2014). Identifying good group homes: Qualitative indicators using a quality of life framework. *Intellectual and Developmental Disabilities, 52*(2), 348–366. doi:10.1352/1934-9556-52.5.348

Bigby, C., Knox, M., Beadle-Brown, J., & Clement, T. (2015). "We just call them people": Positive regard as dimension of culture in group homes for people with severe intellectual disability. *Journal of Applied Research in Intellectual Disabilities, 28*(4), 283–295. doi:10.1111/jar.12128

Brydon-Miller, M., Kral, M., Maguire, P., Noffke, S., & Sabhlok, A. (2011). Jazz and the banyan tree: Roots and riffs on participatory action research. In N. K. Denzin & Y. S. Lincoln (Eds.), *The SAGE handbook of qualitative research* (4th ed., pp. 387–400). Thousand Oaks, CA: Sage.

Bryman, A. (2012). *Social research methods* (4th ed.). New York, NY: Oxford.

Charmaz, K. (2014). *Constructing grounded theory: A practical guide through qualitative analysis* (2nd ed.). London: Sage.

Clement, T., & Bigby, C. (2010). *Group homes for people with intellectual disabilities: Encouraging inclusion and participation.* Melbourne: Jessica Kingsley.

Davis, S. R., Durvasula, S., Merhi, D., Young, P. M., Traini, D., & Bosnic-Anticevich, S. Z. (2015). The role of direct support professionals in asthma management. *Journal of Intellectual & Developmental Disability, 40*(4), 342–353. doi:10.3109/13668250.2015.1041100

Department of Health and Human Services. (2016). *Senior Practitioner report 2015–2016.* Retrieved from https://dhhs.vic.gov.au/publications/senior-practitioner-report-2015-2016

Felce, D. (1989). *The Andover project: Staffed housing for adults with severe or profound mental handicaps: Summary report of a DHSS funded research project.* Kidderminster: BIMH.

Foucault, M. (1972). *The archaeology of knowledge and the discourse on language.* New York, NY: Pantheon Books.

Frie, R. (2011). Situated experience: Psychological agency, meaning, and morality in worldly contexts. *International Journal of Psychoanalytic Self Psychology, 6*(3), 340–351. doi:10.1080/15551024.2011.582935

Garfinkel, H. (1967). *Studies in ethnomethodology.* Los Angeles, CA: Prentice-Hall.

Hamilton, L. (2014, November). *Beyond the file note: Making group homes genuine homes.* Paper presented at the 49th Annual Australasian Society for Intellectual Disability conference, Fremantle, Western Australia.

Laragy, C., Ramcharan, P., Fisher, K., McCraw, K., & Williams, R. (2013). *Making it work: A workforce guide for disability service providers.* Retrieved from http://www.ndis.gov.au/document/522

Levinson, J. (2010). *Making life work: Freedom and disability in a community group home.* Minneapolis, MN: University of Minnesota Press.

Liamputtong, P. (2007). *Researching the vulnerable: A guide to sensitive research methods.* London: SAGE.

Lipsky, M. (1980). *Street-level bureaucracy: Dilemmas of the individual in public services.* New York, NY: Russel Sage Foundation.

Lyon, D. (2001). *Surveillance society: Monitoring everyday life.* Buckingham: Open University Press.

Mansell, J., & Beadle-Brown, J. (2012). *Active support: Enabling and empowering people with intellectual disabilities.* London: Jessica Kingsley.

Mansell, J., Felce, D., Jenkins, J., de Kock, U., & Toogood, S. (1987). *Developing staffed housing for people with mental handicaps.* Tunbridge Wells: Costello.

McEwan, J., Bigby, C., & Douglas, J. (2014). What are Victoria's disability service standards really measuring? *Research and Practice in Intellectual and Developmental Disability, 1*, 148–159. doi:10.1080/23297018.2014.956385

Mills, J., Bonner, A., & Francis, K. (2006). Adopting a constructivist approach to grounded theory: Implications for research design. *International Journal of Nursing Practice, 12*(1), 8–13.

Nunkoosing, K., & Haydon-Laurelut, M. (2011). Intellectual disabilities, challenging behaviour and referral texts: A critical discourse analysis. *Disability & Society, 26*(4), 405–417. doi:10.1080/09687599.2011.567791

Poppes, P., Van der Putten, A. A. J., & Vlaskamp, C. (2014). Addressing challenging behaviour in people with profound intellectual and multiple disabilities: Analyzing the effects of daily practice. *Journal of Policy and Practice for Intellectual Disability, 11*(2), 128–136. doi:10.1111/jppi.12078

Quilliam, C., Bigby, C., & Douglas, J. (2015). Paperwork in group homes for people with intellectual disability. *Journal of Intellectual and Developmental Disability, 40*(3), 286–296. doi:10.3109/13668250.2015.1034255

Quilliam, C., Bigby, C., & Douglas, J. (2017). Being a valuable contributor on the frontline: The self-perception of staff in group homes for people with intellectual disability. *Journal of Applied Research in Intellectual Disabilities.* Advance online publication. doi:10.1111/jar.12418

Spirituality and social networks of people with intellectual and developmental disability

Precious N. Sango and Rachel Forrester-Jones

ABSTRACT

Background: Researchers contend that religious and spiritual communities may provide a conduit to friendship for people with IDD. This research explored the interface between social networks and spirituality for individuals with IDD living in either a faith or non-faith based service.

Method: A mixed-methods approach was used including semi-structured interviews, the Social Network Guide and the Spiritual Belief Inventory-15R with individuals with IDD (or staff members who provided their opinions of what individuals who lacked capacity to consent would say if they had capacity). These findings were corroborated with extensive field notes generated from participant observation.

Results: The faith-based group had a higher network size ($m = 78$) compared to the non-faith based group ($m = 44$). Those with larger social networks also reported higher SBI-15R scores.

Conclusion: Findings highlight the possible role of social, religious and spiritual activities for expanding individuals' social networks.

Spirituality and religion are generally used interchangeably, yet spirituality may be defined as faith in the "sacred" and finding a personal relationship with God or a supreme power (see Baker, 2003) whereas religion can denote a state of adherence to specific institutional beliefs and practices (see Argyle & Beit-Hallahmi, 1975). Spirituality is increasingly viewed as an important aspect of holistic and person-centred care (Potter, 2002) and features as a variable in the World Health Organization Quality of life assessment (see Group, 1998). However, studies have shown that the religious and spiritual aspects of the lives of people with intellectual and developmental disability (IDD) tend to be ignored in care services, because the spiritual needs are unacknowledged, or carers feel unprepared to constructively deal with them (see Swinton, 2002).

It has been suggested that faith-based communities can create environments in which individuals including those with IDD feel accepted and experience self-worth (Swinton, 2002). Such environments have also been shown to help people with IDD overcome feelings of stigma, low self-esteem with spiritual and religious activities providing social and psychological support (Culliford, 2002; McNair & Leguti, 2000). Faith-based organisations are defined as "*any organization that refers directly or indirectly to religion or religious values and functions as a welfare provider or as a political sector*" (Dierckx, Vranken, & Kerstens, 2009, p. 1). In Walls and Zarit's (1991) study of 98 older adults without IDD from African American churches in urban Pennsylvania, 50% reported that their closest friends were family members while 40% considered church members to belong to this category. Social networks which facilitate participation in spiritual and religious activities have also been shown to be important aspects of quality of life for people with IDD (see Forrester-Jones et al., 2006).

Alternatively, religious communities can create barriers to integrating people with IDD due to the abstract nature and discourse of some beliefs. For example, Scientology assumes a cognitive basis for spirituality with an intellectual response required to certain verbal formulations which may serve to exclude people with IDD, not because they are less spiritual, but because of the ways in which spirituality is defined (Swinton, 2002). Nevertheless, it has been proposed that access to a religious or spiritual community may provide a conduit to developing and maintaining friendships for people with IDD (Gaventa, 1993) since such communities operate in a way which recognises the spiritual needs of "all" individuals forming an integrated community, which wider society may lack (Swinton, 2002).

Aim and research question

The aim of this paper is to report on a study which explored the interface between social networks and spirituality for individuals with IDD living in a faith-based (pseudonym, Adam's House (AH)) and a non-faith based (pseudonym, Greenleaves (GL)) service. The main research question was: To what extent does the opportunity to exercise religion and spirituality mediate the social lives of individuals with IDD?

Methods

Study design

The study was exploratory. Mixed-methods were chosen since spirituality is a complex phenomenon which cannot be explored using a single research method (Sandelowski, 2000). Quantitative and qualitative data were collected simultaneously, analysed independently and combined to gain a deeper understanding of participants' perspectives (Creswell, Klassen, Plano Clark, & Smith, 2011); pragmatism being the philosophical underpinning of this methodological triangulation (Tashakkori & Teddlie, 1998).

Ethics

The study gained ethical approval from the United Kingdom's (UK) National Health Service Ethics Committee (Ref: 13/LO/0594). No funding was available to pay participants; their participation was voluntary without inducement. Each participant received either a plain English or easy read information sheet explaining the nature, reason and voluntary aspect of the study, and an assurance of anonymity and confidentiality. The first author also visited each service to explain the research and answer questions. For those who lacked capacity to consent (17 service users), the Mental Capacity Act (MCA) 2005 applied. Managers identified either a personal consultee (e.g., family member or advocate) or a nominated consultee (e.g., care manager or other professional or lay person who knew the potential participant well and who had no connection with the project). Personal and nominated consultees' roles were to consider the risks and benefits of the individual participating in the research and whether the participant would want to participate if they were able to consent in line with section 32 (4) (a) and (b) of the MCA 2005. The voluntary nature of the research was made clear to all potential participants, consultees and nominated consultees and that non-participation would not affect residency, care provision or staff status and that no reason was required for declining the invitation to participate.

Table 1. Service users' ($n = 36$) demographic data.

	Adam's house	Greenleaves	Overall
Sample number	18	18	36
Gender			
Male	9	16	25
Female	9	2	11
Age			
Mean	48.72	45.28	47
Median	54.00	49.50	51.75
Range	21–71	23–67	21–71
ID condition			
Mild	2	7	9
Moderate	8	2	10
Severe	6	5	11
Profound	2	4	6

Note. ($n = 36$) is the total number of participants.

Sample

A purposive sampling method was used, the aim being to recruit 40 individuals with IDD (20 in AH; 20 in GL) so that statistical comparisons could be made. After agreement was gained from managers of both services, all residents (19 living in GL; 22 in AH) were invited to participate. Of the total number of service users approached (n= 40); 36 ($n = 18$ in AH; $n = 18$ in GL) agreed to take part. All had a diagnosis of IDD; case files revealed that more individuals in AH had moderate to severe IDD while GL mainly had individuals with either mild or profound IDD (see Table 1). The total group were predominantly male ($n = 11$ females; 25 males) with ages ranging from 21 and 71. The whole group were White British and just under 40% had lived in their respective service for over 10 years.

Setting

AH and GL were both located in Southern England, UK and regulated by their local authority (LA). The services were purposefully selected to explore both a stated faith-based service (AH) and a service stating no faith (GL). AH consisted of nine supported living houses (with a total of 22 service users; between three and six residents with IDD in each house) with 24 hour care provided by "live-in" paid staff and volunteers. A couple of the houses had "live out" staff, helping individuals when necessary. According to in house policy documents and discussions with service managers, AH's care philosophy centred around notions of "sharing", "relationships", and "simplicity"; specifically setting out to support individuals to explore their spiritual lives. Service users' access to AH was mainly via their local social networks. For those with more severe or profound IDD, family members together with the LA care manager would decide on whether AH was an appropriate environment.

GL consisted of three residential houses (between 3 and 11 residents with IDD living in each house) with a 24 hour care system. None of the staff lived in the residence. GL's mission statement was based on "Valuing People 2011" with a focus on Person Centred Plans. The decision to reside at GL was generally made by family members or the LA.

Both AH and GL had residences located in rural and urban areas. While the two services were not identical in nature and direct comparisons could not be made, the purpose of the study was not to compare the services *de facto*; rather, to explore the interface between religion and spirituality and social networks. The study was also non-experimental; the sample of care organisations and participants being non-random. Therefore, causal inferences from the quantitative data could not be made and care ought to be taken when interpreting the findings. Nevertheless, the explorative mixed-methods approach chosen, offered a more holistic picture to emerge as regards a rather "fuzzy" topic. The quantitative measures provided a structure to the research and guided the interview data collection process, while qualitative methods enabled an in-depth comparison of participant's perspectives.

Materials and procedure

The first author engaged in participant observation (PO) for six months in each service; joining in with daily activities; aiding volunteers and staff to support service users in various social and spiritual and religious activities including dance, music, monthly house meetings, communal lunches and dinners, church, and "community spiritual gatherings" (organised by staff and service users) in AH and helping out at meal times, social clubs (usually taking place in local pubs and church halls), woodwork, and cooking classes at a nearby college in GL.

Quantitative methods included the Adaptive Behaviour Scale (ABS) short form (Hatton et al., 2001) to measure individual's adaptive and social behaviour using three factor scales: personal self-sufficiency; community self-sufficiency; and personal social responsibility. This was completed by the researcher with each service user either alone or with support from their carer, depending on their communication abilities. The Cronbach's alpha for the three ABS factors was 0.86 indicating a high level of internal consistency, with high construct validity. The Social Network Guide (SNG; see Forrester-Jones, Jones, Heason, & Di'Terlizzi, 2004; Forrester-Jones et al., 2006) was used to map individuals' social relationships including the structural (size and membership), interactional (reciprocity, frequency and duration) and functional (e.g., personal, household, material support) aspects of their social networks. The SNG invites participants to name or provide the contact's network membership (e.g., staff, friend, family etc) from 10 possible areas of life. In some cases, participants indicated the number of people they knew in the different areas of life by counting with their fingers, often pausing to think before giving a number.

The Spiritual Belief Inventory-15R (SBI-15R; Holland et al., 1998) measures Beliefs in a Supreme Being and Practices (Subscale 1, ten items) as well as social support gained from religious and spiritual affiliation (Subscale 2, five items) as a potentially mediating variable in coping with life conditions and quality of life. An example of questions about belief and practices being "*Religion is important in my day-to-day life*" and of social support being "*I enjoy attending religious functions held by my religious group*". Responses coded from "strongly disagree" to "strongly agree" were adapted with smiley faces with questions simplified to aid understanding. An analysis of SBI-15R by Holland et al. (1998) found high internal consistency for data: Cronbach's alpha 0.93 (for all the 15 items); Cronbach's alpha 0.92 for Subscale 1; Cronbach's alpha 0.89 for Subscale 2.

The above applied measures were carried out via face-to-face interviews with 10 individuals with IDD from AH and 9 from GL who were verbally capable. For the other 17 individuals who lacked capacity, staff were asked to give their opinion based on what they knew about the individuals (following the MCA, 2005). Administered during the second month of fieldwork, these applied instruments were followed by semi-structured open-ended interviews concerning individual's beliefs during PO which not only maximised data corroboration but also allowed a good rapport and trust to develop between the researcher and participants. It also afforded the researcher with an extended understanding of the cultural context of the field. All interviews were audio-recorded and transcribed verbatim.

While there was the possibility of "researcher bias" (i.e., the first author's Christian belief biasing data collection and analyses), descriptive and interpretive validity steps were taken to mitigate this risk. Descriptive validity refers to the factual accuracy of the researcher's account of observations and interviews by the audio recording of all interviews and the immediate writing up of field notes post-observations. Recorded interviews were transcribed verbatim, creating an accurate, unbiased account of what respondents said. To ensure interpretive validity, (i.e., how well participants' perspectives rather than researcher's perspective was understood, described and represented) the first author (rather than anyone else) transcribed audio recordings of all interviews, thereby approaching thematic analysis with knowledge of each interviewee's vocal inflections, speech modulation and in some cases body language. This process contributed to a more accurate understanding and description of each participant's perspective. The second author then independently analysed half of the transcripts, comparing and cross-checking codes and themes with those of the first author. A final discussion between both authors followed until themes were saturated and agreed upon. In subsequent analyses, interpretive validity was ensured by staying close to the transcripts at all times and grounding all interpretations in direct quotes and phrases capturing respondents' own words.

The self-report instruments used risked being prone to the social desirability effect (e.g., exaggerating responses regarding the number of members in a network) to portray themselves, or their care service in a positive light. It is hoped that the effective use of triangulation including interview responses being double checked with PO (Creswell, 2013) will have reduced this effect and increased data reliability.

Analysis

Using SPSS V22, quantitative data were subjected to descriptive analysis and a non-parametric Man Whitney U test. Spearman Rho correlation was used to test for any relationship between the SBI-15R and SNG data. The effect sizes for both significant and non-significant P values (Tables 3 and 4) were manually calculated using the non-parametric formula of $r = Z/\text{square root } (N)$. Cohen's (1988 in Dunst & Hamby, 2012) effect size estimates were used to interpret the strength of the relationship or effect size, where "insignificant" was up to 0.19, "small" 0.20 to 0.49, "medium" 0.50 to 0.80, and "large" 0.80 onwards (see Dunst & Hamby, 2012).

NVivo V10 (QSR International, 2012) was used to manage and initially sort the qualitative data. This was followed by in-depth thematic analysis by the first author following Braun and Clarke's (2006) process of familiarisation with the data (via transcription, reading and re-reading transcripts and noting down initial ideas); generating initial codes across the entire data set; searching for and collating of codes into potential themes while gathering quotes relevant to each potential theme; and reviewing of themes by checking if the identified themes worked in relation to the coded extracts and the entire data set. This stage was facilitated through the generation of thematic "spider like" maps. As stated above, the second author independently analysed half of the transcripts, comparing codes and themes with the first author until saturation. In this final stage, identified themes were named and vivid, and compelling extract examples were selected and analysed in the context of the research and literature (see Braun & Clarke, 2006).

Results

Adaptive behaviour scores for factors A, B and C

Statistical analysis for Factor A (i.e., personal self-sufficiency) revealed no significant differences between the two groups (see Table 2) indicating that individuals across the study had similar abilities in terms of self-care including the use of a knife and fork, toileting, bathing and dressing, and personal mobility. Similarly, no significant differences were found between the groups for Factor B (i.e., community self-sufficiency) or Factor C (personal-social responsibility including being aware and considerate and being able to interact and socialise with others).

Participants' Spiritual Belief Inventory-15R (SBI-15R) score

Table 3 shows the total sample scores for the SBI-15R (Holland et al., 1998) which simultaneously measured "belief in a supreme being" "practices towards such belief" and social support gained from religious and spiritual community. Significant statistical differences were found; individuals from AH reporting higher levels of spiritual beliefs and practice, as well as reporting the likelihood of gaining support from their religious and spiritual community compared to individuals from GL.

Table 2. ABS (short form) data for both services ($n = 36$).

	Adam's House	Greenleaves	Mann-Whitney U test
ABS Factor A: Personal self-sufficiency			
Mean	23.61	25.28	$U = 191.500$
Median	26.00	30.50	$p = 0.355$
Range	0–33	10–33	
ABS Factor B: Community self-sufficiency			
Mean	22.00	28.67	$U = 214.500$
Median	25.50	34.50	$p = 0.097$
Range	2–41	4–47	
ABS Factor C: Personal -social responsibility			
Mean	19.56	18.89	$U = 154.500$
Median	21.00	19.50	$p = 0.815$
Range	3–27	4–28	

Note. The two samples presented here generally show lower average levels of adaptive behaviour than the normative sample.

Table 3. Service users' ($n = 36$) SBI-15R scores.

	Adam's House	Greenleaves	Mann-Whitney U test	Raw effect size (r)
Beliefs & Practices				
Mean	21.22	11.28	$U = 69.000$	−0.49
Median	20.50	8.00		
Range	6–30	0–29	$p = 0.003$**	
Support from spiritual community				
Mean	10.56	5.83	$U = 69.000$	−0.49
Median	11.00	4.50		
Range	5–15	0–14	$p = 0.003$**	

Note. **Significant at the 0.05 level; ($n = 36$) is the total number of participants.

Table 4. Service users' ($n = 36$) social network guide.

	Adam's House	Greenleaves	Mann-Whitney U test	Raw effect size (r)
Social Network Size				
Mean	78.00	44.06	$U = 19.500$	−0.75
Median	69.00	43.50	$p = 0.000$**	
Range	56–135	21–66		

Note. **Significant at the 0.05 level; ($n = 36$) is the total number of participants.

Qualitative data: emergent themes

Three interlinking themes were inducted from the qualitative data; corroborating the SBI-15R findings, especially the "belief and practice" SBI-15R subscale. The first two themes: "*perceptions of death*", and "*importance of prayer*" characterised over half of the total sample, while the third theme "*expressions of belief*" was unique to core members from AH.

Theme 1: perceptions of death

This theme depicts individuals' understanding of what happens and where people go when they die. One person felt that the deceased were "*asleep*" as illustrated below:

> **S:** He doesn't mention him [Tyre's dead brother] but I know that if you talk about him or you are looking through photos he says "he's asleep". (GL staff)

Others understood death to mean that the deceased "had gone to heaven":

> **Katia:** … [I am] upset … because she is going to heaven and [I] am going to be by myself.
> **Researcher:** What will she do in heaven?
> **Katia:** She will be with my dad, my Dad is up there, they will be together. (Service user, AH)

Here, Katia expressed grief and also her conviction that heaven existed. Jethro, from GL also indicated a belief in an after life; describing it as "up there":

> **Jethro: [prayer]** - yeh, very important, so is my Dad … .Dad is up there.

Theme 2. The importance of prayer

While this theme emerged from both services, AH service users appeared more able to express the importance of prayer in their lives than their GL counterparts; citing healing, buffering worry, and mediating hope. For example, Rose from AH, described how she believed that praying to "Jesus", and the prayers of her family, friends and church members contributed to the healing of her epilepsy such that she no longer depended on medication, which improved her quality of life:

> **Rose:** I prayed to Jesus and said "oh could you heal me of my seizures?" … Mum and Dad prayed as well and I was at school one day and yeh I felt like I was going to go into one [a fit] and no I did not go into one and ever since then I have been like "wow" and coming off the medication I feel more brighter because before I was like really tired and exhausted …

The importance of prayer for helping loved ones, and providing comfort in difficult times was also highlighted by AH core members George, Katia and Rose:

> **Researcher:** What sort of things do you say to God?
> **George:** Friends, family … to help someone poorly.
> **Katia:** Make my Mum well. It helps, when [I] am down I go to the garden, sit there, talk to God by myself … I pray and pray, like a tunnel with a light going through the tunnel every day.
> **Rose:** I believe in God and that He can sort everything. If you got a problem you can pray to Him and He can sort that situation out and you do not have to worry about it and you can just sing to Him …
> **Researcher:** Does this help you?
> **Rose:** Yea, especially when I am stressed …

The importance of prayer was also noted in the context of aiding mental health and self-esteem:

> **Camille:** being confident in myself, I believe in myself, because I had that problem not believing in myself when I was younger and sometimes I still, but sometimes I don't get it now so much.. I ask him, I tell him, "God could you help me believe in myself, help me to be strong and grow in wisdom".

Camille also described how God helped her through daily challenges such as the absence of a favourite member of staff:

> **Camille:** with God and my needs, well if I say "[I] am finding this hard" … he will listen to me … I say "Oh God can you help me next week because [a staff that lives with Camille] is going to be away for a whole week" he will answer me …

Talking "to Jesus" also helped and guided Camille to make new friends:

> **Camille:** I pray three times a day. I ask him to help me to do this, or help me with this meeting tomorrow.
> **Researcher:** Give me an example?
> **Camille:** … I had a friend who didn't want to be friends with me, and I asked Jesus could He help me to be friends with this other person, and I kept asking and asking, it took a while but yeh …

The importance of prayer for individuals from GL (as shown below by Micah and Silas) appeared to be mainly rooted in the desire to pray for and longing to remain spiritually connected with their deceased parents:

> **Micah:** I pray sometimes.
> **Researcher:** Who or what do you pray to?
> **Micah:** Couple of years ago my Mum died … so something like that really.
> **Researcher:** Who do you pray to?

Micah: My mum mostly.
Silas: I pray.
Researcher: what do you pray about?
Silas: My dad, passed away.

Theme 3. Expressions of belief

This theme, unique to those living at AH, referred to individuals' expression of their knowledge of doctrinal aspects about God and church:

Researcher: What else do you do when you go to church?
Clifford: Holy Communion sometimes
Researcher: What is Holy Communion?
Clifford: wine and bread
Researcher: What is Holy Communion?
Katia: Like bread, you cut it up in pieces and give it to people

With some individuals demonstrating some understanding of what might be regarded as fairly sophisticated doctrinal understandings of Jesus as helper, and God and Jesus as One:

Researcher: Tell me about God?
Paterson: God [is] like Jesus (AH service user with moderate ID and limited verbal ability).
George: Jesus
Researcher: Who is he?
George: Helper. Helps us (AH service user with moderate ID and limited verbal ability).
Camille: I believe in God because He is Jesus as well, God is Jesus, God is not one man and Jesus is another.
Researcher: Why do you believe this?
Camille: [deep breath and smiles] It's hard to say … you have to believe Jesus is God, you can't say "no, Jesus is one man God is another", it doesn't work like that, other people think it works like that but I don't. I believe Jesus is God and God is always there, whatever you do, God is always there, always. And if I go to college or do my laundry or my cleaning, or my room or I am eating, God is there. God follows you and in fact God is in your heart every day and night.

Such relative complex beliefs were illuminating especially in relation to individuals like Camille who required daily assistance with her personal care and domestic chores. This particular theme did not emerge from the GL data.

These themes contextualised the SBI-15R data, further contributing to an understanding of service users' spirituality.

Social networks: size

Mean social network size was significantly higher for the AH group (average = 78) compared to those in GL (average = 44) (Table 4). A significant positive correlation was found between social network size, beliefs and practices (rho = 0.422; $p = 0.01$) and social support from a spiritual community (rho = 0.418; $p = 0.01$) indicating that individuals with larger sized networks reported more spiritual belief and practice and gained more social support from their spiritual community.

Social network membership

Staff made up the largest membership category of individuals' networks in both services (paid staff: GL = 303 (38.3%); AH = 384(27.3%)). Other membership groups included other people with IDD (GL = 231(29.2%); AH= 123(8.8%)), and other family (GL= 90(11.4%); AH = 108 (7.7%)). Individuals in AH reported more social acquaintances (AH = 335(23.8%); GL = 20 (2.5%)), other friends without IDD (AH = 233(16.6%); GL = 80(10.1%)), and employer or colleague (AH = 97 (6.9%); GL = 0%) compared to their GL counterparts.

Social support

The frequency of social support provided by network members was categorised either as "hardly" or "never" (score 0) and "always" or "sometimes" (score 1).

Personal support

No significant differences in personal support (e.g., washing, dressing) were found between services though GL participants received slightly more (27.5%) than those in AH (24.6%). Personal support was mainly provided by paid staff.

Household support

Overall, both groups received similar amounts of household support (HS) (around 27%), mainly from paid staff although (90% in AH vs 70% in GL) This difference may be explained via the fact that, as highlighted by Z (AH staff) and the field note below, household tasks (including cleaning of bedrooms, laundry, food shopping), were always carried out jointly between staff and service users:

Z: Whether it's one core member or two, you are doing activities with them, cleaning the house and their bedroom … they are helping.
Field note 07.11.2013 … an assistant asked me to help them with the weekly shopping … with Charlie, a core member and two assistants. Elise, another core member joined us … Charlie and Elise took charged of pushing the trolley and picked items from the shelves … we all unpacked the shopping at the residence …

Material support

Individuals living in AH received significantly (U= 684,382.500; $p = 0.000$) more material support (31% including provision of gifts) than those from GL (8%) which, for both groups was provided mainly by paid staff (AH = over 50%; GL = 80%), other friends without

IDD; family and club or church members. Observations indicated that there were more opportunities for reciprocal gift giving in AH than in GL. For example, in AH, staff and service users' birthdays were always celebrated via jointly organised birthday parties.

Decisions and feedback

More network members (28.5%) provided decision-making and feedback for individuals in AH than for those in GL (23.9%). In AH this support was provided by paid staff (over 60%); "club or church" members; "household" members, "other friends" without IDD, "other family", and "visiting professionals". In GL, paid staff (over 90%) mainly provided this support.

Confiding

Confiding (concerning private matters, hopes and aspirations) was significantly ($U = 623{,}327.500$; $p = 0.000$) provided by more network members (28.8%) of those living in AH compared to GL (16.8%). In AH, confidants varied, including paid staff (over 40%); other friends without IDD (over 10%) and club or church members (over 10%). In GL, confidants were reported to be mainly paid staff (over 70%).

Companionship

Most individuals with IDD (98.7% for both AH and GL) reported that they enjoyed and received companionship (including talking, shopping, group card making, group singing). GL participants reported having little company from neighbours, probably because they had little, if any contact with their local neighbours, apart from other people with IDD, whom they did not necessarily wish to associate themselves with.

Invisible

This related to people who may not have been physically present but whom individuals with IDD felt "watched out for" or "kept an eye" on them. More network members belonging to those living in AH (98%) significantly ($U = 709{,}677.00$; $p = 0.000$) provided invisible support compared with GL (29.5%). Invisible support was provided by over 40% of paid staff in GL versus around 20% in AH. Both study groups also reported that they obtained invisible support from club or church members; other family; other friends without IDD; day centre or evening club members and household members. Only those from AH received invisible support from social acquaintances (over 20%) and people from their place of work (a little below 10%).

Critical

None of the participants from AH reported that their social contacts were critical of, or upset them while around 3% of the total network members belonging to individuals in GL were reported as critical, including other service users and family members (circa 50% for both network members). Observations and interviews indicated that a few individuals with IDD in GL did not always get along with their colleagues, as illustrated in the quote below by a member of staff talking about Joshua who was non-verbal. The service users referred to by S, often argued with each other due to personal dislikes:

> **S (staff for Joshua):** He gets on with all the staff, [but] can have a few problems with some of the people he lives with ... [they] don't get on .... arguing, shouting at each other, [it] can become physical. They just have a dislike for each other.

As indicated below, a few individuals from GL sometimes felt that their families were critical of, and upset them. For example Saul had quarrelled with his sister, refusing to speak to her because she was critical of him:

> **Field note 04.07.2014** During the interview, **SH** (staff) intervenes asking Saul "have you made up with your sister yet?" **Saul**: "No I am not going to speak to her, she upset me".

Reciprocity

Reciprocal relationships were mostly evident in AH (AH = 28.3% vs GL = 11.2%). While in GL, reciprocal relationships were mainly between participants and paid staff (over 50%); other family (over 20%) and household members (over 15% fellow service users), in AH reciprocal relationships were more wide spread across members (staff only accounted for approximately 35% of reciprocal relationships). The type of reciprocal relationships evident within AH is illustrated below:

> **Researcher:** So you visit Tamar (another core member) often?
> **Camille:** Yeh, or Tamar comes here. She has been a good friend for years now.
> **Researcher:** How has she been a good friend?
> **Camille:** Because she always gives me stuff and I give stuff back to her ... earlier this morning she put a hand bag outside the door. I said "oh is that for me?", She said "Yeh". And she will often do that - leave something outside the house, or ring my bell, or come in for [a] drink and watch telly with me.

Frequency of interaction

Individuals from GL interacted with their network members daily or weekly (69.3%) compared to those from AH (57.4%). In GL, these network members mainly consisted of paid staff (circa 50%), and other service users (over 20%). Individuals from AH mainly interacted daily or weekly with paid staff (40%) as well as club or church members (circa 20%). Individuals from AH often met up with their social acquaintances during community gatherings (monthly events celebrating various religious and non-religious occasions including Christmas, Easter or "family day" visits). This was emphasised by N, Z, Ht and J (staff from AH) stating:

> **N:** It's nice when we all come together ... assistants from other houses. On community gathering, you see the whole community and it's nice to meet other people.
> **Z:** We have general community gatherings every month or two months. Either a little disco or the [plant garden] opening. Houses have their own parties so we frequent other houses.
> **Ht:** So within the system, they've got the opportunity to pray on Wednesdays and during the community gathering.
> **J:** Its quiet nice and there are some community gatherings sometimes devoted to prayer.

Such gatherings also potentially allowed service users opportunities to expand their social networks:

> **L:** ... there is extra things happening in people's lives because of that, community events, the parties, the whole network of people which opens up to people being part of [AH].

Duration of relationships

More individuals with IDD in AH had known their network members for more than five years (67.6%) compared to those in GL (26.5%).

Type of relationship

More participants from AH perceived various network members (7%) as their "best friends" (including staff; other core members, club and church members, other friends and family) than participants from GL (0.1%) who generally only considered family members to be their "best friends" (over 95%).

The combination of quantitative and qualitative data appears to highlight not only how the study group understood their spirituality and religion through their beliefs around death, and their ability to express doctrinal concepts such as prayer, Holy Communion and the Trinity, but also illustrates how spirituality and religion relates to the types of social networks participants had.

Discussion

Previous studies (e.g., Swinton, 2002; Turner, Hatton, Shah, Stansfield, & Rahim, 2004) did not report on adaptive abilities, only reporting the degree of individuals' conditions (i.e., mild, moderate or severe). Therefore, this study provided a more detailed breakdown of group skills, showing no significant differences with both samples displaying generally lower than average levels of daily living skills (mean = 138.01; median = 157). This mean was slightly higher than for those living in residential campuses (mean = 103.9) in Robertson et al.'s 2001 study but lower than those living in village communities (mean = 195.4) or in dispersed housing (mean = 150.2) and also lower than those in Forrester-Jones et al. (2004) study where participants scored a total ABS mean of 269.5 pre-employment. This research has demonstrated that despite skills deficits, our sample could and did engage with spiritual activities to various degrees; service users in AH generally displaying higher levels of individual spiritual belief and being in receipt of more spiritual and social support from their care service than GL participants.

The average social network size for the two groups (AH = 78; GL = 44) was small compared to ordinary population studies which report around 124 network members (Hill & Dunbar, 2003). Compared to previous studies of the social networks of people with IDD using the same measure, our sample were faring. For example, O'Callaghan and Murphy (2002) found a mean network size of 20.6 for 60 adults with IDD residing in Kent and a London suburb and Forrester-Jones et al. (2006) reported a mean network size of 22 for people with an IDD living in services across England. Nevertheless, sharp differences between the two services were evident, with AH participants enjoying a much higher average number of contacts compared to their GL colleagues. One explanation for this is that individuals in AH were in paid or voluntary employment (e.g., card and candle making, etc) compared with those in GL. Employment may have provided avenues for AH individuals to acquire social contacts (Forrester-Jones et al., 2004). Alternatively, individuals in AH who attended spiritual and religious activities (e.g., regular prayer and group meetings and church attendance), may have been in a better position to gain more network members (see Bekelman et al., 2007).

The impact of spirituality on the social well-being of people with IDD has also been advocated by Swinton (2002); Minton and Dodder (2003) and Turner et al. (2004) who all reported that if given the opportunity to participate, many individuals with IDD enjoy the accepting atmosphere at religious services as well as secondary outcomes of friendships and acquaintances including "other friends without IDD". Therefore, the importance of participation in spiritual and religious events in addition to social and work-based (paid or voluntary) activities for providing effective opportunities to develop social relationships should not be underestimated.

That residents in GL received more personal and household support from staff compared to their AH counterparts may have reflected more of a dependency model of care (Forrester-Jones et al., 2006) in GL despite the similar levels of adaptive behaviour of both groups. Support in AH was carried out in the spirit of "partnership" between staff and service users, presenting a picture of a more balanced staff role, which in turn could be more facilitating of individual independence; positively impacting on self-esteem and QOL (see Gabriel & Bowling, 2004). Such a "partnership-support model" also appeared to play an important role in facilitating social network development through the provision of spiritual and religious activities.

The emergent qualitative themes corroborated the quantitative data and highlighted how spiritual and religious practices can meliorate psychological well-being including reducing symptoms of worry, (see Meisenhelder, Schaeffer, Younger, & Lauria, 2013; Young, Cashwell, & Shcherbakova, 2000) as well as scope for improving self-esteem and confidence. The themes also rebut previous notions that people with IDD have no understanding of spiritual matters (see Bassett, Perry, Repass, & Silver, 1994; Swinton, 2002; Turner et al., 2004 for further discussion). Instead, they corroborate Forrester-Jones's (2013, 2014) work depicting how individuals with IDD understand dying, death and funeral rituals in the context of spirituality. Similarly, the current findings clearly indicate that some people with IDD have spiritual beliefs which they will practice when provided with opportunities to do so. What differed between the study groups was only the level and intensity of expression of spiritual belief; with those from AH appearing to have a means and language in which to express their ideas and thoughts within an openly spiritual environment, compared to those from GL. It might also be argued that increased spiritual and religious participation may in turn, increase the communication and vocabulary of some individuals; consequently equipping them with the verbal tools to enter spiritual discourse with others, though this would need to be tested out with further research.

Study limitations

In addition to those discussed within the methods section above, further study limitations are outlined as follows. The initial aim was to recruit 40 individuals with IDD (20 in each service) for statistical comparative analysis. Eighteen individuals in each service (36 in total) agreed to take part meaning that the sample is relatively small, mainly consisting of females, making generalisations difficult. Our study was also restricted to the Christian faith. After a long period of initial scoping, a Jewish service was recruited, but withdrew part-way through the study due to "staffing issues". An Islamic community service was also sought, but personal communications with this community in the UK during the research time-scale led the authors to decide that such a service for people with IDD could only be found outside of the UK (and funding was unavailable to expand the study in this way). Therefore, our findings are not necessarily transferrable to other similar settings. Yet while transferability, is primarily the responsibility of the one doing the generalisation (Bitsch, 2005,) our findings, which were enhanced through the detailed descriptions of the research context and purposeful sampling method (see Bitsch, 2005, p. 85) may be applied to other settings. Ultimately though, individuals wishing to "transfer" our results to a different context are responsible for making their judgment regarding how sensible the transfer is.

Conclusion and recommendations for future research and practice

This research has shown that spirituality is at least as important as other quality of life dimensions for people with IDD, and also has implications for the development and maintenance of social networks. Previous literature on the topic has been generally philosophical or autobiographical than empirical; our study thereby makes important contributions to the field. The following recommendations aim to expand this area of study and practice:

Recommendations for practice

- Health and social care organizations should facilitate spiritual support to individuals with IDD to enhance their quality of life.

Recommendations for research

- The current findings should be used to adapt and enhance existing measures of spirituality to be more relevant to people with IDD.
- The link between spiritual and religious practices and social relationships should be researched more widely within the field of IDD, incorporating services operating from different religious backgrounds.

Disclosure statement

No potential conflict of interest was reported by the authors.

References

Argyle, M., & Beit-Hallahmi, B. (1975). *The social psychology of religion*. London: Routledge.

Baker, D. C. (2003). Studies of the inner life: The impact of spirituality on quality of life. *Quality of Life Research, 12*, 51–57.

Bassett, R. L., Perry, K., Repass, R., & Silver, E. (1994). Perceptions of God among persons with mental retardation: A research note. *Journal of Psychology and Theology, 22*, 45–49.

Bekelman, D. B., Havranek, E. P., Becker, D. M., Kutner, J. S., Peterson, P. N., Wittstein, I. S., … Dy, S. M. (2007). Symptoms, depression, and quality of life in patients with heart failure. *Journal of Cardiac Failure, 13*, 643–648. doi:10.1016/j.cardfail.2007.05.005

Bitsch, V. (2005). Qualitative research: A grounded theory example and evaluation criteria. *Journal of Agribusiness, 23*, 75–91.

Braun, V., & Clarke, V. (2006). Using thematic analysis in psychology. *Qualitative Research in Psychology, 3*, 77–101. doi:10.1191/1478088706qp063oa

Cohen, J. (1988). *Statistical power analysis for the behavioral sciences* (2nd ed.). Hillsdale, NJ: Erlbaum.

Creswell, J. W. (2013). *Research design: Qualitative, quantitative, and mixed methods approaches*. Thousand Oaks, CA: Sage.

Creswell, J. W., Klassen, A., Plano Clark, V., & Smith, K. (2011). *Best practice for mixed methods research in the health sciences*. Bethesda, MD: Office of Behavioral and Social Sciences Research, National Institutes of Health. Retrieved from https://tigger.uic.edu/jaddams/college/business_office/Research/Best_Practices_for_Mixed_Methods_Research.pdf

Culliford, L. (2002). Spirituality and clinical care: Spiritual values and skills are increasingly recognised as necessary aspects of clinical care. *British Medical Journal, 325*, 1434–1436.

Department of Health. (2005). *Mental capacity act*. London: HMSO.

Dierckx, D., Vranken, J., & Kerstens, W. (2009). *Faith-based organisations and social exclusion in European cities*. National Context Reports. Leuven/Den Haag: Acco.

Dunst, C. J., & Hamby, D. W. (2012). Guide for calculating and interpreting effect sizes and confidence intervals in intellectual and developmental disability research studies. *Journal of Intellectual & Developmental Disability, 37*, 89–99. doi:10.3109/13668250.2012.673575

Forrester-Jones, R. (2013). The road barely taken: Funerals and people with intellectual disabilities. *Journal of Applied Research in Intellectual Disabilities, 26*, 243–256. doi:10.1111/jar.12022

Forrester-Jones, R. (2014). Loss and people with autism. In S. Read (Ed.), *Supporting people with intellectual disabilities experiencing loss and bereavement* (pp. 165–174). London: Jessica Kingsley.

Forrester-Jones, R., Carpenter, J., Coolen-Schrijner, P., Cambridge, P., Tate, A., Beecham, J., … Wooff, D. (2006). The social networks of people with intellectual disability living in the community 12 years after resettlement from long-stay hospitals. *Journal of Applied Research in Intellectual Disabilities, 19*, 285–295. doi:10.1111/j.1468-3148.2006.00263.x

Forrester-Jones, R., Jones, S., Heason, S., & Di'Terlizzi, M. (2004). Supported employment: A route to social networks. *Journal of Applied Research in Intellectual Disabilities, 17*, 199–208. doi:10.1111/j.1468-3148.2004.00199.x

Gabriel, Z., & Bowling, A. (2004). Quality of life from the perspectives of older people. *Ageing and Society, 24*, 675–691. doi:10.1017/S0144686X03001582

Gaventa, W. (1993). Gift and call: Recovering the spiritual foundations of friendships. In A. Amado (Ed.), *Friendships and community connections between people with and without developmental disabilities*. (pp. 41–66). Baltimore: Brookes.

Group, T. W. (1998). The World Health Organization quality of life assessment (WHOQOL): Development and general psychometric properties. *Social Science & Medicine, 46*, 1569–1585.

Hatton, C., Emerson, E., Robertson, J., Gregory, N., Kessissoglou, S., Perry, J., … Hillery, J. (2001). The adaptive behavior scale-residential and community (part I): Towards the development of a short form. *Research in Developmental Disabilities, 22*, 273–288. doi:10.1016/S0891-4222(01)00072-5

Hill, R. A., & Dunbar, R. I. M. (2003). Social network size in humans. *Human Nature, 14*, 53–72.

Holland, J. C., Kash, K. M., Passik, S., Groner, M. K., Sison, A., Lederburg, M., … Fox, B. (1998). A brief spiritual beliefs inventory for use in quality of life research in life-threatening illness. *Psychooncology, 7*, 460–469. doi:10.1002/(SICI)1099-1611(199811/12)7:6<460::AID-PON328>3.0.CO;2-R

McNair, J., & Leguti, G. (2000). The local church as an agent of natural supports to individuals with developmental disabilities. *Issues in Transition, 2*, 11–16.

Meisenhelder, J. B., Schaeffer, N. J., Younger, J., & Lauria, M. (2013). Faith and mental health in an oncology population. *Journal of Religion and Health, 52*, 505–513. doi:10.1007/s10943-011-9497-1

Minton, C. A., & Dodder, R. A. (2003). Participation in religious services by people with developmental disabilities. *Journal Information, 41*, 430–439.

O'Callaghan, A. C., & Murphy, G. H. (2002). *Capacity to consent to sexual relationships in adults with learning disabilities*. Final report to the Nuffield Foundation, UK. Tizard Centre, Canterbury, Kent.

Potter, D. (2002). Spirituality and people with learning disabilities. *Tizard Learning Disability Review, 7*(4), 36–38. doi:10.1108/13595474200200038

QSR International. (2012). NVivo 10 (version 10) [computer software]. Doncaster: Australia QSR International Pty Ltd.

Robertson, J., Emerson, E., Gregory, N., Hatton, C., Kessissoglou, S., Hallam, A., & Linehan, C. (2001). Social networks of people with mental retardation in residential settings. *Mental Retardation, 39*, 201–214. doi:10.1352/0047-6765(2001)039<0201:SNOPWM>2.0.CO;2

Sandelowski, M. (2000). Focus on research methods-whatever happened to qualitative description? *Research in Nursing and Health, 23*, 334–340. doi:10.1002/1098-240X(200008)23:4<334

Swinton, J. (2002). Spirituality and the lives of people with learning disabilities. *Tizard Learning Disability Review, 7,* 29–35. doi:10.1108/13595474200200037

Tashakkori, A., & Teddlie, C. (1998). *Mixed methodology: Combining qualitative and quantitative approaches.* Thousand Oaks, CA: Sage Publications.

Turner, S., Hatton, C., Shah, R., Stansfield, J., & Rahim, N. (2004). Religious expression amongst adults with intellectual disabilities. *Journal of Applied Research in Intellectual Disabilities, 17,* 161–171. doi:10.1111/j.1468-3148.2004.00192.x

Walls, C. T., & Zarit, S. H. (1991). Informal support from black churches and the well-being of elderly blacks. *The Gerontologist, 31,* 490–495. doi:10.1093/geront/31.4.490

Young, J. S., Cashwell, C. S., & Shcherbakova, J. (2000). The moderating relationship of spirituality on negative life events and psychological adjustment. *Counselling and Values, 45,* 49–57. doi:10.1002/j.2161-007X.2000.tb00182.x

Reasons for marriage of educated Bedouin women to Bedouin men with intellectual disability from the point of view of the women

Iris Manor-Binyamini

ABSTRACT
Background: The aim of this study was to explore how educated Bedouin women perceive the causes and meaning of their marriages to Bedouin men with intellectual disability (ID).
Methods: In-depth semi-structured ethnographic interviews were utilised in data collection from 15 educated Bedouin women who were married to Bedouin men with ID. The interviews were recorded, transcribed verbatim, and then translated into English. Themes were generated using thematic analysis.
Results: Six main reasons are presented: the need for independence; age; family and societal pressures; receiving social protection of the husband or man; destiny; and the desire for children.
Conclusions: The research findings offer an intra-cultural insight into the reasons for marriages from the point of view of the women. These reasons have a cultural and community basis. These results provide a valuable conceptual understanding of the phenomenon of the marriage of educated Bedouin women to Bedouin men with an ID.

Marriage of educated Bedouin women to men with intellectual disability (ID) exists in the Bedouin community. However, the dimensions of this phenomenon are unknown, and it has also not yet been investigated in the Bedouin community in the Negev.

This study joins the few studies conducted worldwide on the subject of marriage of people with disabilities and people without disabilities, such as Edgerton's (1967) classic study "Cloak of Competence" where, from a population of ex-hospital patients, all regarded marriage as a significantly positive achievement and half of the women married non-disabled men whom the participant-observers considered generally benevolent but occasionally secluding, over-controlling, and exploitative. Studies such as the one presented in this paper, may deepen our understanding of what Bogdan and Taylor referred to as the "sociology of acceptance" (Bogdan & Taylor, 1987).

The Bedouin community in the Negev

The Bedouin community in the Negev is similar in some of its socio-demographic and cultural characteristics to the other Bedouin Arab communities in the Middle East (e.g., marriage between relatives, polygamy, extended family as the most basic social unit), but it is unique in other aspects. Part of the Bedouin community in the Negev live in unrecognised settlements, inhabiting structures such as shacks and tents, without the supply of basic services (e.g., electricity, running water, a sewage system, telephone lines, or paved roads) and without access to convenient public transportation, health, or education services. (For a broad overview of the characteristics of the Bedouin community, see Manor-Binyamini (2013).)

Israel's Bedouin population is nearly 140,000 people, of which approximately 45,000 are women aged 18 and older (Manor-Binyamini, 2013).

Traditionally, the Bedouin-Arab, who are Muslim, were nomadic people, but today they are undergoing a rapid and dramatic process of transition and change caused by sedentarisation, urbanisation, and the influences of modernisation. Bedouin-Arab society is highly gender segregated and patriarchal. Men lead the household and dominate the polity and economy. The culture controls women through such constructs as family honour, shame, female virginity, female sexuality, and, in some instances, female genital mutilation (Al-Sadawi, 1985; Shalhoub-Kevorkian, 1997).

The roles and social class of the individual in the tribal Bedouin community vary according to one's age and gender. From childhood, different social paths are set for men and women, and there is a clear division of roles at every organisational level. While the status of women is considered lower than that of men, it is also subject to change over the course of their lives in conjunction with the different roles they must fulfil. Their sense of identity and, for the most part, their supportive social networks as well are built on a tribal basis, and the tribe constitutes an affiliation group (Aharoni, 2004).

Women in the Bedouin community in the Negev

The minority group (18%) of Bedouin women in the Negev are integrated into the Israeli employment market (The Knesset Research and Information Center, 2015). In 2010, the number of Bedouin women who completed their studies at an institution of higher education reached 303. On the other hand, according to reports by the civil society in the Negev, more than 75% of women in the unrecognised Bedouin villages who are over the age of 35 are illiterate (Rozinsky, 2011). Additionally, it is estimated that 35% of all Bedouin families live in polygamy (Manor-Binyamini, 2013).

Bedouin women significantly benefit neither from the secular or civil rules in their community in regard to their personal status nor from their rights according to Sharia (Islamic law); their lives are generally governed by the laws of the tribal tradition (Sharia law) and a patriarchal judicial system (Gahashan, 2005). Despite the above, the Bedouin woman in Israel lives in a world of contradictions, between the trend for modernisation and change and forces of conservatism and traditionalism. These forces operate in opposite directions and are influenced by many factors, for example, slow changes are seen in the traditional gender roles (Abu-Rabia-Queder, 2008; Meir & Gekker, 2011). More women are now being allowed to study and attain higher education (Abu-Rabia-Queder, 2011), enabling them to work outside the home and have some contact with the dominant Jewish culture. Marriages of educated women to men with ID should be understood within the unique context in which these women live in Israel, that is created by the dynamics that exist among several categories, among which are nationality, status, culture, social, and gender background (Mohanty, 1991). Most researchers point out that Bedouin women are at the bottom of the socio-economic ladder among Israeli citizens and are subject to double, and even triple, oppression, based on ethnicity and gender: they belong to non-Jewish people in the Jewish state, and in addition, they also live in a patriarchal society (Karkabi-Sabah, 2009; Yonay & Kraus, 2009). The Bedouin society, which is Muslim, is a collectivist society. Like other Muslim and collectivist societies in the Middle East, marriage is considered a supreme social value. The encouragement to marry appears in the Koran, in the Hadith and the Sunna, and is unrelated to economic or social status. Marriage is perceived as a public, social matter, and not as a personal and private matter. Alongside the social and religious importance attributed to marriage, to the establishment of a family, and to birthing children, among the Bedouin in Israel, the importance of the institution of marriage is of additional importance because of its national and demographic value. Therefore, Bedouin women who do not marry are perceived as having failed to fulfil their obligations, on all the levels mentioned above.

The marriage process is considered and defined as a social contract between two families as well as an event for the entire family rather than a private event relating to the two individuals concerned. For that reason, choosing partners is determined in close consultation with all family members.

The status of Bedouin women in marriage and the choice of their spouse are based on Islam. In Islam, a woman has the right to approve or reject any potential spouse. It is forbidden to force a woman to marry a man she does not want to marry. However, the woman is not entitled to make the initial choice about the husband, without asking for the opinion of the person responsible for her, usually her father.

People with ID in the Bedouin community

In Israel today, there are more than 1.6 million people with disabilities, constituting 22% of the population; the proportion of people with ID among the entire Arab population in Israel (7.5 per thousand) is significantly higher than among the Jewish population (3.9 per thousand). The proportion of people with severe ID among the general Arab population is three times higher than among the Jewish population (14% versus 5%, respectively) (The Knesset Research and Information Center, 2015). In addition to the prevalence of disabilities in the Bedouin community, people with disabilities in this society are subject to double or even triple difficulties: as people with disabilities who do not receive full equality in the general population, as people who are excluded from the community in which they live, and as Bedouin citizens and residents of Israel who suffer from ongoing discrimination in the allocation of resources and the granting of rights. This double discrimination places people with disabilities from this society in a problematic situation because they suffer from failures in systems that are not customised to their needs: education, employment, housing, and transportation systems are neither adapted nor accessible. A low level of awareness of their own rights, which is caused, among other things, by the fact that the information available to the public does not exist in the Arabic language, and from the lack of Arabic-speaking professionals in certain professions and positions (Commission for Equal Rights for People with Disabilities in Israel, 2011).

Based on the unique characteristics of the Bedouin community, the reasons why educated women marry men with ID are interesting, especially in light of the fact that no study has attempted to explore the local cultures to explain the causes of this phenomenon. Thus, the purpose of the present study was to explore how educated Bedouin women perceive the causes and meaning of their marriages to Bedouin men with ID.

Methodology

Study site

The interviewees were found using a "snowball" approach. It began with the story of Salma (alias), a social worker who has worked with the author of this article, who asked her to speak up. Based on Salma's story, a request was made to the Services for Intellectual Disability in the Southern Region and to the National Service, the main institutions in charge of the care of people with ID in Israel; neither of these offices had any information about the phenomenon.

Study participants

Each interviewee filled out a demographic questionnaire.

All interviewees had an academic background: 8 had a master's degree and 7 had a BA degree, 6 were teachers, 3 were social workers, 3 were psychologists, 3 were school counsellors, and 1 was a nurse. All were married and the marriage age range was 30–37 years. The range of years of marriage was 2–11 years, almost all had children, and the range of children was 1–4; 8 lived in unrecognised settlements and 7 lived in permanent residence.

Sampling procedures

The study began with an interview with Salma, at the end of which Salma referred the researcher to two other women, and the other women did the same. A request was made to each of the women; only women who agreed to be interviewed and whose husbands were diagnosed and recognised by the Services for Intellectual Disability as persons with ID were interviewed. Of the 32 women contacted, 15 were interviewed. Each woman received 50$ for participation in the study.

With regard to the definition of the severity of the husbands' disabilities, based on the Welfare Law of 1969 and the definition of the APA (2013), out of the 15 men, 8 were diagnosed with a mild ID, 5 were diagnosed with a mild to moderate ID, and 2 were diagnosed with a moderate ID.

Data collection methods

First, ethical approval for the research was received from the ethics committee of the University. All participants signed informed consent forms before the interview, were told that participating in the study was voluntary and that there were no consequences for refusal or withdrawal. The women were assured that the interviews were completely confidential and that their names would be replaced by numbers.

Next, in-depth, semi-structured ethnographic interviews were conducted; in the first part, demographic questions were presented, while the second part included open-ended questions (see the Appendix).

Data were collected with respect to the following research question: How do Bedouin women who are married to a man with ID describe, perceive, and assign meaning to their experiences of being married to a man with ID in their social and cultural context?

The interviews relied on two main types of questions: descriptive and structured (Spradley, 1979). Due to the sensitivity and "silence" that surrounds this issue within the Bedouin community, as well as the need to protect the details of the women's lives, all the interviews were conducted by the author; the interview guide facilitated the conversation, while allowing for flexibility to let the participants raise issues of interest and ask clarifying questions. The interviews took place at the participant's tent or home and lasted from 1–3 hours. The interviewing phase of the study took 13 months.

Data were collected by means of tape-recorded ethnographic interviews transcribed verbatim (Spradley, 1979). The interviews and preliminary analysis were given to the women, who were then asked to read the description of the interview and the first analysis, and to relate to them.

With regard to the language in which the interviews were conducted, each of the interviewees was presented with two options: being interviewed in Arabic, by a Bedouin student for a master's degree in psychology, or to be interviewed in Hebrew by the researcher. They all chose to be interviewed by the researcher, and in Hebrew. It is important to note that all of the interviewees have studied for their degrees in Hebrew-speaking universities in Israel, and most of them use Hebrew in their work on a daily basis. The interviewees indicated that the ability to speak with someone from outside the community, and in Hebrew, seemed to create what in research term is known as defamiliarisation for them. This defamiliarisation seemed to help the interviewees

Data storage and analysis

A thematic analysis of the interviews was performed by the author using familiarisation, highlights, and techniques for writing memos or notes (Burnard, 1991). Familiarisation involves repeated listening to recordings and transcript readings and the documentation of first impressions.

Thematic analysis was applied as a multiple-stage procedure, with the first step involving the interpretation of individual interviews. Themes were then developed based on this analysis and were then cross-checked and compared with other interviews, thus enabling a comparison between the individual and the collective understanding. Some categories that were not raised in other interviews were merged with a broader theme as subcategories. This procedure allowed for the comparison of the theme generated in each individual interview with other participants from the group. This process of combining the experiences of individual participants into one group provided an overview of the women's experiences as a whole.

Narralizer software was used for data management and the organisation of transliterations of the interviews.

In the process of generalising the themes and categories, the author carefully followed coding practices (Burnard, 1991), reflecting the main message of the data while maintaining the study participants' original wording as much as possible. This coding system was then tested by member checking to achieve reliability by double-blind coding of two colleagues who did not take part in the study. Then, apparent validation was performed (Atkinson, Coffey, Delamont, Lofland, & Lofland, 2001).

The analysis of the data was carried out from a constructivist standpoint, it is an attempt to use these data to construct a grounded theory that could be applied in immediate and specific situations, a theory that gives a theoretical explanation for a specific and particular phenomenon which is located in the context of a people, a time and a place, as unique and unusual as the phenomenon presented in this article (Charmaz, 2000). The goal was not to diminish the complexity by dividing it into variables but to increase the complexity by including the context, that is, the analysis procedure was anchored in a field-based theory (Flick, 1998).

Positioning

In the studies that I conduct in the Bedouin community, I wear "four hats": a professional in the field of special education, a researcher, a Jewish person who studies a Muslim community, and a woman who does research in a patriarchal society.

Results

Six themes were constructed to represent the experience of the Bedouin educated women to marry men with ID and the meanings they assign to these reasons. The reasons that were uncovered in the study are the need for independence, age, family and societal pressures, protection of the husband or man, destiny, and the desire for children. The theme that is the focus of this study was the most common; it was brought up by all the interviewees and was referred to at length during the interviews. For reasons of confidentiality, the interviews in the study are presented chronologically and according to serial number, without names or any identifying details.

Reasons for marriage

The need for independence

The need for independence was raised by all 15 interviewees; it was expressed as the desire to continue their employment. The women described their struggle to acquire education and to be allowed to work because according to their tradition, as described by the interviewees, the role of the Bedouin woman, indeed their entire world, revolves around the home. After acquiring and obtaining education, these women said that they are unwilling to let go of these accomplishments:

> Here, in the Bedouin community, most women do not study; they give up school after the 6th grade. A Bedouin woman who is married and wants to work outside the tribe must go back home immediately after work ... she is constantly being monitored. I do not have this problem, my husband doesn't monitor me. (Interviewee 9)

> I married him because I wanted to keep my job, keep running my own life .... (Interviewee 4)

> ... Me, because I am a married woman ... I am free to behave as I choose. I, for example, because of my profession, I can come in to other families' homes. I can come home late ... only my husband can tell me to come back home early. (Interviewee 7)

According to the interviewees, they use their marriage to a man with ID as a means of keeping their right to work and their independence. They behave in keeping with the expected female model according to the Bedouin society, and so they are able to gain legitimacy for keeping their employment and being out in public in a professional capacity without threatening the image of the female model they are expected to portray according to their culture's codes of acceptable behaviour.

The interviewees spoke at length about marriage as a means of maintaining their independence:

> ... I am not the normal Bedouin woman. I drive a car, I have a job, I make a living. I do not want to be a slave to anybody. I want my independence ... and this marriage allows me to be independent .... He doesn't tell me what to do. He doesn't interfere with household matters .... (Interviewee 1)

Most of the women also referred to their independence in terms of financial independence:

> ... I have been working for many years. I love the work I do, it's important to me because I get to support children and help them but also because I earn money. I want to continue to be able to work and buy what I want, so that no man can tell me what I can buy and what I can't ... it's important to me to have my own money that way .... (Interviewee 11)

Some of the interviewees explained their need for independence by comparing the single women to the married women in the tribe in the context of freedom and autonomy; they said that married women are perceived as having more freedom than single women. The unmarried woman is more limited in her ability to make her own choices freely and in her own free will, and she is exposed to the criticism of her family and society:

> ... The married woman, once she is married, no one looks at her, no one talks about her. When she's single, the people of the tribe are constantly looking at her ... they have something to say about everything she does ... Why is she coming home to the tribe after working so late? Where does she go? What does she do? ... Talking, all the time, a lot of talking ... But if she's married, no one talks about her, no one tells her what to do, no one asks her questions; only her husband can control her, no one else has any rights over her ... and people stop intervening and she can do whatever she wants ... she is independent .... (Interviewee 6)

> the unmarried woman is constantly accountable to everyone; her father, her brothers, everybody supervises her ... she isn't really free ... a married woman can do what she wants ... (Interviewee 16).

Age

Another reason that most of the study's interviewees gave for marrying a man with ID is their age at the time of marriage. Women who spent many years studying and working reached an age that is considered old for marriage in the Bedouin community because of all the time they devoted to their studies and their work.

All of the women interviewed in this study were still unmarried after the age of 30 because their education and their professional life made it difficult for them to find a suitable partner for marriage, they said. According to the existing norms in the Bedouin community, when a woman reaches the age of 30, she is considered an "old maid," and therefore her ability to find a man to marry decreases. However, she can become a married man's second or third wife, since polygamous marriages are an acceptable norm in the Bedouin community. Every one of the interviewees who commented on this issue expressed opposition to polygamous marriages:

> ... I wouldn't agree under any circumstances to be a second wife .... I did not want to share my life with another woman and raise other people's children .... (Interviewee 12)

> I'd rather marry a man who has mental retardation than have to be a second wife .... (Interviewee 15)

> I know that the fact that I married a retarded man means that I am constantly forced to make concessions ... but I did not want to stay a single woman and I did not want to become a second wife, so this was the best option for me. (Interviewee 6)

Family and societal pressures to marry

The interviewees spoke about the importance of marriage in the Bedouin community and about the relentless pressure under which they were put to get married. According to the interviewees, marriage gives women in the community their status:

> You can live with your parents and your family ... but at a certain age you need to get a husband and a house and children ... The role of the woman is to be in the house in this community and the men make sure to keep them in this role .... (Interviewee 5)

> ... I worked, for many years I really loved my job I put a lot into it. And that entire time I lived at home; for many years, I stayed at home alone, all my brothers and sisters got married, and there are 15 of us children ... What about me? .... I felt the pressure to get married .... (Interviewee 13)

> Your parents, your brothers and sisters and the people around you, begin to pressure you a great deal. And around here, in the tribe, everyone was constantly asking questions: What happened? Why haven't you gotten married yet? ... You need to have your home .... (Interviewee 5)

One interviewee spoke about the pressure put on her by the husband's family and the people close to her to agree to marriage:

> They came and talked with my father ... they sent people, you know, like my husband's brothers ... They came around and they talked with my parents. At first my parents were reluctant ... My mother used to say that

> they would never agree to give their daughter away, but you know what, they were relentless, they just hung around all the time. They would not leave, they heard our initial answer and that was it: they stayed glued to us, and they sent respected people from the tribe to our house, this man and that man, very important people in the village ... it went on for months. (Interviewee 14)

> There were delegations that came over ... for years ... someone came to request my hand in marriage from my father ... and I refused ... When I turned 30 my father told me it was time to marry. I refused; my father kept mentioning it over and over .... (Interviewee 13)

> If I hadn't gotten married people would think that I was crazy, abnormal, that something was wrong with me ... I was 35 years old. (Interviewee 6)

According to Bedouin norms, an unmarried woman – one who never married or who is divorced – is considered abnormal.

> ... There was intervention by the Sheiks, an entire delegation of dignitaries from several tribes had arrived .... (Interviewee 3)

Some of the interviewees agreed to marry a man with ID because, according to them, they did not want to disappoint their fathers, since their fathers were the ones who gave them the rare freedom to study and then work. Most of them are the only educated women in their tribes. And so they have come to accept their fathers' will to avoid any further pressures.

> I grew tired of all the fights; before it was my studies, my degree, four difficult years; later there were fights about me going to work ... I have no strength left in me for another fight, so I decided to get married .... (Interviewee 8)

Receiving social protection of the husband or man

One of the topics raised repeatedly in the interviews was the need for women in the Bedouin community to be under the protection of a man or of his family. Bedouin society requires women to be under the protection of a man. This protection affords affiliation, for the man is the head of the family and controls the family structure. The existence of the entire family and of the woman in particular is validated just by being affiliated with the man. As explained by some interviewees,

> What is important in our culture is to whom you belong, to which tribe, to which family you belong. When Bedouin meet, the first question is: Which tribe do you belong to? (Interviewee 2)

> In our culture you are under the protection and supervision of the man at all times; before it was my father, my brothers; now it's my husband ... I wanted to leave home, so I got married, and now I'm under the protection of my husband; that's how it appears from the outside ... so that society would leave me alone and let me manage my own life .... (Interviewee 4)

> You know that it's funny ... I am under the protection of my husband ... What protection? He can't protect me because he is a man with ID, but the community doesn't care as long as I belong to some man ... and that's why I married him .... (Interviewee 11)

The mere presence of a man and protection that he gives is what is important in the Bedouin community, and according to the interviewees, this does not depend on anything the man does or on his cognitive capability. This protection is given to the woman simply by virtue of being married to a man; it is given to the married woman through her husband's masculine essence. About half of the interviewees mentioned the protection of the husband's family. The social status of the husband's family, according to the women interviewed, was an important factor in their decision to marry a man with ID.

> When I heard what tribe and what family he is from, I decided to marry him. They are a large tribe ... they are not slaves: they are farmers. This is a distinguished family ... their status .... (Interviewee 7)

> My father asked about his family, my father made enquiries about them, he did not want me to marry into a non-respectable family ... that ... they came to the village, here, many times, he asked ... He asked, many people, there is no one who did not ask. Every time he would ask about the family, he was told the same things: they are a respectable family, my father asked about my husband. They told him he was a good man, his family were good people who do not make trouble, they never slander other people, never inconvenience others and that people like them and that the young man is a good man. (Interviewee 15)

Destiny

Some of the interviewees claimed that the reason for their marriage to a man with ID is destiny, a type of divine sentence that the woman must accept.

> This is how God wrote it to be ... this is what God sent for me, this is my destiny ... God has determined that I am to marry a man with intellectual disability .... (Interviewee 13)

One interviewee consented out of resignation to destiny, a destiny that is an expression of divine will:

> I thought he had a speech impediment, but I told myself that it didn't matter: God made him that way ... what can I do about it? I didn't say no; I said yes, I wanted to take him on. I wanted to get married, it was important to me to get married, it was me who chose him, I'm the one ... My parents asked me whether I agree so we can get back to them with an answer. I answered yes, that I

> wanted him; nobody put any pressure on me and nobody forced me. They told me that I get to decide, and I told my father that I trust in God, and to answer them in the affirmative. (Interviewee 6)

Another interviewee said:

> I saw him and I spoke to him before we were married. Four times. He came over to my parents' house and I said yes, I wanted him. I told my parents about him ... when I sat with him, I felt that he had a speech impediment but I decided that I was going to accept him ... I felt that he had a problems functioning. When I decided I thought about a sentence from the Koran ... I thought I wanted to do something good for God because it was my destiny .... (Interviewee 8)

Desire for children

One of the reasons for marrying that every one of the interviewees brought up was children. Some of the interviewees expressed their desire to have children. They explained that in the Bedouin community, which is a society that operates within a traditional framework, getting pregnant out of wedlock is a serious and unacceptable offence.

> I was already 30 years old, I wanted children of my own, I didn't want to be a second wife and raise other people's children, but there is no chance of having children here if you are not married ... I would have been murdered if I did anything like that ... This way I could have children ... It was the only way. (Interviewee 13)

> The only thing that was important to me was whether he could have children. (Interviewee 8)

Discussion

This study has examined a social phenomenon in the Bedouin community that has never been studied in Israel: the marriage of educated Bedouin women to men with ID.

The focus of the study is on the reasons for and the meaning that these women give to their marriages. The participants in the study mentioned six main reasons for marriage: the need for independence, age, family and societal pressures, protection of the husband or man, destiny, and the desire for children.

The findings of the study reveal that, from their own point of view, women were able to create a space for themselves in which they could be independent. This meaning, assigned by the interviewees to the need to create an independent space, is one of liberation from social oppression without exceeding the cultural, social, and gender limits of the Bedouin community, which is a traditional and patriarchal society. Most of the interviewees stated that through their marriage to a man with ID, they got to be a "first wife." They said that they were maintaining their independence to keep their employment and that they enjoyed greater freedom than other women.

It seems that marriage to a man with ID is perceived by these women as the only way to realise an independent life. These marriages constitute a form of protection, one that ensures that the women obtain respect from a society that sees the ideal woman as one who submits to the control of a man (Abu-Rabia-Queder, 2006). This finding shows that even in situations of oppression, people still look for ways to express their capabilities and maintain their agency.

Crenshaw's concept of structural intersectionality provides a possible explanation for the complex phenomenon women in this study described because it renders visible phenomenological experiences of people or women who face multiple forms of oppression without fragmenting those experiences through categorial exclusion (Carastathis, 2014).

In a nontraditional way, intersectionality enables us to stretch our thinking about gender and feminism to include the impact of context and to pay attention to interlocking oppressions and privileges across various contexts, in our case educated Bedouin women.

Intersectionality calls on us to consider women as whole beings, to recognise that not all women experience their womanhood in the same ways, many women face multiple forms of oppression, and not all women are rendered powerless.

In this context, another possible explanation can be Exchange Theory for the phenomenon studied in this research. This theory explains how people perform exchanges to advance their personal interests, a process in which they give up certain things (such as intellectual capabilities) in exchange for other things (such as independence) (Klein & White, 1996). This decision is seen by some of these women as an expression of living with dignity within the society and without too much interference from others in their lives.

The study findings show how patriarchal ideology emphasises the dominance of men over women. Most of the women in this study spoke of family and societal pressures as a reason for their marriage; in Bedouin and Arab societies, marriage is considered one of the most important topics in family life (Blackmore, 1999). Even the process of modernisation that has begun to permeate the Bedouin community over the last decade has not lessened the importance of marriage for women (Hason & Abu-Asba, 2004).

According to Abu-Rabia-Queder (2011), Bedouin women maintain constant negotiations with both the Bedouin society and the Israeli society, and their ways of coping also reflect social and political power structures that operate outside the Bedouin society. Exposure to the Israeli society and to Western ideas expands the repertoire of power sources and the coping mechanisms that they have at their disposal. Sometimes the split and the cracks between the two cultures and the identities create a third space of coping that not only contains a great deal of difficulty but also combines the sources of power that they receive from the different places to which they are exposed.

It is possible that the women in this study adopt the norms of resistance that is dictated by their culture, and that is how they succeed in changing their culture and their positioning, without threatening the men and without endangering their conservative image as respectable women who are subject to the male power. The women accomplish this through education. Abu-Saad (2001), and Passate-Schubert (2005) note that education is a tool that enables and promotes the ability to get out of subordination to traditional norms and ethnic and gender marginality. They argue that education can provide tools for the struggle to improve the status of women within the family and to be a factor of social and national empowerment and mobility.

According to the interviewees, the pressure to get married is also associated with their age; they believe that the older an unmarried woman is, the less her chances of getting married. These findings reinforce those of other studies that indicate about a third of women in the Arab world reach the age of 30 unmarried.

In addition, the findings of this study reveal some information about the place of men with ID within the Bedouin community. The Bedouin society is a Muslim society, and according to the laws of Islam (Sharia law), it is permissible to arrange for the marriage of a man with ID, if he shows signs of affection and interest towards women, and a desire for physical contact with them. Under these conditions, the father is the guardian who gives his consent for the son's marriage, and it is the father that must obtain the consent of the judge of the Sharia court; the clerics view the marriage of people with ID as a way of integrating them into the society and releasing them from the effects of their disability. Marriage provides a response to their physical and mental needs because their partners serve as a source of support and care (Sayid, 2009). I suggest that the attitudes towards certain disabilities at a given point in time mirror essential tenets and characteristics of the society which abide by that law.

Limitations of the study

This study examined a phenomenon whose dimensions and prevalence are unknown, making it difficult to assess. Thus, the findings may not be applicable to people of excluded counties or of other counties in Israel. I did not establish the socio-economic status of the participants, which might have influenced these women's decision to get married. Another limitation of the current study is that it did not examine the perspective of men with ID. For example, it is important to examine whether the marriage was forced, from the perspective of the men. In countries such as England, forced marriages of people with ID are against the law and can be seen as an abuse of human rights, a form of domestic abuse, and a form of violence against the person (Rauf, Saleem, Clawson, Sanghera, & Marston, 2013, p. 135)

Another limitation of the current study is that it did not examine the results or effects of these marriages on the children of these couples. The study also failed to examine the perceptions of experts working in the Bedouin community regarding the causes of this phenomenon to obtain a deeper understanding of the phenomenon.

Implications

The results of this study may have implications for professionals working in the Bedouin community in the field of ID. There is a need to raise awareness of the topic of ID in the community.

Conclusions

The research findings offer an intra-cultural observation of the phenomenon of the marriage of educated Bedouin women to Bedouin men with an ID and highlight the reasons for these marriages from the point of view of the women, reasons that have a cultural basis. These results provide a valuable conceptual understanding of the phenomenon under study and can dapper our understanding of a sociology of acceptance perspective.

Disclosure statement

No potential conflict of interest was reported by the author.

Acknowledgements

The author would like to thank all of the women who participated in this research. The author also would like to thank the three reviewers, for their important comments that have improved the quality of the article.

References

Abu-Rabia-Queder, S. (2006). Between tradition and modernization: Understanding the problem of female Bedouin dropouts. *British Journal of Sociology of Education*, *27*, 3–17. doi:10.1080/01425690500376309

Abu-Rabia-Queder, S. (2008). Does education necessarily mean enlightenment? The case of higher education among Palestinian-Bedouin women in Israel. *Anthropology & Education Quarterly*, *39*, 381–400.

Abu-Rabia-Queder, S. (2011). Higher education as a platform for cross-cultural transition: The case of the first educated Bedouin women in Israel. *Higher Education Quarterly*, *65*, 186–205.

Abu-Saad, L. (2001). Education as a tool for control vs. development among indigenous peoples: The case of Bedouin Arabs in Israel. *HAGAR: International Social Science Review*, *2*, 241–261.

Aharoni, R. (2004). Navadut be medina modernit: Bedouin bemedinat Israel [Nomads in a modern country: Bedouin in the state of Israel (1948–2004)]. *Mifne*, *25*, 29–35.

Al-Sadawi, N. (1985). Growing up female in Egypt. In E. W. Fernea (Ed.), *Women and the family in the Middle East: New voices of change* (pp. 111–120). Austin, TX: University of Texas Press.

American Psychiatric Association - APA. (2013). *Diagnostic and statistical manual of mental disorder* (5th ed.). DSM 5. Lake St. Louis, MO: American Psychiatric Association .

Atkinson, P., Coffey, A., Delamont, S., Lofland, J., & Lofland, L. (2001). *Handbook of ethnography*. Thousand Oaks, CA: SAGE Publications.

Blackmore, J. (1999). *Troubling women: Feminism, leadership and educational change*. Buckingham: Open University Press.

Bogdan, R., & Taylor, S. J. (1987). Toward a sociology of acceptance: The other side of the study of deviance. *Social Policy*, 18, 34–39.

Burnard, P. (1991). A method of analyzing interview transcripts in qualitative research. *Nurse Education Today*, *11*, 461–466. doi:10.1016/0260-6917(91)90009-Y

Carastathis, A. (2014). The concept of intersectionality in feminist theory. *Philosophy Compass*, *9*(5), 304–314.

Charmaz, K. (2000). Grounded theory: Objectivist and constructivist methods. In N. K. Denzin, & Y. S. Lincoln (Eds.), *Handbook of qualitative research* (2nd ed. pp. 509–535). London: Sage Publications.

Commission for Equal Rights for People with Disabilities in Israel. (2011). State of Israel.

Edgerton, R. B. (1967). *The cloak of competence: Stigma in the lives of the mentally retarded*. Berkeley: University of California Press.

Flick, U. (1998). *An introduction to qualitative research*. London: Sage Publications.

Gahashan, T. (2005). Bedouin women and the rights of personal status. In H. Sana, R. Ratcliff, & C. Parizor (Eds.), *The Arab woman in the Negev: Realities and challenges* (pp. 20–37). Beer Sheva: Ma'an.

Hason, S., & Abu-Asba, H. (2004). *Jews and Arabs in Israel in a changing reality: Problems, trends, scenarios and recommendations*. Jerusalem: Floersheimer Center for Policy Studies.

Karkabi-Sabah, M. (2009). The base of organization of the clan and the position of the Arab woman. In A. Azaiza (Ed.), *Arab women in Israel: A current situation and a look toward the future* (pp. 47–79). Tel-Aviv: University of Haifa, Arab-Jewish Center.

Klein, D. M., & White, J. M. (1996). *Family theories: An introduction*. Thousand Oaks, CA: Sage Publications.

The Knesset Research and Information Center. (2015). *Employment among Arab women*. A report submitted to the Knesset on July 14, 2015.

Manor-Binyamini, I. (2013). *School-parent collaboration in indigenous communities: Providing services for children with disabilities*. New York, NY: Springer.

Meir, A., & Gekker, M. (2011). Gendered space, power relationships, and domestic planning and design among displaced Israeli Bedouin. *Women's Studies International Forum*, *34*, 232–241.

Mohanty, C. T. (1991). Under western eyes: Feminist scholarship and colonial discourses. In C. T. Mohanty, A. R. Russo, & L. Torres (Eds.), *Third world women and the politics of feminism* (pp. 51–80). Indiana: Indiana University Press.

Passate-Schubert, A. (2005). Changing from the margins: Bedouin women and higher education in Israel. *Women`s Studies International Forum*, *26*(4), 285–298.

Rauf, B., Saleem, N., Clawson, R., Sanghera, M., & Marston, G. (2013). Forced marriage: Implications for mental health and intellectual disability services. *Advances in Psychiatric Treatment*, *19*, 135–143.

Rozinsky, A. (2011). *The Bedouin Society in the Negev changes in the age of urbanization*. Bear-Sheva: The Abraham Foundation.

Sayid, M. (2009). *Marriages of persons with mental disabilities in Palestinian society in Jerusalem*. Jerusalem: The Palestinian Center for Counseling.

Shalhoub-Kevorkian, N. (1997). Wife abuse: A method of social control. *Israel Social Science Research*, *12*, 59–72.

Spradley, P. J. (1979). *The ethnographic interview*. London: Holt, Rinehart and Winston.

The Welfare Law. (1969). *Treatment of the Mentally Retarded*.

Yonay, Y., & Kraus, V. (2009). Culture or opportunity structure: Why do Palestinian women rarely join the labor market? In A. Azaiza (Ed.), *Arab women in Israel: A current situation and a look toward the future* (pp. 20–37). Haifa : University of Haifa, Arab-Jewish Center.

Appendix. The interview guide.

1. Tell me about the background to your marriage?

What were your reasons for marrying?
What were your reasons for marrying a man with an intellectual disability?
What was the most significant thing that led you to marry a man with an intellectual disability?
What influenced your decision to marry a man with an intellectual disability?
What did you know about people with intellectual disabilities before your marriage?
What motivated you to marry a man with an intellectual disability? (Were the motives personal/social/emotional?)
How did the idea of marrying a man with intellectual disability come up?
How long did it take you to decide?
Did you have any doubts?
Were there any family pressures, social pressures, religious pressures to get married, or were these pressures a part of your decision to marry?
Were there any people who helped you, people you consulted with about the marriage? Who are they? What were their positions?

2. Tell me about your married life
Describe your marriage to me
How do you perceive your marriage?
How do you explain/interpret your marriage to a man with intellectual disability?
What does your marriage mean to you?
What does your marriage mean to your children? (Asked only of women who are mothers)
What does your marriage mean for your family?
Has anything changed in your society's attitudes towards you after your marriage?

BOOK REVIEW

Phallacies: historical intersections of disability and masculinity, edited by Kathleen M. Brian and James W. Trent Jr., New York, Oxford University Press, 2017, 368 pp., £38.99 (hardback), ISBN: 9780190458997

Since Judith Butler (1993), it has become somewhat cliched to say that bodies matter. As this edited volume nevertheless shows, in a moment when President Trump's "promise to 'Make America Great Again' is devoted to reclaiming and restabilising the normative privileges of white heterosexual Christian masculinity" (p. 7), bodies – specifically those which, however impaired, are understood as masculine – matter at least as much as ever.

The contributors present a range of historical analyses that demonstrate the intricate and variable connections between masculinity and disability. Masculinity of course depends upon its alter, femininity, just as notions of disability and impairment implicate and require, at least implicitly, notions of the normal. But none of these constructs are entirely homogenous, each intersects with webs of other constructs, and these intersections differ and change over time and between places: hence the intricacy and variability.

The core theme of masculinity recurs throughout, and is frequently appraised through contrasts with ideas of femininity as (for example) weaker, more capricious, or more lascivious. In some chapters, both masculinity and femininity are linked to ideas and practices of reproduction: within a (predominantly American and hence rugged individualist) capitalist economy for the masculine; and sexually, or within the domestic sphere, for the feminine. The interplay of stereotypically masculine and feminine traits and desires is therefore prominent, appearing, for example, in Linker and Laemmli's consideration of saucy cartoons about men with paraplegia and pin-up style nurses; in Serlin's invocations of sexualised images of bodies of gay men with disabilities; and in Simpson's analysis of desire, gender roles, and impairment in Russ Meyer's (1960s) grindhouse film "Faster Pussycat! Kill! Kill!"

The normal is also a core theme, one considered in particularly compelling detail by Creadick in her discussion of the Normman (as in "norm-man") and Norma statues produced in America shortly after the Second World War. Physically instantiating both anthropometric norms and data from studies of sexology and childbirth, Creadick shows how these quite literally perfectly normal statues have inescapable eugenic overtones or connotations. Like other analyses in the book, Creadick's illustrates how normal bodies get instantiated as such through their relations with other influences and potentials – cultural, social, political, institutional, economic – as well as through their physical characteristics. The normal is continuously contingent upon other intersecting regimes of knowledge and practice: in both the economic and the domestic spheres, but also with respect to notions of race and sexuality, as well as impairment or disability. So when ideas of the normal body get formulated they are always contingent upon a cultural formation that necessarily positions some other bodies as abject, inferior or abnormal.

Frequently, the analyses in this book deal primarily with the symbolic aspects of bodies classed as impaired. For example, and in addition to those summarised above, Kinder analyses how the war-damaged bodies of male veterans were symbolically mobilised and exploited in American advertising, showing how normative concerns with conventional attractiveness still permeate these practices. Likewise, Bogdan presents a fascinating analysis of his own collection of historical photographs of people with disabilities, showing how these performances (in the sense that they were staged, framed, featured props, etc.) symbolised and reproduced well-worn distinctions between the deserving and undeserving poor, while at the same time they blurred distinctions between charity and gainful employment.

Given the centrality of symbolism to many of the contributions it is impossible not to wonder at the symbolism attaching to the book's treatment of intellectual disability. Only two chapters deal with this issue – which gets coded here as feeble-mindedness – at any length. One is Simpson's analysis of Russ Meyer's film, wherein one character is a man with an intellectual disability called "Vegetable." The other is George and Trent Jr.'s analysis of the murder in 1940s America of an infant with Down Syndrome by his father, who was himself physically impaired after contracting polio.

Meyer's film features a trio of voluptuous, confident and sexually assertive women who interact with, and are frequently contrasted against, men who are for the most part relatively weak (although this proto-feminist dynamic gets continuously undercut, Simpson notes, by Meyer's objectifying camerawork). Among them are the wheelchair-using "Old Man" and his son "Vegetable" – a massive man whose size gets blamed for the death of his mother in childbirth. Simpson describes how Vegetable is largely mute and mostly asexual "which the audience is invited to regard as the result of his intellectual disability," such that "intellectual disability means the lack of adulthood and determination" (p. 83). It seems, then, that Meyer's film plays into a familiar stereotypical bifurcation of the sexuality of men with intellectual disabilities: they are either sexually rapacious, dangerous and unpredictable, or else they are asexual innocents, eternal children.

John Noxon's murder of his son Lawrence, who had Down Syndrome, occurred in 1943 in Pittsfield, Massachusetts. Its analysis here emphasises how wealth, privilege, connection, and class shaped the lives of key players in the subsequent legal proceedings: Noxon was initially convicted of murder and sentenced to death, but his sentence was later commuted to six years imprisonment. The authors note how the legal proceedings occurred contemporaneously with dawning awareness in America of the horrors of the Nazi Holocaust and its program of deliberate slaughter (which began well before the Second World War, with people with intellectually disability among its first victims [Lifton, 1986]). Hinting at a broadly psychoanalytic explanation for the murder – John Noxon perhaps killed his son with a disability to erase a persistent reminder of his own impaired masculinity – George and Trent Jr. show how social capital determined the subsequent legal outcome, and conclude that:

> disability, like class, gender, status and power, is in this story stratified. And for those at the bottom end of the strata, the best outcome is "mercy killing" … the rhetoric of the time, usually subtle and implied but at other times explicit – suggests that "crippled" Noxon had every right to kill "mongoloid" Lawrence. A triumphant disability represents a life worth living, a hopeless one does not. (p. 230)

In this book, then, the bodies of men with intellectual disabilities feature in depressingly familiar ways: either as infantilised and sexually sanitised, or as unproductive, hope-destroying burdens, life unworthy of life. While we might hope for something more positive this is, perhaps, a reasonable reflection of what is probably the dominant strand of the historical record. So this book should not be read for its novel insights into the embodiments of men with intellectual disabilities, and still less for any related message of change, optimism, or self-determination. As a timely, detailed, and scholarly exploration of masculinity and disability more generally, though, it is both erudite and entertaining.

References

Butler, J. (1993). *Bodies that matter: On the discursive limits of sex.* New York: Routledge.

Lifton, R. J. (1986). *The Nazi doctors: Medical killing and the psychology of genocide.* New York: Basic Books.

John Cromby

OPEN ACCESS

Comparing costs and outcomes of supported living with group homes in Australia*

Christine Bigby, Emma Bould and Julie Beadle-Brown

ABSTRACT

Background: Supported living is perceived as more flexible than group homes for people with intellectual disability. This study identified costs and factors associated with quality of life (QOL) in supported living and compared this with group homes.

Method: Thirty-one residents in supported living participated in a survey incorporating measures of service user characteristics and QOL. Participants in supported living were compared to a sample of 397 people in 96 group homes, and QOL outcomes compared for a matched sample of 29 people in supported living and group homes.

Results: QOL differed little, supported living was cheaper, and 30–35% of both groups had similar support needs. Being younger, having autism, better health, family support, and participation in structured activities were associated with better outcomes in supported living.

Conclusions: Supported living holds potential for group home residents, but greater support is required in domains such as health and interpersonal relationships.

Introduction

Since the late 1970s, shared supported accommodation that combines housing with 24-hour staff support, usually in the form of group homes, has been the primary service to replace large institutions for people with intellectual disability who do not live with their families in Australia and the United Kingdom (UK). A significant body of research shows that overall the quality of life (QOL) outcomes in these services exceeds those of institutional or clustered arrangements (Kozma, Mansell, & Beadle-Brown, 2009; Mansell & Beadle-Brown, 2009). However, the outcomes between services are variable, with severity of disability, and staff and managerial practices the key determinants (Bigby & Beadle-Brown, 2016).

Concern about the limitations of group homes has generated a search for alternative models that might have greater potential to deliver, choice about with whom to live, flexible individualised support, and good QOL outcomes. One of the most common of these is generically known as "supported living" (Kinsella, 1993). In this model, housing is separated both financially and organisationally from support, which is focused on one person at a time, can be tailored to anyone regardless of their level of disability, and is concerned with building social connections (Howe, Horner, & Newton, 1998; Stainton, Brown, Crawford, Hole, & Charles, 2011). This model reflects the intent of service system reforms in the UK and Australia to deliver greater person-centred support. As these reforms use social care markets, consumer-driven demand, and individualised self-directed funding mechanisms to replace block-funding of services, the availability of supported living models are likely to increase.

From a policy perspective, supported living represents a more efficient use of resources, for some people (Felce et al., 2008). Several studies suggest that a sizeable proportion of people living in group homes do not require 24-hour support and could live more independently with the right support arrangements (Mansell, Beadle-Brown, & Bigby, 2013; Stancliffe & Keane, 2000). Some people have already moved from group homes; for example, an initiative in Victoria, Australia, supported approximately 150 group homes residents to move to supported living between 2002 and 2009 (Department of Human Services [DHS], 2010).

There is, however, less research about supported living than group homes, particularly about outcomes and factors that make it successful, such as types of

*This paper is based on the following report, which was prepared to meet the requirements of the funding body: Bigby, C., Bould, E., & Beadle-Brown, J. (2015). *'Not as connected with people as they want to be' – Optimising outcomes for people with intellectual disabilities in supported living arrangements.* Melbourne, Australia: Living with Disability Research Centre, La Trobe University. Available at http://hdl.handle.net/1959.9/505173

support arrangements or communities (Mansell & Beadle-Brown, 2010). UK and United States research comparing QOL outcomes in supported living to group homes, controlling for individual service user differences, found a mixed picture. Supported living had better outcomes on domains of choice, frequency, and range of recreational or community-based activities, and was significantly more cost-effective, but had poorer outcomes in terms of safety (vulnerability to exploitation), frequency of scheduled activities, health, and money management (Emerson et al., 2001; Felce et al., 2008; Howe et al., 1998; Perry, Firth, Puppa, Wilson, & Felce, 2012; Stancliffe, 1997). Similar findings were evident in the first Australian study that used a matched sample of 27 people from group homes and supported living (Stancliffe & Keane, 2000). A large survey in Canada found the advantages of supported living only on the domain of choice and control (Stainton et al., 2011).

Research about group homes points to the significance of service characteristics and staff practice to good outcomes (Bigby & Beadle-Brown, 2016). Few studies have systematically investigated the characteristics of communities, or formal and informal support arrangements associated with better outcomes in supported living. Locality is suggested as important by Emerson et al. (2001). Stainton et al. (2011) speculated about the importance of having informal support from family, and a recent Australian study identified the importance of family support in moving to supported living (Wiesel et al., 2015). A small study found some support for propositions in the KeyRing model about the benefits of a locality-based peer networks and explicit assistance to build social connections (Bigby, Anderson, & Bould, 2015). An evaluation of innovative housing services suggested attention to collective as well as individual needs are important in supported living arrangements when people shared accommodation (Fyffe, McCubbery, & Bigby, 2007).

Managing self-directed funding and coordinating support arrangements are more challenging for people with intellectual disability than those without cognitive impairment, particularly in the absence of a strong network of informal support (Neely-Barnes, Graff, Marcenko, & Weber, 2008). To realise the potential cost and anticipated QOL advantages of supported living, more knowledge is required about the factors associated with good outcomes to inform service development, commissioning, and funding bodies.

We aimed to investigate the QOL of people with intellectual disability in supported living, identify the cost and configuration of support arrangements, factors associated with good outcomes, and finally compare the QOL of people living in supported living with those in group homes. The research questions were as follows:

(1) What are the QOL outcomes for people with intellectual disability living in supported living arrangements who receive disability-funded support, and how do they compare to the outcomes of people with comparable support needs living in group homes?
(2) What individual characteristics and support arrangements are associated with good QOL outcomes in supported living?
(3) What is the average cost of disability-related support in supported living arrangements?

Method

Design

The study had several elements and used a mixed methods approach. A survey was used to collect self-report and proxy data on characteristics, QOL, costs, and support arrangements of people with intellectual disability in supported living arrangements who receive disability-funded support. Inferential statistics were used to identify factors associated with better QOL outcomes for this group. A sample of group home service users was selected from an ongoing longitudinal study and matched to supported living service users on key characteristics. Corresponding data about QOL outcomes and indicative costs were compared across the matched samples (service users in supported living and service users in group homes) and inferential statistics used to identify differences.

Recruitment and description of participants

Supported living participants

A sample of 31 participants in supported living were recruited through advertisements circulated to disability service providers in Victoria inviting services that supported people in supported living arrangements to contact the research team and participate in the study. Additionally, a letter was sent by the Victorian Department of Human Services to people who had moved out of group homes to supported living inviting them to participate in the study. As many of these people were no longer their clients, it was uncertain how many letters actually reached the addressee. Many of the supported living participants were recruited from the earlier qualitative stage of the study, which had used a similar method of recruitment (as reported in Bigby, Bould, & Beadle-Brown, 2016).

The criteria for inclusion were people aged 18 years or over, self-identification as a person with intellectual disability, in receipt of a disability service funded by the Department of Human Services, and a supported living arrangement (i.e., living alone, or with no more than two other people who were not parents or siblings, where housing and support were separated). This latter inclusion criterion was based on Kinsella's (1993) conceptualisation of supported living, as separating housing and support, and Emerson et al.'s (2001) definition as being a household of three or fewer people.

Sample of group home service users

We identified service users in group homes from a longitudinal study of group homes in Australia being conducted by the research team and colleagues (Mansell et al., 2013). This study included 397 service users in 96 group homes across three states in Australia. Comparable data had been collected about the characteristics of service users and elements of QOL to that collected in the survey of service users in supported living.

Matched sample

Samples of 29 service users in group homes and 29 in supported living matched on key characteristics were derived from the supported living and group home samples.

Data collection instruments

The design of the survey for supported living participants was informed by the literature, qualitative data about the experiences of living in supported accommodation (as reported in Bigby et al., 2016), and valid and reliable measures that had been used extensively in research on group homes, thus enabling QOL comparison to be made with other studies. The first part of the survey was designed to be completed by a support worker nominated by the participant, without the participant being present. This was because most of these measures were designed to be completed by a person who knew the participant well. This part of the survey collected data about participant characteristics, community inclusion, and formal support arrangements. It drew on the "People we support questionnaire" (Mansell et al., 2013) and included the short form of the Adaptive Behavior Scale Part I (ABS; Hatton et al., 2001), the Aberrant Behavior Checklist (ABC; Aman, Burrow, & Wolford, 1995), the Index of Participation in Daily Living (Raynes, Wright, Shiell, & Pettipher, 1994), and the Choice Making Scale (Conroy & Feinstein, 1986). Open-ended questions were also included about support, tenancy, and living situation of participants.

The second part of the survey was designed to be conducted as a face-to-face interview with the service user and a nominated support worker who knew them well. It comprised a modified version the Index of Community Involvement (Raynes, Sumpton, & Pettipher, 1989), Observed Secondary Health Conditions (Koritsas & Iacono, 2011), the Social Capital Questionnaire (Onyx & Bullen, 2000), and open-ended questions about experience of their living arrangements.

Procedures

The Human Research Ethics Committee of La Trobe University approved the study, and all participants gave either written or verbal informed consent to participate in the study. Surveys were sent to each participant's nominated support worker to be completed by them and collected at the time of the face-to-face interview with the participant to complete the second part of the survey. All the interviews were conducted by the same member of the research team, lasted between 15 and 60 minutes, and were recorded and fully transcribed.

Analysis

The matched sample was compiled by comparing levels of disability between people in supported living and the group home samples. The resultant samples were matched on the basis of age, level of disability (score on the ABS), physical disability, presence of autism, presence of social impairment, and presence of challenging behaviour (score on the ABC). Comparisons between the two samples were conducted using Mann–Whitney *U* and chi-square. As Table 1 shows, there were no significant differences on any of these attributes in the matched samples of 29 people. An inspection of the attributes (percentage with epilepsy, mental health problems, visual impairment, hearing impairment, and showing more than five severe behaviours on the ABC) other than those on which they were matched identified no significant differences at the $p < .01$ level.

Schalock et al.'s (2002) eight QOL domains – social inclusion, interpersonal relationships, personal development, physical wellbeing, emotional wellbeing, material

Table 1. Characteristics on which the supported living and group home samples were matched.

		Supported living	Group home
	N/*n*	29	29
Age (years)	*M*	46	42
	Range	24–64	23–65
Percentage male		(*n* = 13) 45%	(*n* = 16) 55%
Part I ABS score	*M*	242	239
	Range	166–282	210–263
Total score on the ABC	*M*	12	11
	Range	0–41	0–25
Percentage socially impaired		(*n* = 7) 24%	(*n* = 10) 35%
Percentage with a physical impairment		(*n* = 9) 31%	(*n* = 4) 14%

wellbeing, self-determination, and civil rights – were used as the framework to measure QOL. Items from the survey were extracted and used as indicators for each domain; these are set out in Table 2 together with the schema used to rate them. The choice of items used to score QOL was made by the research team based on knowledge of Schalock et al.'s framework and pragmatism given the limited number of relevant corresponding items between the two samples.

Data were entered into SPSS and analysed using both descriptive and inferential statistics. For each domain, each included survey item was rated as either Good or Poor, and scores were then combined at the domain level into one of three ratings categories: Good, Mixed, or Poor (see Table 2).

Based on domain scores, an overall category of QOL was calculated for all the sample of participants living in supported arrangements and the matched group home sample. Initially, QOL was categorised into one of four groups on the following basis: Good–Mixed (at least five of eight domains good, some mixed, no poor) $n = 0$, Mixed–Good (at least two domains good, remainder mixed, no poor) $n = 14$, Mixed (at least five of eight domains mixed or good, fewer than three domains poor) $n = 16$, Poor (no good, at least five of eight domains poor) $n = 1$. To ensure sufficient numbers for analysis, these four categories were collapsed, so that each person was categorised into one of two groups: Mixed–Good ($n = 14$) or Mixed–Poor ($n = 17$). Depending on level of measurement and whether other parametric assumptions were met, comparisons between the two groups were conducted using t tests, Mann–Whitney U and chi-square. As the study was primarily exploratory, Bonferroni adjustments were not used in order to reduce the risk of Type II errors. However, as the number of comparisons conducted was more than 20 (but less than 100), $p < .01$ was reported for significance of main effects. Cohen's (1988) guidelines were also used to report effect sizes where appropriate.

Estimating support costs

Neither participants nor their nominated support workers had a detailed understanding of the arrangements and costing that underpinned provision of direct support or attendance at day support or other services. Based on the qualitative data from the open-ended questions (see Table 3), we estimated a total weekly and annual cost for each participant in supported living. These are indicative figures, as some agencies receive funding as part of historic or locally negotiated agreements that does not reflect the current funding schema. For example, an organisation supporting a study participant received a mix of negotiated funding for infrastructure and individualised packages to support a flexible number of people that did not reflect either current items or rates. We used the Victorian Department of Human Services funding rates, current at the time of the analysis,[1] for outreach support and flexible day support level 3 to estimate cost using the following logic:

- Outreach or ISP support @ $42.68 an hour (DHS hourly rate)
- Any type of day support, such as attending a day program, volunteer, or supported work @ $84.25 a day (DHS flexible day support level 3, calculated from annual rate of $19,378 based on 46 weeks a year)
- Attendance at social group or self-advocacy group @ $42.13 a group (based on cost of 0.5 day of day program support)
- KeyRing support @ $113.40 a week (based on local negotiated funding of $5,896 a person a year).

For example, one participant received 2 hours of outreach support (2 × $42.68), regularly attended a social group ($42.13), attended a day program 3 days a week (3 × $84.25), and attended a self-advocacy group ($42.13), making a total estimated weekly support cost of $422.37 ($85.36 + $42.13 + $252.75 + $42.13), and an annual cost of $21,963.24. Costs such as the Home and Community Care program, employment, or allied health services were not included in cost estimates, as they are not funded directly by disability services and unit cost figures are not available or are too general to be useful.

Results

Participant characteristics

Supported living participants were predominately female (58%), had a mean age of 46 years (range: 26–63 years), and an average score of 239 on the ABS (range: 166–282). The lowest score on this scale of 166 was higher than the 151 normally used as an indicator of a severe level of intellectual disability. Every participant had one or more health conditions, with a mean number of 6. The most common health problems were associated with physical fitness or conditioning, vision, weight, joint and muscle pain, and dental (see Table 7). Sixteen percent of participants ($n = 5$) had mental health problems and 29% ($n = 9$) a physical impairment.

Over half the supported living participants lived alone ($n = 17$, 57%), in some form of rented social housing ($n = 22$, 71%). On average they had lived in their

Table 2. Quality of life domains, indicators of outcomes, and domain scores.

Quality of life domain	Survey questions used as indicators	Scores (Good, Mixed, or Poor outcomes)
Emotional Wellbeing	1. Survey Part 2, Social Capital Questionnaire. Q2. Are you satisfied with your life? • Good outcome (Score of 3 or 4) 2. Survey Part 1. Q26.1. Possible Problem Behaviour = Total score on the ABC • Lowest average score in the literature 15.7 • Good outcomes (Score of < 16) 3. Survey Part 1. Q26.1. Possible Problem Behaviour • Good outcome (outcome (Stereotypic factor score < = 2)	• Good outcomes (all good) • Mixed outcomes (either satisfaction is good OR level of CB = good) • Poor outcomes (at least satisfaction good and one CB measure poor)
Interpersonal Relations	1. Survey Part 2. Q4. Do you have regular contact with your family? • Good outcomes (Yes) 2. Survey Part 2. Q1. Had friends or family in for a meal OR Had guests to stay OR Been on an overnight stay to family or friends. • Good outcomes (At least one of the above = YES) 3. Survey Part 2. Q3b = YES (ever have social contact with the neighbours) AND contact is once a week or more. • Good outcomes (Yes and Once a week) 4. Survey Part 2. 2ic. The people I met spoke to me rather than a worker who was with me. • Good outcomes (4–5, True) 5. Survey Part 2. Q2h. I experienced negative attitudes or actions from others in the community. • Good outcomes (1–3, Not True) 6. Survey Part 2. Q5. Do you have contact with friends? • Good outcomes (Yes) 7. Survey Part 2. Q6a. Number of friends outside the home. • Good outcomes (2 or more friends outside of the home) 8. Survey Part 2. Q6b. Number of friends without intellectual disability. • Good outcomes (1 or more friend without intellectual disability) 9. Survey Part 2, Social Capital Questionnaire. Q17. How many people did you talk to yesterday? • Good outcomes = spoke to at least someone yesterday – a score of 2 or above	• Good outcomes (majority of outcomes [6 or more] good and none poor) • Mixed (roughly equal number of good/ poor) • Poor outcomes (no more than two good, remainder poor)
Material Wellbeing	1. Survey Part 2. Q1. Been to a cinema OR Been to pub OR Been to concert/play OR Been on holiday. • Good outcomes (At least one of the above = YES) 2. Survey Part 2. Q2. I used public transport while out in the community. • Good outcome (3, 4, or 5) 3. Survey Part 1. Q40. Are they renting their accommodation? • Good outcomes (No; i.e., they own) 4. Survey Part 1. Q43. What is their current income? • Good outcomes ($45,000 and above) 5. Survey Part 2. 2id. I handled money (e.g., paying for purchases) during the activity. • Good outcomes (4–5, True) 6. Survey Part 2. Q8. Any full-time or part-time paid employment. • Good outcomes (Yes)	• Good outcomes (majority of outcomes [5 or more] good and none poor) • Mixed (roughly equal number of good/ poor) • Poor outcomes (no more than one good, remainder poor)
Personal Development	1. Survey Part 1. Q28.1. Participation in Daily Life. Index of Personal Development. • Mean Total Score = 75; • Good outcomes (Score 76 >) 2. Survey Part 2. Q8a.1; Q8a.2; Q8a.3; Q8a.5; Q8a.6; Q8a.8; Q8a.9 • Poor outcomes (If any Yes) 3. Survey Part 2. 2ia. I participated in the activity with others rather than simply being present. • Good outcomes (4–5, True) 4. Survey Part 2. 2ik. The activity/ies helped me to develop skills in some way. • Good Outcomes (4–5, True) 5. Survey Part 2. Q8. Any employment or other structured daytime activities occurring at least once a week (or 5 or more times in a month). • Good outcomes = yes AND number of attendances 4 or greater.	• Good outcomes (majority of outcomes [3 or more] good and none poor) • Mixed (roughly equal number of good/ poor) • Poor outcomes (no more than one good, remainder poor)
Physical Wellbeing	1. Survey Part 2, Social Capital Questionnaire. Q6. Do you feel safe walking down your street after dark? • Good outcome (score of 4) 2. Survey Part 2, Extent of health condition – Overall Health Score • Mean Overall Score = 12; • Good outcomes (Score of <= 12) 3. Survey Part 2. Q7b. Do you have a regular GP? And/or Q7c. Does the district nurse visit you? • Good outcomes (Either Yes) 4. Survey Part 2, Extent of health condition. Q1. Weight Problems • Good outcomes (0–1, No problem–Mild)	• Good outcomes (majority of outcomes [3 or more] good and none poor) • Mixed (roughly equal number of good/ poor) • Poor outcomes (no more than one good, remainder poor)

(*Continued*)

Table 2. Continued.

Quality of life domain	Survey questions used as indicators	Scores (Good, Mixed, or Poor outcomes)
Self-Determination	1. Survey Part 1. Q28.2 to Q28.7. Choice Making Scale. • Looking at scores above and below 50 (midpoint of scale); • Good outcomes (Score 49 >) 2. Survey Part 2, Social Capital Questionnaire. Q21. If you need information to make a life decision, do you know where to find that information? • Good outcome (score of 3 or 4)	• Good outcomes (both good) • Mixed (one good/one poor) • Poor outcomes (both poor)
Social Inclusion	1. Survey Part 2, Index of Community Involvement, • Mean Total Score = 54; • Good outcomes (Score 55 >) 2. Survey Part 2. Q3a. How many neighbours in the area know you by name or do you know by name? • Good outcomes (1 or more) 3. Survey Part 2. Q3b. Do you ever have social contact with the neighbours, other than saying hello? • Good outcomes (Yes) 4. Survey Part 2. 2if. I took part in an activity that contributed to the community in some way (e.g., volunteering, looking after someone's garden or pet, helping out someone). • Good outcomes (4–5, True) 5. Survey Part 2. 2ig. I took part in ordinary activities, not just special activities for people with disability. • Good outcomes (4–5, True) 6. Survey Part 2, Q2c. Did you interact with anyone other staff/or other people with intellectual disability who live in the same house or nearby? • Good outcomes (Yes) 7. Survey Part 2, Social Capital Questionnaire. Q1; Q13; Q14; Q15; Q20; • Good outcome (If two or more of the above questions have a score of 3 or 4)	• Good outcomes (majority of outcomes [6 or more] good and none poor) • Mixed (roughly equal number of good/poor) • Poor outcomes (no more than two good, remainder poor)
Rights	1. Survey Part 2. 2ib. I was treated with dignity and respect by others in the community. • Good outcomes (4–5, True) 2. Survey Part 2. Q7. Do you have an advocate? • Good outcomes (Yes) 3. Survey Part 2, Social Capital Questionnaire. Q5; Q23; Q24; Q25; Q26; • Good outcome (If one or more of the above questions have a score of 3 or 4) 4. Survey Part 2. 2ij. I was able to physically access all the facilities visited without any difficulties. • Good outcomes (4–5, True)	• Good outcomes (majority of outcomes [3 or more] good and none poor) • Mixed (roughly equal number of good/poor) • Poor outcomes (no more than one good, remainder poor)

current home for 5 years (range: 3 months to 10 years). Participants lived in various locations around metropolitan Melbourne and in two regional towns. The disability support pension was their main source of income, and no one had an income more than the Australian minimum wage, at that time, of A$33,326 per annum.

Support and participation

Table 3 summarises the types of support participants in supported living received and their involvement in various programs supporting social or economic participation. As this table shows, most had support for 8 hours or less a week with tasks of everyday living and

Table 3. Type of support of sample in supported living.

Type of support	*n*	%
Everyday living		
Outreach, max. 2 hours week, regular home visit, on call, support with problem-solving, and at least one other task of daily living.	8	26
Individualised support package or more intensive outreach, 3–8 hours a week, 2–4 home visits a week, on call, problem-solving, and other tasks of daily living.	22	71
Individualised support package and case management 42 hours a week, daily visits on call, problem-solving, and other tasks of daily living.	1	3
Home and community care (assistance with cleaning, meals, maintenance).	9	29
Health related		
Regular allied health, such as occupational therapy or physiotherapy, or contact with a medical professional.	4	13
Participation and social support		
Employment service job seeking.	3	10
KeyRing program (mutual support network and assistance with social connections).	10	32
Disability day program such as day service, volunteer, or supported employment, or combination 5 days a week.	9	29
Disability day program such as day service, volunteer, or supported employment, or combination 3 days a week.	18	58
Regular attendance at social group attendance disability or mainstream.	21	68
Self-advocacy group.	9	29

problem-solving from a disability worker who visited their home. One person was exceptional, having daily visits and 42 hours of support a week. On average (omitting the exceptional person), participants received 4 hours a week of this type of support, with a range from 30 minutes to 8 hours. Only one person received a case management service.

As Table 3 shows, all but four participants were involved in at least 3 days a week of structured activity through a day program, volunteering, or supported employment. In addition, 68% ($n = 21$) regularly attended a disability-specific or mainstream social group, such as a women's group attached to a self-advocacy group or a social group in a community centre, and 29% ($n = 9$) were members of a self-advocacy group that met fortnightly.

Scores on the Index of Participation in Daily Life ($M = 76$, range: 12–100) and Index of Community Involvement ($M = 54$, range: 19–94) indicated that participants were very involved in the tasks of everyday living and frequently made use of at least some community facilities. Scores on the Choice Making Scale were relatively high, with a mean of 76% but a wide range from 44 to 100%.

Most people ($n = 23$, 77%) had social contact with family and friends on a regular basis. Over three-quarters ($n = 19$, 86%) had weekly contact with a family member by phone, saw a family member at least monthly, and had regular contact with friends outside their home. Most of their friends were people with an intellectual disability, but just under half of the participants reported having contact with a friend without intellectual disability. Just over half ($n = 17$, 55%) had someone other than a paid staff person whom they saw as an advocate, which in most cases was a family member.

Costs of support

Table 4 shows that the estimated mean weekly cost of disability support of the sample living in supported arrangements rounded to the nearest Australian dollar was $585, and ranged from a low of $213 a week to a high of $1,877. If the person with an exceptional level of support is omitted from the calculations, the estimated weekly cost is $542 – an annual figure of $28,196.

Table 4. Estimated support costs of sample in supported living.

	Weekly			Annual		
	M	Lowest	Highest	*M*	Lowest	Highest
All sample	$585	$213	$1,877	$30,435	$11,068	$97,595
Sample outlier omitted	$542	$213	$750	$28,196	$11,068	$38,985

Quality of life

As described earlier, each participant in supported living was rated as Good, Mixed, or Poor on each QOL domain (see Table 2), and then rated across all domains as Mixed–Good or Mixed–Poor (Mixed–Good, with at least two domains good, remainder mixed, no poor; and Mixed–Poor, with at least five domains mixed). Participants fell fairly evenly across the two groups, with 45% ($n = 14$) categorised Mixed–Good and 55% ($n = 17$) Mixed–Poor, which suggested overall that participants experienced a mixed rather than good QOL.

Table 5 shows that participants did relatively better on the domains of emotional wellbeing (42%) and self-determination (39%), but even on these domains more were rated as having mixed rather than good outcomes. Ratings were particularly low on physical health and personal development, and no one rated good on domains of interpersonal relationships or material wellbeing.

A comparison of the Mixed–Good with the Mixed–Poor group on a range of different individual and contextual dimensions found very few statistically significant differences. This may be explained by the small sample size and the degree of similarity between groups. As Table 6 shows, a Mixed–Good QOL was associated

Table 5. Participant QOL by domain and categorisation of sample in supported living.

Categorised by QOL outcomes	Mixed–Good QOL	Mixed/Poor QOL	All sample	
QOL domain	%	%	*n*	%
Emotional wellbeing				
Good	43	41	13	42
Mixed	57	47	16	52
Poor	0	12	2	6
Interpersonal relations				
Good	0	0	0	0
Mixed	100	94	30	97
Poor	0	6	1	3
Material wellbeing				
Good	0	0	0	0
Mixed	100	94	30	97
Poor	0	6	1	3
Personal development				
Good	50	0	5	16
Mixed	50	71	19	62
Poor	0	29	7	22
Physical wellbeing				
Good	7	0	1	3
Mixed	93	41	20	65
Poor	0	59	10	32
Self-determination				
Good	43	35	12	39
Mixed	57	59	18	58
Poor	0	6	1	3
Social inclusion				
Good	7	6	2	6
Mixed	93	71	25	81
Poor	0	24	4	13
Rights				
Good	21	6	4	31
Mixed	79	59	21	68
Poor	0	35	6	19

Table 6. Individual and contextual characteristics of sample living in supported living by QOL outcomes associated with better QOL.

		Mixed–Good	Mixed–Poor	*p*
Age (years)	*N*/*n*	14	17	
	M	40	50	$p = .02$
	Range	24–57	23–63	
Percentage with autism		($n = 3$) 21%	($n = 0$) 0%	$p = .045$
Family are closely involved in the individual's life, support, and decisions		($n = 11$) 79%	($n = 7$) 44%	$p = .05$
Any day service, supported voluntary work experience, or supported employment (or combination) at least 3 days week		($n = 14$) 100%	($n = 13$) 77%	$p = .05$

with younger age, having autism, participation in regular structured activities, such as paid or volunteer work or attendance at a day program for at least three days a week, and having closely involved family members. However, these factors were not significant at the $p < .01$ level. As Table 7 shows, a Mixed–Poor QOL was associated with significant or chronic health conditions, particularly problems with physical fitness and conditioning, fatigue, contractures, vision problems, or mobility. Wilson's (2001) effect size calculator was used to calculate Cohen's *d*, and, as shown in Table 7, the effect sizes were all large (range: 0.9969–1.8615).

Overlap of supported living and group home service users

To compare people in supported living and group homes in terms of severity of disability, we looked at the mean and range of ABS scores for each group. As Table 8 shows, there is a wider range of severity of disability among people in group homes compared to those in supported living. There is, however, some overlap between the two groups: 30–35% of people in group homes were in the same ABS range as those in supported living.

Comparison of QOL in supported living and group homes

As Table 9 shows, comparison of the matched samples showed very few significant differences on the QOL measures or the Indexes of Participation in Daily Living and Community Involvement. The only significant difference was on access to a social club, in the direction of those in supported living having more access than those in the group homes. Wilson's (2001) effect size calculator was used to convert the *p* value from the chi-

Table 7. Percentage of health conditions rated as mild/infrequent–significant/chronic by QOL category of sample in supported living.

	Mixed–Good ($n = 14$)		Mixed–Poor ($n = 17$)			
	N/*n*	%	*N*/*n*	%	*p*	Cohen's *d*
Weight problems	6	43	13	76	$p = .056$	–
Physical fitness and conditioning problems	6	43	16	94	χ^2 9.79 $p = .002$	1.3345
Dental/oral problems and hygiene	6	43	14	82	$p = .022$	–
Respiratory problems	1	7	5	29	$p = .118$	–
Fatigue	3	21	13	76	χ^2 9.31 $p = .002$	1.3345
Joint and muscle pain	6	46	14	82	$p = .037$	–
Contractures	0	0	6	35	χ^2 6.13 $p = .013$	0.9969
Balance problems/dizziness	2	14	9	53	$p = .025$	–
Bladder problems	2	14	8	47	$p = .052$	–
Pressure sores	0	0	1	6	$p = .356$	–
Bowel problems	2	15	5	29	$p = .368$	–
Vision problems	6	43	15	88	χ^2 7.24 $p = .007$	1.1073
Hearing problems	1	7	8	47	$p = .015$	–
Problems with mobility	2	14	11	65	χ^2 8.02 $p = .005$	1.1676
Seizures	1	7	0	0	$p = .263$	–
Average score across health conditions	.40		1.13		Z -3.58 $p = .001$	1.6155
Mean number of health conditions (mild to chronic)	3.14		8.12		Z -3.7 $p = .001$	1.8615
Mean number of mild/infrequent problems	1.36		2.47		$p = .1$	–
Mean number of moderate/occasional problems	1.00		2.47		Z -2.96 $p = .003$	1.1646
Mean number of significant/chronic problems	.79		3.18		Z -3.47 $p = .001$	1.2463

Table 8. Percentage of overlap in level of disability of supported living and supported accommodation samples.

	Supported living sample	Group home samples			
		Year 1	Year 2	Year 3	Year 4
Part I ABS score (range)	239 (166–282)	154 (39–253)	144 (31–277)	139 (22–263)	148 (22–263)
% Overlapping		30% (166–253)	35% (166–277)	30% (166–263)	31% (166–263)
% Supported accommodation sample below 166 (lowest score of supported living sample)		54%	61%	60%	58%
% Supported living group score above the highest score of group home sample		16% (above 253)	4% (above 277)	10% (above 263)	11% (above 263)

Table 9. Comparison of indicators of quality of life outcomes for matched samples.

		Supported living	Group home	*p*
	N/*n*	29	29	
Score on the Index of Participation in Daily Life	*M*	74.27%	65.5%	$p = .285$
	Range	11.5–100	19.2–100	
Score on the Index of Community involvement	*M*	53.68	56.60	$p = .662$
	Range	18.8–93.8	31.3–100.0	
Score on the Choice Making Scale	*M*	76.22	69.17	$p = .981$
	Range	44–100	2.78–100	
Regular family contact		79%	83%	$p = .664$
Contact with friends		76%	83%	$p = .504$
Have an advocate		65%	68%	$p = .653$
Advocate – family member		70%	82%	$p = .201$
Family are closely involved in the individual's life, support, and decisions		57%	68%	$p = .359$
Any type of work (paid or unpaid)		48.3%	52.6%	$p = .768$
Attended some form of day program		41.4%	47.4%	$p = .683$
Accesses a social club		44.8%	5.4%	χ^2 8.7 $p = .003$

square test to Cohen's *d*, and the effect size for this association was large (0.9481).

Discussion

This is the first Australian survey of people with intellectual disability in supported living arrangements. Participants were predominantly middle-aged people, without a severe level of disability, living alone in social housing. They received drop-in outreach support with practical tasks and problem-solving for a mean of 4 hours a week. Despite claims about the greater potential of supported living, their QOL was comparable to people with similar characteristics living in group homes. Overall participants' QOL can be characterised as a "mediocre," falling into either a Mixed–Good or Mixed–Poor range. The consistent advantage of community living in terms of greater choice and control, found in international studies, was reflected in relatively high scores on the Choice Making Scale. Nevertheless, this appeared to have little overall impact on QOL. On the QOL domain of self-determination a higher proportion was rated as mixed than good, and there was no significant difference in scores on the Choice Making Scale between the matched samples from supported living and group homes. This finding was not consistent with the strong sense of choice and control expressed by many focus group participants in the first stage of the study, who asserted that this was a key point of difference in supported living compared to either group homes or with family (Bigby et al., 2016).

Participants' mediocre QOL made it difficult to draw conclusions about factors associated with good outcomes. A different research design that includes a more targeted sample of people with an identifiable good QOL may be necessary to do this. However, although not significant at the $p < .01$ level, some factors were associated with better outcomes: being younger, having autism, better health status, having strong family support, and participation in regular structured activities. These findings support the proposition that informal support from family is a factor enabling good outcomes (Stainton et al., 2011).

Contrasting with other studies of supported living, the present study found a high level of engagement in regular structured activity, through disability-specific day programs, volunteering, or supported employment. The pattern may be explained by the emphasis on attendance at day programs in Victorian deinstitutionalisation programs (Bigby, Cooper, & Reid, 2012). Given regular structured activity as one of the factors associated with better outcomes, the question arises: How and by whom is such participation facilitated for people in supported living? In Australia, this may be particularly pertinent as the dominance of traditional day programs diminishes and block-funding ceases, replaced by individualised funding for things such as "community access" through the National Disability Insurance Scheme. Several recent studies have demonstrated the skilled support often required to negotiate and support participation in volunteer work or membership of mainstream social groups (Bigby et al., 2014; Craig & Bigby, 2015; Stancliffe, Bigby, Balandin, Wilson, & Craig, 2015; Stancliffe & Keane, 2000).

These studies suggest that facilitative and episodic support is necessary to negotiate and sustain participation in community groups. Together with the findings from the present study, this suggests that support for regular structured activities should be a component of individualised support packages for people in supported living. This is not always the case. Notably, in this regard, Stancliffe and Keane (2000), in the only published Australian study with a comparable definition of supported living, did not include the cost of type of support in their calculation of support costs.

Comparison of group homes and supported living found few differences between the two models; a mediocre QOL in both. The findings suggest that 30–35% of people in group homes have the potential to live more independently, given the similarity of their level of disability to those living in supported living. This lends further support to previous Australian studies that have concluded a proportion of residents in group homes may not need such a high level of support and could achieve similar or better outcomes living more independently (Mansell et al., 2013; Stancliffe & Keane, 2000).

Our study suggests significant differences in the cost of support between supported living and group homes. The estimated average annual cost for supported living, including day support, was $30,435 compared to the estimate of at least $80,000 per person, plus day program support, of approximately $19,000 for group homes. Such cost differentials are similar to Stancliffe and Keane's (2000) matched sample study. The characteristics of their participants differed slightly from the present study (they were younger, lived in their current home less time, and part of larger households). Comparison of estimated support costs between studies is hampered by the differing value of money over time and inclusion of different items, such as the omission of day support, and the unit used to calculate costs (household or individual). Nevertheless, both studies found the estimated cost of living in group homes was much higher than that of supporting living arrangements.

Supported living may be a preferable option to group homes economically and have some potential advantages in terms of increased choice and control. There are, however, important further considerations pointed out by Stancliffe and Keane (2000): "Although outcomes for the two groups were mostly similar, this did not imply that the outcomes were satisfactory. Conceivably, they could have been equally poor" (p. 299). This appeared to be the case from the data in the present study, which suggest that people in supported living would benefit from greater support, particularly in regard to health, material wellbeing, personal development, and social relationships.

Similar to other studies, our findings show that people in supported living were using local facilities and participating in a range of leisure and community activities, and unlike other studies were also engaged in regular structured activities. Despite this, there are indications (low levels of social capital, low rating on domain of interpersonal relationships, just over half of the sample not having any friends without intellectual disability) that these activities were not sufficient as pathways to wider social connections or friendships with community members. This suggests a more proactive approach is required to support building and maintenance of social connections or friendships. However, little evidence exists about the processes and costs of deliberate strategies, such as matching and formation of circles of support (Amado, 2014; Fyffe & Raskin, 2015; Poll, 2007; Simons, 1998). It is also not clear with whom the role of enabling friendships should lie; whether it should be with outreach workers who provide practical support with everyday living or differently skilled workers with enabling friendships as their primary focus.

The challenges of supporting people with intellectual disability to lead healthy lifestyles, access quality health care, and manage chronic health conditions are well documented (Emerson & Hatton, 2013). Many of the problems lie in the failure of the healthcare system to adjust or be responsive to the needs of people with intellectual disability (Ouellette-Kuntz et al., 2005). However, as the current cohort of middle-aged people in the study get older and experience age-related health and physiological changes, the challenges of maintaining good health will increase. As well as systemic change, individual support through case management, practice nurses, or clinical care coordination models may be necessary for people living more independently whose health is not regularly monitored by staff. A majority of participants in this study relied on social housing and many preferred living alone. This suggests that a major obstacle to the expansion of supported living may be the already identified shortage of affordable housing (Wiesel, 2015).

The limitations of this study relate to its small scale and coverage of only one Australia state. Despite repeated advertisements to disability service providers, and letters sent by the Victorian Department of Human Services, the size of the study was limited by the number of people who contacted us to participate. This may reflect the constraints on the time of disability support workers to discuss and support the people they support to be involved in research, and perhaps poor experiences with researchers in the past. Consequently, the small sample limits the power in the statistical analysis given both the size of the dataset and the type of data collected. The absence of data about housing and support arrangements for people with intellectual disability as a specific group also makes it difficult to judge representativeness of the sample. Costs of support are indicative only due to the variation of funding between organisations for similar services as a result of historic or negotiated arrangements, and absence of detailed knowledge by informants about costs of individualised support. Finally, although items were available across all eight domains corresponding to Schalock et al.'s (2002) conceptualisation of QOL, a validated QOL scale was not used.

Conclusion

This study has added new knowledge about supported living arrangements for people with intellectual disability in Australia, and to the wider literature. It has identified some of the factors associated with better outcomes, shortcomings of current support arrangements, and the challenges to be met if supported living expands in the future.

The significant cost differential between supported living and group homes and minimal differences in QOL for service users between these two models should inform commissioning, funding, and service development policies, and be considered in individualised planning decisions. The potential identified for a sizeable minority of people in group homes to live more independently suggests the need for initiatives to provide information about alternative options to people living in group homes and a more individualised approach, accounting for age, whereby people have the option to move into supported living arrangements should they choose to try this option.

Note

1. http://www.dhs.vic.gov.au/about-the-department/plans-programs-and-projects/plans-and-strategies/key-plans-and-strategies/department-of-human-services-policy-and-funding-plan-2012-2015

Acknowledgements

We acknowledge the contributions of Sue Slade and Williams Crisp who collected some of the data for the study.

Disclosure statement

No potential conflict of interest was reported by the authors.

Funding

This study was funded with assistance from a funding grant offered under the National Disability Research and Development Agenda, jointly implemented by disability representatives from Commonwealth, State, and Territory governments. However, the information and views contained in this research are not intended as a statement of the Australian Government or any jurisdictional policy, and do not necessarily, or at all, reflect the views held by the Australian Government or jurisdictional government departments.

ORCID

Christine Bigby http://orcid.org/0000-0001-7001-8976
Emma Bould http://orcid.org/0000-0003-3108-2072
Julie Beadle-Brown http://orcid.org/0000-0003-2306-8801

References

Amado, A. N. (2014). Building relationships between adults with intellectual disabilities and community members: Strategies, art, and policy. *Research and Practice in Intellectual and Developmental Disabilities*, *1*, 111–122. doi:10.1080/23297018.2014.941968

Aman, M. G., Burrow, W. H., & Wolford, P. L. (1995). The Aberrant Behavior Checklist - Community: Factor validity and effect of subject variables for adults in group homes. *American Journal on Mental Retardation*, *100*, 283–292.

Bigby, C., Anderson, S., & Bould, E. (2015). *"I might need a hand with that": Enabling mutual support & social connections for people with intellectual disabilities: A report on the Marillac Neighbourhood Connections Programme*. Bundoora, Australia: Living with Disability Research Centre, La Trobe University. Retrieved from http://hdl.handle.net/1959.9/319804

Bigby, C., & Beadle-Brown, J. (2016). Improving quality of life outcomes in supported accommodation for people with intellectual disability: What makes a difference? *Journal of Applied Research in Intellectual Disabilities*. Advance online publication. doi:10.1111/jar.12291

Bigby, C., Bould, E., & Beadle-Brown, J. (2016). Conundrums of supported living: The experiences of people with intellectual disability. *Journal of Intellectual & Developmental Disability*. Advance online publication. doi:10.3109/13668250.2016.1253051

Bigby, C., Cooper, B., & Reid, K. (2012). *Making life good in the community: Measures of resident outcomes and staff perceptions of the move from an institution*. Melbourne, Australia: Department of Human Services.

Bigby, C., Wilson, N. J., Stancliffe, R. J., Balandin, S., Craig, D., & Gambin, N. (2014). An effective program design to support older workers with intellectual disability participate individually in community groups. *Journal of Policy and Practice in Intellectual Disabilities, 11*, 117–127. doi:10.1111/jppi.12080

Cohen, J. (1988). *Statistical power analysis for the behavioral sciences* (2nd ed.). Hillsdale, NJ: Erlbaum.

Conroy, J. W., & Feinstein, C. S. (1986). *The Choice Making Scale*. Philadelphia, PA: Conroy and Feinstein Associates.

Craig, D., & Bigby, C. (2015). "She's been involved in everything as far as I can see": Supporting the active participation of people with intellectual disability in community groups. *Journal of Intellectual & Developmental Disability, 40*, 12–25. doi:10.3109/13668250.2014.977235

Department of Human Services (DHS). (2010). *Evaluation of outcomes for people with a disability moving from group homes to community living* [Tender]. Melbourne, Australia: Author.

Emerson, E., & Hatton, C. (2013). *Health inequalities and people with intellectual disabilities*. Croydon, UK: Cambridge University Press. doi:10.1017/CBO9781139192484

Emerson, E., Robertson, J., Gregory, N., Hatton, C., Kessissoglou, S., Hallam, A., … Walsh, P. N. (2001). Quality and costs of supported living residences and group homes in the United Kingdom. *American Journal on Mental Retardation, 106*, 401–415. doi:10.1352/0895-8017(2001)106<0401:QACOSL>2.0.CO;2

Felce, D., Perry, J., Romeo, R., Robertson, J., Meek, A., Emerson, E., & Knapp, M. (2008). Outcomes and costs of community living: Semi-independent living and fully staffed group homes. *American Journal on Mental Retardation, 113*, 87–101. doi:10.1352/0895-8017(2008)113[87:OACOCL]2.0.CO;2

Fyffe, C., McCubbery, G., & Bigby, C. (2007). *Evaluation of the housing innovations project grants*. Melbourne, Australia: Department of Human Services.

Fyffe, C., & Raskin, L. (2015). Design and implementation of a leisure buddy program. *Research and Practice in Intellectual and Developmental Disabilities, 2*, 83–91. doi:10.1080/23297018.2015.1004224

Hatton, C., Emerson, E., Robertson, J., Gregory, N., Kessissoglou, S., Perry, J., … Hillery, J. (2001). The Adaptive Behavior Scale-Residential and Community (Part I): Towards the development of a short form. *Research in Developmental Disabilities, 22*, 273–288. doi:10.1016/S0891-4222(01)00072-5

Howe, J., Horner, R. H., & Newton, J. S. (1998). Comparison of supported living and traditional residential services in the state of Oregon. *Mental Retardation, 36*, 1–11. doi:10.1352/0047-6765(1998)036<0001:COSLAT>2.0.CO;2

Kinsella, P. (1993). *Supported living: A new paradigm*. Manchester, UK: National Development Team.

Koritsas, S., & Iacono, T. (2011). Secondary conditions in people with developmental disability. *American Journal on Intellectual and Developmental Disabilities, 116*, 36–47. doi:10.1352/1944-7558-116.1.36

Kozma, A., Mansell, J., & Beadle-Brown, J. (2009). Outcomes in different residential settings for people with intellectual disability: A systematic review. *American Journal on Intellectual and Developmental Disabilities, 114*, 193–222. doi:10.1352/1944-7558-114.3.193

Mansell, J., & Beadle-Brown, J. (2009). Dispersed or clustered housing for adults with intellectual disability: A systematic review. *Journal of Intellectual & Developmental Disability, 34*, 313–323. doi:10.3109/13668250903310701

Mansell, J., Beadle-Brown, J., & Bigby, C. (2013). Implementation of active support in Victoria, Australia: An exploratory study. *Journal of Intellectual & Developmental Disability, 38*, 48–58. doi:10.3109/13668250.2012.753996

Mansell, J., & Beadle-Brown, J., with members of the Special Interest Research Group on Comparative Policy and Practice. (2010). Deinstitutionalisation and community living: Position statement of the Comparative Policy and Practice Special Interest Research Group of the International Association for the Scientific Study of Intellectual Disabilities. *Journal of Intellectual Disability Research, 54*, 104–112. doi:10.1111/j.1365-2788.2009.01239.x

Neely-Barnes, S., Graff, J. C., Marcenko, M., & Weber, L. (2008). Family decision making: Benefits to persons with developmental disabilities and their family members. *Intellectual and Developmental Disabilities, 46*, 93–105. doi:10.1352/0047-6765(2008)46[93:FDMBTP]2.0.CO;2

Onyx, J., & Bullen, P. (2000). Measuring social capital in five communities. *The Journal of Applied Behavioral Science, 36*, 23–42. doi:10.1177/0021886300361002

Ouellette-Kuntz, H., Garcin, N., Lewis, M. E. S., Minnes, P., Martin, C., & Holden, J. J. A. (2005). Addressing health disparities through promoting equity for individuals with intellectual disability. *Canadian Journal of Public Health/Revue Canadienne de Santé Publique, 96*(Suppl. 2), S8–S22. Retrieved from http://www.jstor.org/stable/41994456

Perry, J., Firth, C., Puppa, M., Wilson, R., & Felce, D. (2012). Targeted support and telecare in staffed housing for people with intellectual disabilities: Impact on staffing levels and objective lifestyle indicators. *Journal of Applied Research in Intellectual Disabilities, 25*, 60–70. doi:10.1111/j.1468-3148.2011.00647.x

Poll, C. (2007). Co-production in supported housing: KeyRing living support networks and neighbourhood networks. In S. Hunter, & P. Ritchie (Eds.), *Co-production and personalisation in social care: Changing relationships in the provision of social care* (pp. 49–66). London, UK: Kingsley.

Raynes, N., Sumpton, R., & Pettipher, C. (1989). *The Index of Community Involvement*. Manchester, UK: Department of Social Policy and Social Work, The University of Manchester.

Raynes, N. V., Wright, K., Shiell, A., & Pettipher, C. (1994). *The cost and quality of community residential care: An evaluation of the services for adults with learning disabilities*. London, UK: Fulton.

Schalock, R. L., Brown, I., Brown, R., Cummins, R. A., Felce, D., Matikka, L., … Parmenter, T. (2002). Conceptualization, measurement, and application of quality of life for persons with intellectual disabilities: Report of an international panel of experts. *Mental Retardation, 40*, 457–470. doi:10.1352/0047-6765(2002)040<0457:CMAAOQ>2.0.CO;2

Simons, K. (1998). *Living support networks: An evaluation of the services provided by KeyRing*. Bristol, UK: Pavilion.

Stainton, T., Brown, J., Crawford, C., Hole, R., & Charles, G. (2011). Comparison of community residential supports on measures of *information & planning*; *access to & delivery of supports*; *choice & control*; *community connections*; *satisfaction*; and, *overall perception of outcomes*. *Journal of Intellectual Disability Research*, *55*, 732–745. doi:10.1111/j.1365-2788.2010.01378.x

Stancliffe, R. J. (1997). Community living-unit size, staff presence, and residents' choice-making. *Mental Retardation*, *35*, 1–9. doi:10.1352/0047-6765(1997)035<0001:CLSSPA>2.0.CO;2

Stancliffe, R. J., Bigby, C., Balandin, S., Wilson, N. J., & Craig, D. (2015). Transition to retirement and participation in mainstream community groups using active mentoring: A feasibility and outcomes evaluation with a matched comparison group. *Journal of Intellectual Disability Research*, *59*, 703–718. doi:10.1111/jir.12174

Stancliffe, R. J., & Keane, S. (2000). Outcomes and costs of community living: A matched comparison of group homes and semi-independent living. *Journal of Intellectual & Developmental Disability*, *25*, 281–305. doi:10.1080/13668250020019584

Wiesel, I. (2015). Housing for people with intellectual disabilities and the National Disability Insurance Scheme reforms. *Research and Practice in Intellectual and Developmental Disabilities*, *2*, 45–55. doi:10.1080/23297018.2014.992037

Wiesel, I., Laragy, C., Gendera, S., Fisher, K. R., Jenkinson, S., Hill, T., ... Bridge, C. (2015). *Moving to my home: Housing aspirations, transitions and outcomes of people with disability* (AHURI Final Report No. 246). Melbourne: Australian Housing and Urban Research Institute.

Wilson, D. B. (2001). Practical meta-analysis effect size calculator [Computer software]. Retrieved from https://www.campbellcollaboration.org/escalc/html/EffectSizeCalculator-Home.php

Service receipt of adults with rare genetic syndromes who engage in challenging behaviour

N. Awan, C. Oliver, L. Wilde, K. Eden and J. Waite

ABSTRACT
Background: There is limited research documenting the health and/or psychological services accessed by adults with rare genetic syndromes who engage in challenging behaviour. The study documented service receipt and associations with person characteristics.
Method: Thirty-two parents of adults with rare genetic syndromes completed an adapted version of the Client Service Receipt Inventory. Access to services for general health and challenging behaviour in the last six months were documented. Person characteristics measured were: adaptive behaviour, autism spectrum disorder characteristics, impulsivity and overactivity.
Results: Over half of adults who engaged in challenging behaviour did not receive professional input for behaviours. No association was found between the degree of challenging behaviour and service receipt for challenging behaviour. Total activity score (impulsivity and overactivity) was positively associated, and adaptive ability negatively associated, with accessing professionals.
Conclusions: Service receipt is not appropriately linked to needs. Further research should examine factors that affect service access including individual characteristics and service experience.

Individuals diagnosed with a rare genetic syndrome associated with an intellectual disability (ID) are at heightened risk of displaying challenging behaviour such as aggression, self-injury and destruction of property in comparison to individuals with ID of heterogeneous aetiology (Arron, Oliver, Moss, Berg, & Burbidge, 2011). These behaviours often have a negative effect on the quality of life for the person with ID, as well as the quality of life of those around them (Hastings, 2002). Therefore, there may be a need for professional input to reduce these behaviours (National Institute for Health and Clinical Excellence [NICE], May, 2015). However, there is a dearth of research documenting service receipt for adults with genetic syndromes with associated ID who are living at home, including whether these adults are accessing appropriate services for challenging behaviour, and the influence of individual characteristics on service access.

Prevalence estimates for challenging behaviour in individuals with ID of heterogeneous aetiology range from 1.7% to 41% for self-injury (Cooper, Smiley, Allan, et al, 2009; Emerson et al., 2001a; Saloviita, 2000) and 7% to 27.9% for aggression (Emerson et al., 2001a; Eyman & Call, 1977). Prevalence estimates for self-injury in individuals with specific genetic syndromes such as Cornelia de Lange, Cri du Chat, Fragile X, Lowe, Prader–Willi and Smith–Magenis syndromes are significantly higher than when compared to individuals with ID of heterogeneous aetiology (range: 45–93%; Arron et al., 2011). Therefore, people with genetic syndromes are a high-risk population where access to services is likely to be important for effective interventions to reduce the impact of these behaviours.

Research has shown that challenging behaviour can be maintained via operant reinforcement and thus acquires a function for an individual (Carr & Durand, 1985; Oliver, 1995). There are effective interventions for challenging behaviour (Iwata et al., 1994) and the effectiveness of these interventions is further increased if the function of the behaviour is known (Hurl, Wightman, Virues-Ortega, & Haynes, 2016). Therefore, NICE guidelines for clinicians working to reduce challenging behaviour highlight the importance of assessing the function of behaviour, changing reinforcement contingencies, teaching alternative functional communication strategies and providing education to families about how behaviours are shaped over time (NICE, May, 2015).

Understanding environmental contingencies is important when assessing and intervening with challenging behaviour; however, reinforcement contingencies alone cannot account for all variance in the presentation of behaviour across genetic syndromes and evidence indicates that individual characteristics are associated with behaviour (Oliver, Berg, Burbidge, & Arron, 2009). For example, a diagnosis of autism is associated with self-injury, aggression and destructive behaviours, and receptive communication difficulties are associated with self-injury and aggression (McClintock, Hall, & Oliver, 2003). Being male is also a risk marker for aggression (McClintock et al., 2003). Finally, an association between self-injurious behaviour, repetitive behaviour and impulsivity has been found in rare genetic syndromes, intellectual disability, and autism spectrum disorder (ASD) (Collacott, Cooper, Branford, & McGrother, 1998; Cooper, Smiley, Allan, et al., 2009; Oliver et al., 2009; Richards, Oliver, Nelson, & Moss, 2012; Schneider, Bijam-Schulte, Janssen, & Stolke, 1996). This has led to the hypothesis that underlying behavioural dysregulation may contribute to the development of some topographies of challenging behaviour (Oliver et al., 2009; Oliver & Richards, 2015; Petty & Oliver, 2005; Rojahn, Mateson, Naglieri, & Mayville, 2004).

Despite guidelines for intervening with challenging behaviour and increasing awareness of factors associated with behaviour, longitudinal studies indicate that for a high proportion of individuals, challenging behaviour persists over time (Emerson, Kienan, Alborz, Reeves et al. 2001b). Physical aggression persists in 70% of adults with ID (Totsika, Toogood, Hastings, & Lewis, 2008), with similar findings seen in children with an ID (74%; Emerson, Robertson, Fowler, Letchford, & Jones, 1996). Self-injurious behaviour and destructive behaviour persist in approximately 49–57% and 70% of adults, respectively (Emerson et al., 2001b; Kiernan & Alborz, 1996; Totsika et al., 2008). The reasons for the persistence of challenging behaviour are unclear; particularly, when there is very little research on whether adults who engage in challenging behaviour receive services and interventions. Past research has identified inequalities and unmet needs in general health services for individuals with ID compared to the general population (Howells, 1986; Lennox & Kerr, 1997; Lennox, Diggens, & Ugoni, 1997), despite these individuals being prone to additional physical, mental health and behaviour difficulties (Howells, 1986). Communication difficulties between the patient and professionals (Beange & Bauman, 1990; Cumella, Corbett, Clark, & Smith, 1992; Howells, 1986), communication difficulties between professionals (Cumella et al., 1992) and difficulty in accessing health services (Beange, 1996; Cumella et al., 1992) are some of the barriers facing individuals with ID when accessing general health care. Barriers such as these may explain the persistence of problem behaviours into adulthood.

Studies of children's services indicate that families are not receiving appropriate support with managing challenging behaviour. Kiernan and Alborz (1996) found that the majority of families did not receive any professional support for challenging behaviour displayed by their children. The gap between need and service provision is significant given that children in special schools who show high levels of challenging behaviour are at least 13 times more likely to need services but are only marginally more likely to receive this input (Ruddick, Davies, Bacarese-Hamilton, & Oliver, 2015). McGill et al. (2006) also reported that nearly one-third of families with a child who displays challenging behaviour received no psychological support. Qualitative research has revealed that families have found children's services for challenging behaviours to be insufficient, and the strategies suggested by professionals as ineffective (Wodehouse & McGill, 2009). It is important to note that these studies focus solely on children and little research has documented parents' experiences of services for adults who engage in challenging behaviour.

Knapp, Commas-Herrera, Astin, Beecham, and Pendaries (2005) examined service receipt of adults with ID living in care accommodation and found strong associations between degree of ID, challenging behaviour and service use; however, service use was not appropriately linked to service users' needs. The type of living setting influenced the services that were accessed. Adults living in private or voluntary care accommodation were less likely to use hospital-based day services when compared to adults living in residential accommodation supported by the NHS. These adults were also less likely to see a dietician or an occupational therapist but more likely to see the GP. While this study provides some insight into factors associated with service receipt, the Department of Health (2001) estimates that 60% of individuals with ID live at home with their parents once they reach adulthood, yet very little is known about which services these individuals access if any. Further work is needed to explore service access and the factors that influence it in adults with genetic syndromes who display challenging behaviour.

The first aim of the present study was to document service receipt specifically for adults diagnosed with rare genetic syndromes associated with ID, who display challenging behaviour and still live within the family home. The second aim was to examine the relationship between individual characteristics that are known to be associated with challenging behaviour and service receipt for challenging behaviour. It was predicted that individuals who display more challenging behaviour would spend more time with professionals who typically receive more training in how to reduce challenging behaviour using evidence-based practices (i.e., clinical psychologists, ID nurses and psychiatrists). It was also predicted that individual characteristics typically associated with challenging behaviour (including lower adaptive ability, impulsivity, overactivity and ASD) would be positively associated with accessing these services.

Methods

Ethics

Ethical approval was obtained from the Coventry and Warwick NRES Committee.

Recruitment

Invitation letters were sent to 131 parents inviting them to take part in a broader study about their experiences of challenging behaviour. Participants were selected from an existing database held by the Cerebra Centre for Neurodevelopmental Disorders, University of Birmingham. Participants were invited if their child lived at home, was over 16 years of age and believed to engage in challenging behaviour based on results of a 2011 longitudinal study conducted 8 months before this study. All invited participants had a history of challenging behaviour indicated by the presence of behaviour at one previous time-point during the longitudinal study (either 2006 or 2003).

Forty-two participants (32.06%) expressed an interest in taking part in a follow-up interview about challenging behaviour. Of these participants, two were excluded because their child had moved into residential accommodation; five were excluded due to adjustments to the methodology for the interview (pilot study) and three were unavailable at the time of telephone call due to extraneous circumstances.

Participants

The sample consisted of 32 parents of children with Angelman (*N*=8), Cri du Chat (*N*=1), Cornelia de Lange (*N* = 6); Prader-Willi (*N* = 4); Lowe (*N* = 2); Smith Magenis (*N* = 4) and fragile X (*N* = 7) syndromes. The mean age of the parents was 54.63 years (Range= 42–79). Adults with ID had a mean age of 27.08 years (Range = 18.83–47.17). 18 (56.25%) were male. 12 (37.5%) of the adults were diagnosed by a paediatrician, 18 (56.25%) by a clinical geneticist and 2 (6.25%) by other professionals. 28 (87.5%) of the adults with ID had normal hearing; 24 (75%) had normal vision; 25 (78.13%) were ambulant; 25 (78.13%) were partially able/able in daily living skills such as washing, dressing and feeding; and 23 (71.9%) used some words or sentences.

Procedure

Prior to conducting the interviews, letters were sent to participants explaining that the purpose of this telephone interview study was to explore the services accessed for challenging behaviour. Participants were given information sheets and completed expression of interest and consent forms, online. Following this, participants were contacted via telephone at a scheduled time and the measures were administered.

Measures

Participants completed a telephone interview that included the Challenging Behaviour Questionnaire (CBQ) (Hyman, Oliver, & Hall, 2002) and an adapted version of the Client Service Receipt Inventory (CSRI) (Beecham & Knapp, 1992; Strydom et al., 2010). The CSRI was administered twice to document both overall service receipt and service receipt for challenging behaviour. Participants had completed questionnaires on their child's individual characteristics (adaptive ability, autism spectrum phenomenology and impulsivity/overactivity) 8 months before the start of the current study as part of a broader longitudinal questionnaire study. To reduce burden on participants, and because these measures assessed relatively stable characteristics, these measures were not readministered as part of this study but data were included in the analyses.

Individual characteristics measures

Wessex Scale (Kushlick, Blunden, & Cox, 1973)

The Wessex Questionnaire is an informant questionnaire, which assesses an individual's physical and social adaptive ability. The questionnaire covers vision, mobility, hearing, literacy, speech, continence and self-help. High scores on this measure indicate greater ability. This scale has moderate reliability (Kappa = .62). The self-help score from the Wessex Scale was used in this study along with dichotomous variables ambulatory/nonambulatory and verbal/non-verbal.

The Activity Questionnaire (Burbidge & Oliver, 2008)

This questionnaire was specifically designed for people with an ID. It contains 18 items based on three subscales: impulsivity, impulsive speech and overactivity. Responses are scored on a 5-point Likert scale, which ranges from 0 (never/almost never) to 4 (always/almost always). A high score on TAQ indicates more behaviour. The subscales have good inter-rater and test–retest scores (all correlations >.70).

Social Communication Questionnaire - Current Form (SCQ; Rutter, Bailey, & Lord, 2003)

The SCQ is a screening tool for ASD characteristics. Subscales measure social interaction, communication deficits and repetitive behaviour. A high score on the SCQ indicates more ASD characteristics. The SCQ has good internal consistency ($\alpha = .90$; Berument, Rutter, Lord, Pickles, & Bailey, 1999).

The Challenging Behaviour Questionnaire (Hyman et al., 2002)

The CBQ is an informant-based questionnaire that measures self-injury, aggression and destruction of property. Participants indicate the presence of the behaviour, its severity and frequency on Likert scales. The questionnaire was adapted for this study to include these Likert scales for aggression and destruction of property as these are only included for self-injury on the original measure. A high score on this measure indicates more severe behaviour. The questionnaire has demonstrated good inter-rater reliability (coefficients range from .61–.89).

Client Service Receipt Inventory (Beecham & Knapp, 1992; Strydom et al., 2010)

The CSRI collects comprehensive data on a range of services and demographics including place of residence, accommodation costs, household income and service receipt for health and social care. The CSRI was developed in England; however, it has been adapted into multiple forms and used across the world. The measure was adapted and abbreviated for this study to include only community-based services and services most applicable to adults with ID. Parents were asked whether their child had received input from a list of professionals and were asked to indicate the number of appointments they had with that professional, and the average length of appointments over the last six months. An additional checklist was added to the CSRI for this study to record the types of interventions/input received by professionals for challenging behaviour. Additional items were also added to the measure to gather information on additional support and service experience; however, these were not analysed as part of this study.

Data analysis

Data obtained using the CSRI were analysed first using descriptive statistics. Tests of normality were carried out, which revealed that the scales were not normally distributed; therefore, Spearman's rank correlations were carried out to explore the association between service receipt for challenging behaviour and individual characteristics (degree of challenging behaviour, impulsivity/overactivity, ASD characteristics and self-help score). In addition, Mann–Whitney *U* tests were used to explore differences between ambulant and nonambulant, and verbal and non-verbal participants in the amount of time spent with professionals for challenging behaviour support.

CBQ Composite score

A total score for challenging behaviour based on the CBQ was created by combining the self-injury, aggression and destruction of property scores. This was created for each participant, as the aim was to explore the factors that predict access to services for challenging behaviour including the degree of challenging behaviour displayed by the individual with an ID. Participants who had reported that their child had not engaged in any form of challenging behaviour in the previous month ($N = 2$) were assigned a score of 0 for severity, frequency and duration questions. The raw scores were converted into *z*-scores and an average taken to create a composite score for challenging behaviour (CB Composite). Composite scores were also created for self-injury, aggression and destruction of property.

Professionals groups

The professionals that were included in the abbreviated version of the CSRI are displayed in Table 1. To summarise these data, the professionals were divided into four subgroups following consultation with three clinical psychologists and examination of the NICE (May, 2015) guidelines. The subgroups were: (1) key professionals, who are most likely to have received training in behavioural management; (2) Multi-Disciplinary Team (MDT) professionals, who are most likely to work as part of a team with key professionals and may also support behavioural interventions; (3) wider health professionals; (4) other therapists/support; and (5) hospital-based services (any). See Table 1 for the list of professionals that fell into each of the first four categories. By grouping the professionals, it was possible to explore the type of professionals that the participants had accessed overall for any health issue and specifically for challenging behaviour.

Table 1. List of grouped professionals.

Key professionals	MDT professionals	Wider health professionals	Other therapists/ support
Psychiatrist Psychologist Learning disability nurse Behavioural support team member (general)	Speech and language therapist Physiotherapist Occupational therapist Social worker Paediatrician Nurse (other)	General practitioner Podiatrist Audiologist Optician Dentist Nutritionist/ dietician	Advocate/ counsellor Alternative therapist Art/drama/ music therapist

Table 2. Number of contacts and duration of time spent with each professional group for other health reasons and challenging behaviour (CB) specifically.

Professional group	Contact with professional group: Direct contact with professional group for any reason N (%)	Contact included CB support N (%)	Number of hours with professional group (last six months): Hours with professional per participant not for CB support, when in contact with professional median (IQR)	Hours with professional for CB support, when CB support was received median (IQR)
Key professionals	N = 14 43.75%	N = 9 64.29%	0.75 (7.00)	4.00 (8.00)
MDT professionals	N = 25 78.13%	N = 14 56%	1.5 (4.13)	3.5 (5.69)
Wider health professionals	N = 31 96.88%	N = 4 12.90%	1.33 (2.67)	0.25 (0.48)
Other therapists/ advocates	N = 5 15.63%	N = 0 0%	6.00 (20.08)	0 –
Hospital-based services	N = 13 40.63%	N = 0 0%	1.5 (5.00)	0 –

Results

The first aim of the study was to document services accessed. The number of participants accessing each professional group, and the medians and interquartile ranges (IQR) for hours with each professional group for challenging behaviour support, and other health reasons, are displayed in Table 2. Table 3 shows the descriptive statistics for the type of professional input received for challenging behaviour.

Table 2 shows that 43.75% of the participants accessed the key professionals overall; 64.29% of those participants accessed the key professionals specifically for challenging behaviour. 78.13% of the participants accessed the MDT professionals for any reason and 56% of those participants accessed the MDT professionals specifically for challenging behaviour. 96.88% of participants accessed the wider health professionals and only 12.90% of those participants saw the wider health professionals for challenging behaviour.

Table 3 shows that over half of the participants who reported displaying challenging behaviour had no contact with any professional for help with challenging behaviour in the last six months. None of the participants had received a professional observation of their child's behaviour. Two participants reported their child had received one-to-one therapy and one participant received a written intervention program for challenging behaviour.

Table 3. Descriptive statistics for the type of professional input accessed for challenging behaviour (CB) in last six months.

	Professional conducted observations of CB	Written intervention program for CB	One-to-one therapy for CB	No contact with any professional for CB
N	0	1	2	17
(%)	0	3.13	6.25	53.13

Note. Percentages calculated based on total sample (*N* = 32).

Individual characteristics and service receipt

The second aim of the study was an analysis of the associations between individual characteristics (degree of challenging behaviour, ASD characteristics, impulsivity/overactivity and adaptive behaviour) and service access for challenging behaviour. Descriptive statistics are displayed in Table 4. Associations between challenging behaviour, individual characteristics and hours spent with key and MDT professionals for challenging behaviour are displayed in Table 5.

No associations were found between the degree of challenging behaviour (CB Composite) and hours spent with the professional groups for challenging behaviour in the last six months. This analysis was repeated with the challenging behaviour subscales (self-

Table 4. Descriptive statistics for person characteristics.

Measure	N	Max score	Median	IRQ
CB Composite	32	5	1.78	1.25
Wessex self-help score	32	9	6	2.75
SCQ score	31	39	18	7.00
TAQ score	32	72	39.5	28.35

Note. CB Composite score is displayed without the z-score transformation applied to the subscales, to aid interpretation.

Table 5. Relationship between individual characteristics and hours spent with professionals for challenging behaviour in last six months.

	2.	3.	4.	5.	6.
1. CB Composite	.26	.36*.	−.49**	.17	.25
2. SCQ score		.12	−.22	.08	−.09
3. TAQ score			−.15	−.02	.41*
4. Wessex self-help score				−.33	−.37*
5. Hours with key professionals for CB					.41*
6. Hours with MDT professionals for CB					–

Note. Correlations were not conducted for wider health professionals as these data were heavily skewed due to only a small number of participants being in contact with these services for CB.
$N = 32$
$^{**}p < .01$, $^{*}p < .05$

injury, aggression and destruction of property) and these findings remained consistent.

A higher TAQ score was associated with increased length of time accessing MDT professionals for challenging behaviour. Higher levels of adaptive ability (self-help score) were associated with less time accessing the MDT professionals for challenging behaviour. No significant associations were identified between ASD characteristics and accessing services. Mann–Whitney *U* tests revealed no significant differences between ambulant and nonambulant participants and time spent with the professional groups; nor were any significant differences found for verbal and non-verbal participants (all $ps > .05$).

Discussion

There were two aims of this study; firstly, to document service receipt in adults with a rare genetic syndrome who also display challenging behaviour and live within the family home, and secondly to examine the relationship between individual characteristics and service receipt. We looked specifically at the degree of challenging behaviour, autism characteristics, adaptive ability, mobility and verbal ability, and their relationship with accessing services for challenging behaviour. It was predicted that a higher challenging behaviour score would be associated with access to the main professionals involved with helping to assess and intervene with challenging behaviours (key professionals). It was also predicted that individual characteristics would be associated with service receipt.

Thirty participants reported that their child had displayed challenging behaviour in the previous month; however, less than half of those participants received support from the professionals who are involved with intervening with challenging behaviour. Over three-quarters of the participants saw the MDT professionals; however, approximately half of these participants saw the MDT professionals for reasons other than challenging behaviour. MDT professionals (e.g., speech and language therapist, occupational therapist) work alongside key professionals to help alleviate challenging behaviour or can signpost families to an appropriate professional for intervention, so the number of individuals accessing key professionals for challenging behaviour support appears low given the contact with MDT professionals.

There may be a number of reasons why families did not access support for challenging behaviour including problems in accessing services, such as difficulties in obtaining a referral and long waiting lists to see the appropriate professionals. It is also possible that these individuals accessed services for help with challenging behaviour before the six-month time frame that was examined in this study but found them unhelpful and/or ineffective. The present study focused on documenting the services that these individuals accessed within the previous six months; we cannot ascertain whether these participants accessed any services for challenging behaviour historically. Future research should explore whether individuals with rare genetic syndromes are having difficulties in accessing the services in the first place, or whether they have disengaged due to ineffective and/or unhelpful interventions.

Of the participants who reported displaying challenging behaviour, two participants had received one-to-one therapy for challenging behaviour and only one participant received a written intervention program. No participant reported that a professional had observed the behaviour of the person with ID in the last six months, which appears low given that NICE guidelines indicate that an observation should be considered as part of a thorough assessment of behaviour (NICE, May, 2015).

The second aim of the study was to examine the relationship between individual characteristics and service receipt for challenging behaviour. No association was found between the challenging behaviour score and hours spent with key or MDT professionals. Similarly, the challenging behaviour subscale scores (self-injury, aggression and destruction of property) were also not associated with hours spent with key or MDT professionals. As highlighted previously, difficulties in accessing services or becoming disengaged from services might explain this finding. An alternative explanation is that there may be a poor link between individual needs and service provision. We would expect that individuals with severe and frequent challenging behaviour would require more professional support for dealing with challenging behaviour than those with less severe and infrequent challenging behaviour; however, our findings show no link between degree of challenging behaviour and accessing services. Knapp et al. (2005) found that a higher degree of challenging behaviour increased the probability of accessing the main professionals involved in dealing with such behaviours; however, the living arrangements of the individuals involved in their study also influenced service access. Individuals with ID living in NHS settings were more likely to use NHS day services compared to individuals living in the private/voluntary sector. Knapp et al. suggested that this might be due to services being more easily accessed by individuals living within the same trust. The individuals included in the present study were adults that live within the family home; therefore, the referral process and waiting times may differ for these individuals and they may have become cut-off from professional services over time.

The results also suggest that impulsivity and overactivity may be positively associated with the time spent accessing the MDT professionals for challenging behaviour. Prevalence studies and research examining the risk markers of challenging behaviour in individuals with ID of heterogeneous aetiology and rare genetic syndromes have found that impulsivity is significantly associated with challenging behaviour. It has been suggested that impulsivity is an important factor in the persistence of challenging behaviour in this population (Arron et al., 2011; Oliver & Richards, 2015; Sloneem, Oliver, Udwin, & Woodcock, 2011). Although the present study did not identify any link between the degree of challenging behaviour and service receipt, the findings suggest that impulsivity may represent a particular difficulty for families and may elicit more support from professionals. However, given the possibility of making a type-I error due to multiple tests, these results should be considered preliminary.

A high level of adaptive ability (self-help) was negatively associated with the length of time spent accessing MDT professionals for challenging behaviour. This indicates that individuals with genetic syndromes who have a higher adaptive ability are significantly less likely to access support from MDT professionals for challenging behaviour. Research has identified an association between low adaptive ability and increased challenging behaviour in individuals with ID (Cooper, Smiley, Jackson et al., 2009; Felce & Kerr, 2013). This aligns with our finding that higher levels of adaptive ability decreases the likelihood of seeing the MDT professionals for challenging behaviour and this might be a predictor for service access.

It is important to note the limitations of this study. The sample size was small, and although the study has provided an insight into the services accessed by individuals with genetic syndromes who still live at home, the results cannot be generalised to individuals with genetic syndromes living in other settings. The use of a correlation design also increases the likelihood of a type-I error. Therefore, we must interpret the results with caution. It is also important to note that there may have been a sampling bias, as the individuals who expressed an interest in taking part in this study may be individuals who have received the least support or have had difficulty in accessing services. Finally, individuals with a range of genetic syndromes were included and it may be that there would be differences between the diagnostic groups; however, larger sample sizes would be needed to explore this possibility.

Overall, the results draw attention to the proportion of individuals diagnosed with a rare genetic syndrome and display challenging behaviour who are not receiving any evidence-based professional help for challenging behaviour. The lack of professional support for dealing with challenging behaviour sheds some light on why these behaviours may persist over time. Future research should focus on exploring the factors that influence service receipt including further examination of the role individual characteristics play in service receipt for challenging behaviour. Finally, research examining service experience for adults for ID may also explain the lack of service access for challenging behaviour in this population.

Acknowledgements

We would like to thank Chris Stinton and Jo Moss for help with the collection of data on individual characteristics. Thank you to Hayley Crawford for help with data presentation.

Disclosure statement

No potential conflict of interest was reported by the authors.

Funding

This work was supported by Cerebra.

ORCID

J. Waite http://orcid.org/0000-0002-8676-3070

References

Arron, K., Oliver, C., Moss, J., Berg, K., & Burbidge, C. (2011). The prevalence and phenomenology of self-injurious and aggressive behaviour in genetic syndromes. *Journal of Intellectual Disability Research*, *55*, 109–120.

Beange, H. (1996). Caring for a vulnerable population. *Medical Journal of Australia*, *164*, 159–160.

Beange, H., & Bauman, A. (1990). Caring for the developmentally disabled in the community. *Australian Family Physician*, *19*, 1558–1563.

Beecham, J., & Knapp, M. (1992). Costing psychiatric interventions. In G. Thornicroft, C. Brewin, & J. Wing (Eds.), *Measuring mental health needs* (pp. 179–190). London: Gaskell.

Berument, S. K., Rutter, M., Lord, C., Pickles, A., & Bailey, A. (1999). Autism screening questionnaire: Diagnostic validity. *The British Journal of Psychiatry*, *175*(5), 444–451.

Burbidge, C., & Oliver, C. (2008). *Activity questionnaire: Manual for administration and scorer interpretation*. Birmingham: University of Birmingham.

Carr, E. G., & Durand, V. M. (1985). Reducing behaviour problems through functional communication training. *Journal of Applied Behaviour Analysis*, *18*, 111–126.

Collacott, R. A., Cooper, S. A., Branford, D., & McGrother, C. (1998). Epidemiology of self-injurious behaviour in adults with learning disabilities. *The British Journal of Psychiatry, 173*, 428–432.

Cooper, S. A., Smiley, E., Allan, L., Jackson, A., Finlayson, J., Mantry, D., & Morrison, J. (2009). Adults with intellectual disabilities: Prevalence, incidence and remission of self-injurious behaviour and related factors. *Journal of Intellectual Disability Research, 53*, 200–216.

Cooper, S. A., Smiley, E., Jackson, A., Finlayson, J., Allan, L., Mantry, D., & Morrison, J. (2009). Adults with intellectual disabilities: Prevalence, incidence and remission of aggressive behaviour and related factors. *Journal of Intellectual Disability Research, 53*, 217–232.

Cumella, S., Corbett, J., Clark, D., & Smith, B. (1992). Primary health care for people with a learning disability. *Journal of the British Institute of Mental Handicap (APEX), 20*, 123–125.

Department of Health. (2001). *Valuing People: A new strategy for learning disability for the 21st century a white paper*. London: Author.

Emerson, E., Kiernan, C., Alborz, A., Reeves, D., Mason, H., Swarbrick, R., Mason, L., & Hatton, C. (2001a). The prevalence of challenging behaviors: A total population study. *Research in Developmental Disabilities*, 22(1), 77–93.

Emerson, E., Kiernan, C., Alborz, A., Reeves, D., Mason, H., Swarbrick, R., Mason, L., & Hatton, C. (2001b). Predicting the persistence of severe self-injurious behaviour. *Research in Developmental Disabilities, 22*, 67–75.

Emerson, E., Robertson, J., Fowler, S., Letchford, S., & Jones, M. (1996). The longterm effects of behavioural residential special education on children with challenging behaviours: Changes in behaviour and skills. *Journal of Applied Research in Intellectual Disabilities, 9*, 240–255.

Eyman, R. K., & Call, T. (1977). Maladaptive behaviour and community placement of mentally retarded persons. *American Journal of Mental Deficiency, 82*, 137–144.

Felce, D., & Kerr, M. (2013). Investigating low adaptive behaviour and presence of the triad of impairments characteristic of autistic spectrum disorder as indicators of risk for challenging behaviour among adults with intellectual disabilities. *Journal of Intellectual Disability Research, 57*(2), 128–138.

Hastings, R. P. (2002). Parental stress and behaviour problems of children with developmental disability. *Journal of Intellectual and Developmental Disability, 27*, 149–160.

Howells, G. (1986). Are the medical needs of mentally handicapped adults being met? *Journal of the Royal College of General Practitioners, 36*, 449–453.

Hurl, K., Wightman, J., Virues-Ortega, J., & Haynes, S. N. (2016). Does a preintervention functional assessment increase intervention effectiveness? A meta-analysis of within-subject interrupted time-series studies. *Clinical Psychology Review, 47*, 71–84.

Hyman, P., Oliver, C., & Hall, S. (2002). Self-injurious behavior, self-restraint, and compulsive behaviors in cornelia de lange syndrome. *Journal Information, 107*(2), 146–154.

Iwata, B. A., Pace, G. M., Dorsey, M. F., Zarcone, J. R., Vollmer, T. R., Smith, R. G., … Willis, K. D. (1994). The functions of self-injurious behaviour: An experimental-epidemiological analysis. *Journal of Applied Behaviour Analysis, 27*, 215–240.

Kiernan, C., & Alborz, A. (1996). Persistence and change in challenging and problem behaviours of young adults with intellectual disability living in the family home. *Journal of Applied Research in Intellectual Disabilities, 9*, 181–193.

Knapp, M., Commas-Herrera, A., Astin, J., Beecham, J., & Pendaries, C. (2005). Intellectual. disability and cost in care accommodation: What are the links? *Health and Social Care in the Community, 13*, 297–306.

Kushlick, A., Blunden, R., & Cox, G. (1973). A method of rating behaviour characteristics for use in large scale surveys of mental handicap. *Psychological Medicine, 3*(4), 466–478.

Lennox, N. G., Diggens, J. N., & Ugoni, A. M. (1997). The general practice care of people with intellectual disability: Barriers and solutions. *Journal of Intellectual Disability Research, 41*, 380–390.

Lennox, N. G., & Kerr, M. P. (1997). Primary health care and people with an intellectual disability: The evidence base. *Journal of Intellectual Disability Research, 41*, 365–372.

McClintock, K., Hall, S., & Oliver, C. (2003). Risk markers associated with challenging behaviours in people with intellectual disabilities: A meta-analytic study. *Journal of Intellectual Disability Research, 47*, 405–416.

McGill, P., Papachristofou, E., & Cooper, V. (2006). Support for family carers of children and young people with developmental disabilities and challenging behaviour. *Child: Care, Health and Development, 20*, 37–46.

National Institute for Health and Care Excellence (2015, May). *Challenging behaviour and learning disabilities: Prevention and interventions for people with learning disabilities whose behaviour challenges.*

Oliver, C. (1995). Annotation: Self-injurious behaviour in children with learning disabilities: Recent advances in assessment and intervention. *Journal of Child Psychology and Psychiatry, 36*, 909–927.

Oliver, C., Berg, K., Burbidge, C., & Arron, K. (2009). Self-injurious behaviour in Cornelia de Lange syndrome: I. Prevalence and phenomenology. *Journal of Intellectual Disability Research, 53*, 575–589.

Oliver, C., & Richards, C. (2015). Practitioner review: Self-injurious behaviour in children with developmental delay. *Journal of Child Psychology and Psychiatry, 56*(10), 1042–1054.

Petty, J., & Oliver, C. (2005). Self-injurious behaviour in individuals with intellectual disabilities. *Current Opinion in Psychiatry, 18*(5), 484–489.

Richards, C., Oliver, C., Nelson, L., & Moss, J. (2012). Self-injurious behaviour in individuals with autism spectrum disorder and intellectual disability. *Journal of Intellectual Disability Research, 56*(5), 476–489.

Rojahn, J., Mateson, J. L., Naglieri, J. A., & Mayville, E. (2004). Relationships between psychiatric conditions and behavior problems among adults with mental retardation. *American Journal of Mental Retardation, 109*(1), 21–33.

Ruddick, L., Davies, L., Bacarese-Hamilton, M., & Oliver, C. (2015). Self-injurious, aggressive and destructive behaviour in children with severe intellectual disability: Prevalence, service need and service receipt in the UK. *Research in Developmental Disabilities, 45*, 307–315.

Rutter, M., Bailey, A., & Lord, C. (2003). *Social communication questionnaire (SCQ)*. Los Angeles, CA: Western Psychological Services.

Saloviita, T. (2000). The structure and correlates of self-injurious behaviour in an institutional setting. *Research in Developmental Disabilities*, *21*, 501–511.

Schneider, M. J., Bijam-Schulte, A. M., Janssen, C. G. C., & Stolke, J. (1996). The origin of self-injurious behaviour of children with mental retardation. *The British Journal of Development Disabilities*, *42*, 136–148.

Sloneem, J., Oliver, C., Udwin, O., & Woodcock, J. A. (2011). Prevalence, phenomenology, aetiology and predictors of challenging behaviour in Smith–Magenis syndrome. *Journal of Intellectual Disability Research*, 55, 138–151.

Strydom, A., Romeo, R., Perez-Achiago, N., Livingston, G., King, M., Knapp, M., & Hassiotis, A. (2010). Service use and cost of mental disorder in older adults with intellectual disability. *British Journal of Psychiatry*, *196*(2), 133–138.

Totsika, V., Toogood, S., Hastings, R. P., & Lewis, S. (2008). Persistence of challenging behaviours in adults with an intellectual disability over a period of 11 years. *Journal of Intellectual Disability Research*, *52*, 446–457.

Wodehouse, G., & McGill, P. (2009). Support for family carers of children and young people with developmental disabilities and challenging behaviour: What stops it being useful? *Journal of Intellectual Disability Research*, *53*, 644–653.

What constitutes effective support in obtaining and maintaining employment for individuals with intellectual disability? A scoping review

Cindy Cheng, Jodi Oakman, Christine Bigby, Ellie Fossey, Jillian Cavanagh, Hannah Meacham and Timothy Bartram

ABSTRACT

Background: Employment rates for Australians with an intellectual disability remain low. Effective evidence-based strategies are required to guide future interventions, to enable people with intellectual disability achieve better employment outcomes.

Methods: A literature search of peer-reviewed articles published between 2001 and 2015 was conducted using four electronic databases. Articles were reviewed and sorted according to employment setting and type of support provided.

Results: Twenty-two studies were identified. Four studies of open employment examined workplace level strategies and 17 investigated individual level strategies. A single study of supported employment examined individual level change. Results suggested potential strategies that can be utilised to support people with intellectual disability obtain and maintain employment.

Conclusions: Existing evidence regarding open employment for people with intellectual disabilities could be enhanced through the conduct of rigorous outcomes-focused studies that attend to specific strategies at both individual and organisation levels.

Employment facilitates skill development, and has a range of social and psychological benefits (Ellenkamp, Brouwers, Embregts, Joosen, & van Weeghel, 2016; Sharma, Singh, & Kutty, 2006; Stephens, Collins, & Dodder, 2005). Adults with intellectual disability value paid employment (Ellenkamp et al., 2016; Ferrari, Nota, & Soresi, 2008; Lysaght, Ouellette-Kuntz, & Morrison, 2009), but are more likely to be unemployed and work fewer hours compared to those with other disabilities (Australian Bureau of Statistics, 2012). The labour force participation rate for Australians with intellectual disability is very low: 34.9% of adults with mild to moderate intellectual disability in 2012 compared to 52.8% for all people with disability (2012). The proportion of adults with an intellectual disability employed in the mainstream labour force has not increased since 1995 (Inclusion Australia, 2015; Tuckerman, Cain, Long, & Klarkowski, 2012). The National Council on Intellectual Disability (NCID, 2013) has argued that employment support services need to be informed by evidence about effective strategies if they are to successfully achieve their aims of increasing employment of people with intellectual disabilities.

This scoping review investigates the effectiveness of strategies used by employment services for supporting people with intellectual disability to obtain and maintain employment. To situate this review in disability employment policy, a brief overview of the development of employment supports for people with intellectual disability in Australia is provided, although notably these policies do not necessarily differentiate between people with disabilities and people with intellectual disabilities.

Organised employment support for people with intellectual disability emerged in the 1950s when families established sheltered workshops that were subsequently funded by the Australian government in 1967 (McDermott, Edwards, Abello, & Katz, 2010; Tuckerman, 2002). In the 1970s, the federal government established work preparation centres to provide vocational training for school leavers with intellectual disability (Parmenter, 1999a; Tuckerman et al., 2012). State and federally funded activity therapy centres were also established to address the developmental needs of people with disability for whom participation in sheltered workshops was deemed unlikely (Cocks & Stehlik, 1996). With the growing influence of human rights and normalisation principles during the 1970s and 1980s, the unchallenging work in sheltered workshops, low wages, poor-working conditions, and lack of reliable pathways into paid work in the regular labour market were key concerns, as were issues of rights and choice (Ellenkamp et al., 2016; Parmenter, 1999b; Tuckerman et al., 2012). During this period, evidence of the advantages of integrated employment, including financial and social benefits, as well as employee preference for work in integrated settings, also began to emerge (Jenaro, Mank, Bottomley, Doose, & Tuckerman, 2002; Nord, Lueking, Mank, Kieman, & Wray, 2013). These factors have informed legislative efforts and policy to reform employment support for people with intellectual disability in Australia.

The 1986 Disability Services Act (DSA) introduced two types of employment services in Australia: open employment services and supported employment services (Tuckerman et al., 2012). The term "open employment" typically defines work in the regular workforce for which workers with disability receive wages and conditions of employment commensurate with workers without disability (O'Brien & Dempsey, 2004); internationally, this may be referred to as mainstream or competitive employment (Farris & Stancliffe, 2001). Open employment services provide assistance for job seekers with disabilities to obtain and maintain their employment in the regular workforce through specialist support from outside of the employee's workplace (Anderson, Psychogios, & Golley, 2000). These services in Australia are akin to services internationally referred to as supported employment services and characterised by a "place-and-train" approach with the goal of a real job for regular wages in an integrated setting alongside employees without disability (Brotherton, Stancliffe, Wilson, & O'Loughlin, 2016; Jenaro et al., 2002; Tuckerman et al., 2012). In comparison, "supported employment services" which were recently re-named as Australian Disability Enterprises (ADEs) are characterised by work in settings often formerly described as sheltered workshops, enclaves or work crews; and are usually offered to people who require substantial ongoing support to participate in work (O'Brien & Dempsey, 2004; Tuckerman et al., 2012). Operating as commercial businesses, ADEs attempt to offer employment for people with disability who face barriers to working in the open labour market (McDermott et al., 2010).

The intent of the DSA was to both promote employment options that embraced integration and aligned with the needs and aspirations of people with disability; to transition sheltered workshops to business models of employment more consistent with these goals, and to provide increased levels of on-site support for those with higher support needs (Tuckerman et al., 2012; Wehman, 2012). Subsequent government policy and funding initiatives have been introduced to reinforce the principles enshrined in the DSA. For instance, the 1991 Disability Reform Package (DRP) encouraged work participation by enabling disability support pension recipients to supplement their incomes from part-time work with a partial pension (Dempsey & Ford, 2009); the Disability Discrimination Act (Commonwealth of Australia, 1992) addressed discrimination on grounds of disability; and a supported wages system established in 1994 allowed employers to pay a pro-rata wage to workers unable to work at full productivity, based on an independently assessed productivity rate (Parliament of Australia, 2013; Tuckerman et al., 2012). Furthermore, employment services reforms have included the introduction of a case-based funding model linking the funding of individual needs and outcomes; a quality assurance framework to ensure all government-funded employment services comply with the national standards; and wage determination for supported employees using wage assessment mechanisms based on productivity and competency (Dempsey & Ford, 2009; Tuckerman et al., 2012). More recently, Australia endorsed the Convention on the Rights of Persons with Disabilities (United Nations, 2008), which includes commitments to recognising and protecting the rights of persons with disabilities to work, and to freely chosen, just and favourable working conditions on an equal basis with others.

Notwithstanding considerable progress towards improving employment opportunities and work conditions, national statistics from 1995 to 2010 indicate that the number of adults with intellectual disability participating in open employment services had not increased; and proportionally more adults with intellectual disability work in supported settings (ADEs) than in open employment (Tuckerman et al., 2012). Importantly, average gross weekly earnings of employees with intellectual disability in ADEs are less than one-third of those assisted by open employment services, and pose a significant challenge as to the type of actions required to enhance open employment for adults with intellectual disability (2012). Internationally too, this is a recognised challenge, as is the need to identify specific employment support practices that can improve employment outcomes and career opportunities for people with intellectual disability who can, want to and have a right to work (Nord et al., 2013).

In Australia, the introduction of a National Disability Insurance Scheme has created a new means of providing individualised disability support as it attempts to maximise the economic, education and social participation of Australians with disability (Dowse et al., 2016; Fawcett

& Plath, 2014). In a contemporaneous review of work environment-related factors that contribute to competitive employment for people with intellectual disability, Ellenkamp et al. (2016) identified few studies of relevance and quality over the past 20 years, but concluded employer decisions, job content, workplace culture, and job coaches could influence their work participation. To advance tangible improvements in employment for people with intellectual disability, this scoping review aimed to identify specific strategies used to support adults with intellectual disability to obtain and maintain employment, and their effectiveness in open and supported employment settings.

Method

A scoping review is an initial appraisal of the size and scope of research evidence in the extant literature on a particular topic (Grant & Booth, 2009). This review explores research evidence about strategies used to support people with intellectual disability to obtain and maintain work and follows the methodological framework developed by Arksey and O'Malley (2005).

Four electronic databases: CINAHL, PsycINFO, MEDLINE, and EMBASE, were searched using database-specific subject headings and related keywords, as reported in Table 1. This scoping review defines support as any type of strategy or adjustment made to enable people with intellectual disability to fulfil their work requirements and maintain work. The criteria for inclusion were: (a) peer-reviewed journal articles published in English between 2001 and 2015; (b) studies that included participants above the age of 18; and (c) studies that provided a description of intervention(s) aiming to facilitate the employment of adults with an intellectual disability and specifically reported on the effectiveness of the intervention(s). Exclusion criteria were (a) papers that described the intervention(s) but did not include data about effectiveness; (b) studies that investigated intervention(s) for individuals across a range of disabilities in which data relating to individuals with intellectual disability was inseparable; (c) studies that examined transition from school to work; and (d) opinion papers and reports.

The initial search strategy, outlined in Figure 1 below, returned 10,369 publications: 1,337 from CINAHL, 2,176 from PsycINFO, 1701 from MEDLINE, and 5,155 from EMBASE. After removal of duplicates, CC reviewed 8,548 articles based on their titles. This eliminated many articles that fell outside the review criteria, which were either not relevant to the topic of employment due to broad terms like "support", "program", and "policy" not being combined with work-related terms at an early stage in the original search or did not report research. This resulted in 643 potentially relevant articles, which CC and JO independently assessed for relevance based on the titles and abstracts. Based on this review, 593 further articles were rejected as not meeting the inclusion criteria. Full text articles of the remaining 50 articles were retrieved and independently assessed for eligibility by these two authors. Twenty-eight further articles were eliminated, and were reviewed by CB who confirmed that these articles did not meet the inclusion criteria. Hand-searching was undertaken of reference lists of the 22 included articles to ensure that relevant published articles were not overlooked, none were added to the included studies. For the 22 articles selected, information relating to the purpose of each study, sample size, study design, the type of strategies employed, and the key findings were extracted by CC and checked by JO.

Different strategies used to support people with intellectual disability to obtain and maintain work in open employment and supported employment settings were identified from the included studies. These strategies focused on changes at the level of workplace or individual, and were classified as (a) natural support; (b) employment support services; and (c) instructional approaches. The extracted information presented in Table 2 is organised according to the employment setting and the level at which support was implemented.

Results

Of the 22 articles identified, 20 reported studies conducted in the USA, 1 in the UK, and 1 in Australia. Twenty-one focused on open employment where people with intellectual disability work alongside co-workers without disabilities and one on supported employment where people with intellectual disability work in segregated settings (e.g., sheltered workshop). In terms of data collection, eight studies utilised secondary data (e.g., administrative data sets), nine studies used experiment, three studies used survey, one study used focus groups and employment records, and one study used both interviews and survey. Participant groups varied in their levels of intellectual functioning: one study focused on people with mild intellectual disability, four studies focused on people with moderate intellectual disability and a further two on people with severe intellectual disability, nine studies involved participants with a range of intellectual disabilities. Many studies defined intellectual ability based on intelligence quotient scores; however, three studies did not specify level of intellectual functioning. Of these, three were studies involving employers, employment consultants or family members only.

Table 1. Search terms.

	CINAHL	PsycINFO	MEDLINE	EMBASE
Subject headings	Intellectual disability (explode) Employment of disabled (explode)	Intellectual development disorder (explode)	Intellectual disability (explode) Employment (explode) Employment, supported (explode)	Intellectual impairment (explode) Employment (explode)
Keywords	(1) Employ* or work or supported employ* (2) Intellectual* disab* or intellectual* impair* or intellectual* handicap* or mental* disab* or mental* handicap* or mental* retard* or mental* impair* or learning disab* or learning difficult* or learning disorder or development* disab* or development* impair* (3) Job accommodation* or job adjustment* or job modification* or workplace accommodation* or workplace adjustment* or workplace modification* or workplace train* or job coach* or intervention* or program* or polic* or service* or practice* or support*			

Results are presented according to whether the employment support was provided in an open employment or supported employment setting, as understood in the Australian employment context; and whether the support involved modifying the workplace or support to the individual to enable work participation.

Open employment setting, support at the workplace level

The four studies exploring support at the workplace level investigated the effectiveness of natural support which encompasses existing supports that occur naturally in a workplace, such as co-workers support. The effects of co-worker support varied across the studies. In Farris and Stancliffe's (2001) study, not only did the job placement rate in open employment increase for adults with intellectual disability following the co-worker training, but co-workers and managers also reported positive changes in their attitudes towards individuals with intellectual disability, and higher levels of social involvement with supported employees. In comparison, a single case study combining natural support and employment support services, such as job coach and communication devices, indicated that co-worker support alone may be insufficient to promote social interactions between supported employees and co-workers, without also using a job coach and communication devices (Mautz, Storey, & Certo, 2001). The least promising results were reported in Cimera's (2001) study based on secondary

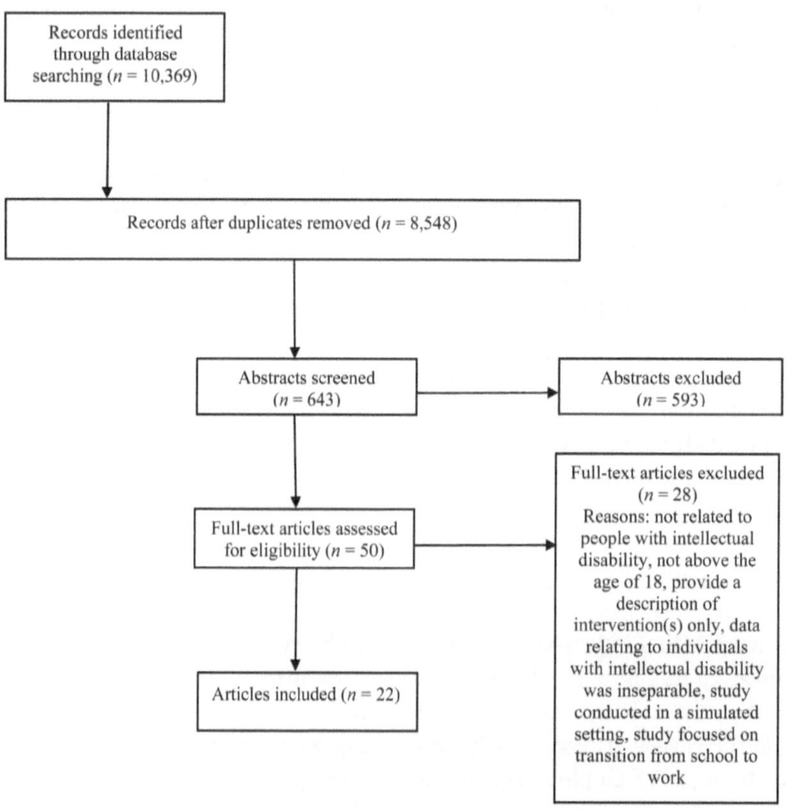

Figure 1. The search strategy.

Table 2. Summary of the included studies.

Author	Purpose of study	Participants/country of origin	Type of study/method	Key findings
Focus on open employment setting (workplace)				
Cimera (2001)	*Natural support* To investigate the impact of involving co-workers in the training of supported employees with intellectual disability	Employees with intellectual disability ($n = 111$); USA	Secondary analysis of state administrative data set	Co-worker support was not significantly associated with wages, hours worked, job retention, and mean length of employment
Farris and Stancliffe (2001)	*Natural support* To examine the effectiveness of training and supporting employees with intellectual disability by co-workers	Co-workers ($n = 12$) and managers ($n = 7$) from KFC restaurants; Australia	Pilot study; Quantitative, survey	Following participation in the co-worker training course, participants placed significantly higher value on persons with a disability in the workplace and supported employees experienced higher levels of involvement with co-workers
Kaehne and Beyer (2013)	*Natural support* To examine the use of co-worker support to deliver supported employment	Families of individuals with intellectual disability ($n = 5$) and employers ($n = 4$); UK	Mixed methods, interviews, and survey	The effectiveness of co-worker support could not be ascertained as many of the advantages reported were generic in nature and specific benefits were not identified
Mautz et al. (2001)	*Natural support and employment support services* To investigate the effectiveness of job modification, natural support, communication devices, job coaches, and co-workers support for social integration in a supported employment environment	Individual with intellectual disability ($n = 1$); USA	Experimental design, multiple baseline design; Qualitative, direct observation	Communication devices, job coach, and co-workers support increased the social interactions of the participant
Focus on open employment setting (individual)				
Moore (2001)	*Employment support services* To compare employment outcomes of African-Americans with Caucasians with intellectual disability	Individuals with mild or moderate intellectual disability who were successfully placed into employment by a state disability employment agency during fiscal year 1997 ($n = 40{,}046$); USA	Ex-post-facto design, secondary analysis of national administrative data set	Participants who received business and vocational training, on-the-job training, job placement, transport services, or maintenance services had a higher chance of being placed into employment
Parsons et al. (2001)	*Employment support services* To examine the effectiveness of an off-site/on-site program to reduce job coach assistance	Individuals with severe intellectual disability and other disabilities ($n = 3$) and job coaches ($n = 2$); USA	Experimental design, a multiple probe design across participants	Job coach support decreased for both onsite and off-site programs in all cases. Work productivity increased for two out of three participants
Moore, Feist-Price, and Alston (2002a)	*Employment support services* To explore the relationship between consumer and service variables and the rehabilitation outcomes	African-American and Caucasian consumers with mild or moderate intellectual disability who were successfully placed into employment by a state disability employment agency during fiscal year 1997 ($n = 253$); USA	Ex-post-facto design, secondary analysis of national administrative data set	When provided with job placement, participants with mild or moderate intellectual disability had a slightly greater chance of obtaining open jobs than participants who were not provided with such service. The provision of services such as transportation and adjustment training were related to the achievement of jobs outside of open employment
Moore et al. (2002b)	*Employment support services* To explore the relationship between race, disability employment services, and the rehabilitation outcomes of persons with severe/profound intellectual disability	African-American and European American consumers with severe or profound intellectual disability who were successfully placed into employment by disability employment agencies ($n = 87$); USA	Same as above	For participants with severe or profound intellectual disability, job placement services seem to contribute significantly to the maintenance of employment
Menchetti and Garcia (2003)	*Employment support services* To investigate the effects of person-centred planning on career choice and employment outcomes	Individuals with intellectual disability ($n = 83$) Employment consultants or job coaches ($n = 6$); USA	Qualitative, focus group and employment records	Eighty-seven percent of participants found employment with a high match to their expectations
Moore et al. (2004)	*Employment support services* To examine disparities in the proportions of open job placements between consumers with mild, moderate, and severe/profound intellectual disability	All consumers with mild, moderate, and severe/profound intellectual disability ($n = 28{,}565$) who were placed into employment by the disability employment system (nationally) during fiscal year 1998; USA	Ex-post-facto design, secondary analysis of national administrative data set	The provision of business training and vocational services resulted in the achievement of open jobs at a significantly higher rate for participants with mild intellectual disability than participants with moderate and severe/profound intellectual disability

(*Continued*)

Table 2. Continued.

Author	Purpose of study	Participants/country of origin	Type of study/method	Key findings
West et al. (2005)	*Employment support services* To examine the effectiveness of the Best Buddies Jobs Program in enhancing social and employment opportunities	Individuals with intellectual disability (*n* = 108) and employers (*n* = 113); USA	Quantitative, survey	Project participants received wages that were 30% to 50% higher than the national wage level for individuals in supported employment in the USA. Hours per week surpassed the national average by about 15%. Job retention was relatively high. Positive feedback from Employers about the program outcomes
Howarth et al. (2006)	*Employment support services* To investigate predictors of successful re-employment following employment discontinuity	Individuals with intellectual disability who received employment services between 2001 and 2003 (*n* = 19,555); USA	Quantitative, survey	Job coaching was associated with re-employment
McInnes et al. (2010)	*Employment support services* To examine the effects of job coaching in promoting stable employment in community settings	Clients from 38 disability boards between years 1999 and 2005 with intellectual disability (*n* = 57,979); USA	Secondary analysis of state administrative data set	Following job coaching, participants are three times more likely to be employed and 1.5 times more likely to be in high-wage jobs than those not coached
Butterworth et al. (2012)	*Employment support services* To examine the effectiveness of a training intervention for employment consultants who assist job seekers with intellectual disability	Employment consultants (*n* = 33); USA	Experimental design, intervention, and control group. Baseline and follow-up surveys	Following training, employment consultants placed 2.3 more job seekers compared to baseline, whereas those in the control group placed 1.1 fewer job seekers than their baseline
Nazarov, Golden, and von Schrader (2012)	*Employment support services* To examine the impact of prevocational services on hourly wages	Consumers participating in supported employment programs (*n* = 20,440), 32.64% intellectual and development disabilities and 14.96% with a learning disability; USA	Secondary analysis of state administrative data set	Participants with prevocational services received wages 7.6% lower than those with no service. Participants with intellectual disability received a 5% reduction in wages following the provision of prevocational services
Austin and Lee (2014)	*Employment support services* Employment outcomes of individuals with intellectual disability and co-occurring psychiatric disabilities who received support from disability employment agencies	Individuals with intellectual disability who received support from disability employment agencies (*n* = 3627); USA	Secondary analysis of national administrative data set	Job-related services (job search assist, on job support, job placement, and job readiness training) were significantly associated with employment outcomes. Personal services (diagnosis, transport, training, and maintenance) was not associated with employment outcomes
Mechling and Ortega-Hurndon (2007)	*Instructional approaches* To examine the effectiveness of video coaching on teaching job tasks	Individuals with intellectual disability (*n* = 3); USA	Experimental design, a multiple probe design across job tasks and across participants	Following video coaching, participants achieved 96.5% correct performance of steps across three job tasks at a job site
Minarovic and Bambara (2007)	*Instructional approaches* To examine the use of sight-word checklists to self-initiate job tasks	Part-time employees with intellectual disability (*n* = 3); USA	Experimental design, single subject multiple probe across participants	After using sight-word checklists, task initiations increased. Job tasks across varied job sequences were initiated only when participants were taught using varied sight-word checklists
Devlin (2008)	*Instructional approaches* To investigate the effect of the self-determined career development model on job performance	University employees with intellectual disability (*n* = 4); USA	Experimental design, multiple baseline across subjects	Following intervention, work-related performances improved. The ability to achieve work-related goals exceeded expectations of supervisors and job coaches
Bennett et al. (2010)	*Instructional approaches* To examine the effects of performance feedback through covert audio coaching	Individuals with intellectual disability enrolled in supported employment programs (*n* = 2); USA	Experimental design, multiple baseline across subjects	Following intervention, work performance across all work tasks improved and lasted several weeks
Goh and Bambara (2013)	*Instructional approaches* To investigate the effectiveness of video self-modelling in teaching job tasks in community-based employment settings	Individuals with intellectual disability receiving services from a university-affiliated supported employment program (*n* = 3); USA	Experimental design, a within participant multiple probe design across job tasks	The effectiveness of video self-modelling in teaching chained job tasks cannot be ascertained
Focus on supported employment setting (individual)				
Bucholz et al. (2008)	*Instructional approaches* To examine the effects of literacy-based behavioural interventions and social stories on work behaviour	Individuals with intellectual disability (*n* = 5); USA	Experimental design, multiple baseline across subjects, and time periods design	Requests for work and work engagement increased significantly. Intervention reduced prompt dependence and increased timely return to work

analysis of data from 111 people with intellectual disability, in which co-worker support was not related to their wages, hours worked, job retention, or mean length of employment.

Open employment setting, support at the individual level

Support at the individual level was investigated in 17 studies, with employment support services being the most common type of support offered to overcome barriers in obtaining and maintaining employment. These services included job search assistance, on-the-job supports, job placement assistance, job readiness training, diagnosis and treatment, vocational rehabilitation counselling and guidance, transportation, job maintenance support, and miscellaneous training. Alternatively, five studies examined strategies related to instructional approaches such as appropriate instructions, prompts, and feedback to allow adults with intellectual disability to perform their work effectively.

Of the studies focused on employment support services, five reported results from secondary data analyses that revealed the diverse impact of these services on employment for adults with intellectual disability. Job-related services such as job search assistance, on-the-job supports, job placement, and job readiness training were generally found to be helpful in gaining open employment (Austin & Lee, 2014). In particular, success in achieving jobs tended to be significantly higher for adults with mild intellectual disability than for adults with moderate and severe intellectual disability when business and vocational training services were provided (Moore, Harley, & Gamble, 2004). Additionally, on-the-job training, job placement, transport services, or maintenance services were found to be important for adults with mild and moderate intellectual disability to maintain open employment (Moore, 2001). For adults with severe intellectual disability, job placement services contributed significantly to the maintenance of employment (Moore, Feist-Price, & Alston, 2002b). Furthermore, when job placement was combined with training and support at the workplace and job maintenance services, the wages, hours of work per week, and job retention rate of adults with intellectual disability appeared better compared to the national average (West, Wehman, & Wehman, 2005). Moreover, results from a qualitative study suggested adults with intellectual disability achieved employment that matched their career preferences when person-centred planning was utilised to determine employment preferences and supports (Menchetti & Garcia, 2003).

The influence of employment consultants and job coaches on employment of adults with intellectual disability was examined in four studies. Based on surveying 33 employment consultants, Butterworth, Nord, Migliore, and Gelb (2012) reported that when given appropriate training and mentoring, employment consultants have a positive impact on the employment outcomes of job seekers with intellectual disability. Job coaching was found to be effective in assisting adults with intellectual disability to achieve employment and high-wage jobs (McInnes, Ozturk, McDermott, & Mann, 2010), as well as regaining employment (Howarth, Mann, Zhou, McDermott, & Butkus, 2006). Conversely, a study using an experimental design involving three individuals with severe intellectual disability and other disabilities showed that work productivity tended to increase when job coach support decreased (Parsons, Reid, Green, & Browning, 2001).

Five other small-scale experimental design studies, involving up to four participants, examined the effectiveness of individual strategies designed to assist adults with intellectual disability to complete their work tasks. Three studies focused on adults with moderate intellectual disability found that their work performance could be improved by teaching job tasks through computer-based video instruction (Mechling & Ortega-Hurndon, 2007); teaching how to set work-related goals, create action plans, solve problems, and self-regulate work behaviour (Devlin, 2008); or use varied sight-word checklists of frequently used words to prompt to self-initiate job tasks (Minarovic & Bambara, 2007). The use of audio coaching as a means to provide performance feedback was also reported to improve work performance of adults with intellectual disability in one study (Bennett, Brady, Scott, Dukes, & Frain, 2010), but no conclusive evidence was found for the effectiveness of using video self-modelling to teach chained job tasks to adults with mild intellectual disability (Goh & Bambara, 2013).

Supported employment setting, support at the individual level

Support at the individual level was examined in one study involving five adults with intellectual disability employed in a sheltered work setting. The social story intervention was used to teach social skills to participants. Results found that the work behaviour and work engagement of participants improved following the use of literacy-based behavioural interventions such as social stories (Bucholz, Brady, Duffy, Scott, & & Kontosh, 2008).

Discussion

This scoping review explored the effectiveness of strategies to assist adults with intellectual disability to gain and maintain employment in open and supported employment settings. Of 22 studies, most were undertaken in the United States, and only 1 Australian study was identified. Three major types of strategies were distinguished: natural support, employment support services, and instructional approaches. Overall, progress in demonstrating the effectiveness of these practices to support adults with intellectual disability into work has been modest in the past 15 years, despite prior research indicating the benefits of integrated employment and natural support (Jenaro et al., 2002; Nord et al., 2013). In the reviewed studies, strategies used were rarely described in detail and most studies either involved small-scale experimental designs or analysis of large administrative data sets. It is difficult to identify effective strategies to assist adults with intellectual disability to obtain and maintain employment based on the existing evidence. A key finding of this review is that the research has predominantly focused on individual level strategies to provide employment-related support rather than workplace environments. This is despite disability discrimination legislation and frameworks, such as the social model of disability, in which an individual's participation is considered a function of both individual and environmental factors (Bigby & Frawley, 2010). This finding is consistent with Ellenkamp et al.'s (2016) recent systematic review, which similarly concluded that little research in the past 20 years has investigated work environment-related factors that might enhance competitive employment outcomes for people with intellectual disabilities.

A workplace level strategy that shows promise is the use of intrinsic natural supports, such as co-workers, to maximise social integration (Storey, 2003; Farris & Stancliffe, 2001). Given social inclusion has consistently been reported as problematic for employees with disabilities, workplace strategies designed to improve social engagement are important (Vornholt, Uitdewilligen, & Nijhuis, 2013). While varied study designs and quality mean that strong conclusions about the effectiveness of natural support in supporting adults with intellectual disability to obtain and maintain employment cannot be drawn, the present evidence suggests natural support is a potentially useful strategy to promote better employment outcomes. Therefore, the links between natural support strategies and employment-related outcomes, such as wages, working hours and job tenure, merit further investigation (Storey, 2003), for which using a tool to survey workplace accommodations and natural supports may be useful (Villotti et al., 2016). In addition, given the importance of social inclusion for people with intellectual disability to sustain employment (Vornholt et al., 2013), the current lack of evidence regarding how to achieve inclusive workplaces is an important area for further research (Lysaght, Cobigo, & Hamilton, 2012). Here, social businesses may have the potential to create inclusive employment with competitive wages, better working conditions and levels of support for people with intellectual disability, and more research regarding best practices in this sector should be encouraged.

Employment services were also identified as potentially important influences on employment for adults with intellectual disability. Some evidence suggests that when employment consultants possess relevant skills and strategies to implement the appropriate career planning and assessment practices, this can positively impact employment rates and quality of jobs obtained by adults with intellectual disability (Butterworth et al., 2012). Furthermore, person-centred career planning is suggested in one study as a viable means through which people with intellectual disability can express career preferences, enabling the achievement of employment that reflects their choices (Menchetti & Garcia, 2003). Future research should investigate how person-centred career planning can best be utilised by employment consultants to enhance employment outcomes for people with intellectual disability. Likewise, job coaching warrants further research, given it can be useful to assist people with intellectual disability to obtain or regain employment following job loss (Howarth et al., 2006; McInnes et al., 2010). Indeed, in practice, person-centred career planning and job coaching may be used to guide effective exploration of individuals' job preferences for job matching and the provision of follow-along coaching and support, each of which are elements of the evidence-based the individualised placement and support (IPS) approach to employment support. Surprisingly, while IPS has well-demonstrated effectiveness in enabling people with persistent mental illness to gain mainstream employment (Bond, Drake, & Becker, 2008; Kinoshita et al., 2013), no rigorous intervention studies of this approach to assist adults with intellectual disability to gain and maintain employment were identified. Such empirical evidence is important to inform employment policy directions, as well as to implement effective supports to maximise meaningful employment outcomes for individuals with intellectual disability.

Several studies noted that the collaboration between employment consultants and employers, especially human resource managers is crucial to the promotion of successful job placement and achievement of sustainable employment for people with intellectual disability

(Luecking, 2011; Migliore, Hall, Butterworth, & Winsor, 2010; O'Brien & Callahan, 2010; Post et al., 2010). Despite this, Ellenkamp et al. (2016) noted that the impact of employers' views and understanding of intellectual disability on hiring decisions and the provision of employment supports are under-explored, as are the views of employees with intellectual disabilities about what might support their success in employment.

Lastly, several instructional approaches were identified as having potential to enhance work task performance, albeit the evidence was predominantly based on small studies involving adults with moderate to severe intellectual disability. A significant issue relating to the heavy reliance on training and workplace-based skill development is that the success of these strategies is dependent on the organisation and type of work undertaken by individuals and the degree to which they can use the learned skills or behaviours (Williams & Mavin, 2012). Nevertheless, in combination with workplace modifications and job coaching, these approaches may be important to support work participation for some adults with intellectual disability and in certain work settings. Bearing this in mind, further rigorous and larger studies seem warranted.

Limitations

There are some limitations to this scoping review. First, given the majority of identified studies were conducted in the USA, its findings may have more limited applicability in countries such as Australia, where local labour market conditions, employment and disability support policy, and service provision are likely to differ. Second, the diverse nature of identified studies and the lack of controlled intervention studies in the area mean that studies were not readily comparable in terms of outcomes. Very few studies have examined the success of interventions in a manner that enables effectiveness to be evaluated. There was also a paucity of longitudinal studies making it difficult to determine the long-term effectiveness of interventions. More comparable data and rigorous empirical studies are thus required for building a knowledge base on ways to enable adults with intellectual disability to obtain and sustain employment.

Conclusion

Improving access to open employment for people with disability has been a priority in Australia for three decades following the enactment of the DSA. Despite this, many adults with intellectual disability remain in supported employment programs, and growth in open employment has been limited (Tuckerman et al., 2012). The challenge facing the Australian government, disability and employment support services is to identify and implement strategies leading to improved open employment participation for adults with intellectual disability. This scoping review identified some potential strategies that might be used to support employment for people with intellectual disability. However, it also highlighted the paucity of Australian research in the area and the limited empirical evidence to guide the development of future interventions to improve the employment outcomes of people with intellectual disability. A particular gap identified is interventions that target changes at the organisational level to enable more tailored job design, and a better fit between employees with intellectual disabilities and the needs of the organisation. More research is urgently required to identify effective mechanisms to enable adults with intellectual disability to obtain and sustain open employment and improve their integration into mainstream society.

Disclosure statement

No potential conflict of interest was reported by the authors.

ORCID

Christine Bigby http://orcid.org/0000-0001-7001-8976

References

Anderson, P., Psychogios, C., & Golley, L. (2000). *Open employment services for people with disabilities 1998–1999*. AIHW cat. No. DIS 20. Canberra: AIHW.

Arksey, H., & O'Malley, L. (2005). Scoping studies: Towards a methodological framework. *International Journal of Social Research Methodology*, *8*(1), 19–32. doi:10.1080/1364557032000119616

Austin, B. S., & Lee, C.-L. (2014). A structural equation model of vocational rehabilitation services: Predictors of employment outcomes for clients with intellectual and co-occurring psychiatric disabilities. *Journal of Rehabilitation*, *80*(3), 11–20.

Australian Bureau of Statistics (ABS). (2012). *Disability and labour force participation, 2012*. Retrieved from http://www.abs.gov.au/ausstats/abs@.nsf/mf/4433.0.55.006

Bennett, K., Brady, M. P., Scott, J., Dukes, C., & Frain, M. (2010). The effects of covert audio coaching on the job performance of supported employees. *Focus on Autism and Other Developmental Disabilities*, *25*(3), 173–185. doi:10.1177/1088357610371636

Bigby, C., & Frawley, P. (2010). *Social work practice and intellectual disability*. New York: Palgrave Macmillan.

Bond, G. R., Drake, R. E., & Becker, D. R. (2008). An update on randomized controlled trials of evidence-based supported employment. *Psychiatric Rehabilitation Journal*, *31*(4), 280–290. doi:10.2975/31.4.2008.280.290

Brotherton, M., Stancliffe, R. J., Wilson, N. J., & O'Loughlin, K. (2016). Supporting workers with intellectual disability in mainstream employment to transition to a socially inclusive retirement. *Journal of Intellectual & Developmental Disability, 41*(1), 75–80. doi:10.3109/13668250.2015.1078878

Bucholz, J. L., Brady, M. P., Duffy, M. L., Scott, J., & & Kontosh, L. G. (2008). Using literacy-based behavioural interventions and social stories to improve work behaviour in employees with developmental disabilities. *Education and Training in Developmental Disabilities, 43*(4), 486–501.

Butterworth, J., Nord, D., Migliore, A., & Gelb, A. (2012). Improving the employment outcomes of job seekers with intellectual and developmental disabilities: A training and mentoring intervention for employment consultants. *Journal of Rehabilitation, 78*(2), 20–29.

Cimera, R. E. (2001). Utilizing co-workers as "natural supports": Evidence on cost efficiency, job retention, and other employment outcomes. *Journal of Disability Policy Studies, 11*(4), 194–201. doi:10.1177/104420730101100401

Cocks, E., & Stehlik, D. (1996). History of services. In J. Annison, J. Jenkinson, W. Sparrow, & E. Bethune (Eds.), *Disability: A guide for health professionals* (pp. 8–33). Melbourne: Thomas Nelson.

Commonwealth of Australia. (1992). *Disability discrimination Act.* Canberra: Australian Government.

Dempsey, I., & Ford, J. (2009). Employment for people with intellectual disability in Australia and the United Kingdom. *Journal of Disability Policy Studies, 19*(4), 233–243.

Devlin, P. (2008). Enhancing the job performance of employees with disabilities using the self-determined career development model. *Education and Training in Developmental Disabilities, 43*(4), 502–513.

Dowse, L., Wiese, M., Dew, A., Smith, L., Collings, S., & Didi, A. (2016). More, better, or different? NDIS workforce planning for people with intellectual disability and complex support needs. *Journal of Intellectual & Developmental Disability, 41*, 81–84. doi:10.3109/13668250.2015.1125868

Ellenkamp, J. J. H., Brouwers, E. P. M., Embregts, P. J. C. M., Joosen, M. C. W., & van Weeghel, J. (2016). Work environment-related factors in obtaining and maintaining work in a competitive employment setting for employees with intellectual disability: A systematic review. *Journal of Occupational Rehabilitation, 26*, 56–69. doi:10.1007/s10926-015-9586-1

Farris, B., & Stancliffe, R. J. (2001). The co-worker training model: Outcomes of an open employment pilot project. *Journal of Intellectual and Developmental Disability, 26*(2), 143–159. doi:10.1080/13668250020054459

Fawcett, B., & Plath, D. (2014). A national disability insurance scheme: What social work has to offer. *British Journal of Social Work, 44*, 747–762. doi:10.1093/bjsw/bsc141

Ferrari, L., Nota, L., & Soresi, S. (2008). Conceptions of work in Italian adults with intellectual disability. *Journal of Career Development, 34*(4), 438–464. doi:10.1177/0894845308316295

Goh, A. E., & Bambara, L. M. (2013). Video self-modeling: A job skills intervention with individuals with intellectual disability in employment settings. *Education and Training in Autism and Developmental Disabilities, 48*(1), 103–119.

Grant, M., & Booth, A. (2009). A typology of reviews: An analysis of 14 review types and associated methodologies. *Health Information and Libraries Journal, 26*(2), 91–108. doi:10.1111/j.1471-1842.2009.00848.x

Howarth, E., Mann, J. R., Zhou, H., McDermott, S., & Butkus, S. (2006). What predicts re-employment after job loss for individuals with mental retardation? *Journal of Vocational Rehabilitation, 24*, 183–189.

Inclusion Australia. (2015). *Designing evidence based transition-to-work and open employment support for people with intellectual disability.* Retrieved from https://engage.dss.gov.au/wp-content/uploads/2015/07/A-New-Framework.pdf

Jenaro, C., Mank, D., Bottomley, J., Doose, S., & Tuckerman, P. (2002). Supported employment in the international context: An analysis of processes and outcomes. *Journal of Vocational Rehabilitation, 17*, 5–21.

Kaehne, A., & Beyer, S. (2013). Supported employment for young people with intellectual disability facilitated through peer support: A pilot study. *Journal of Intellectual Disability, 17*(3), 236–251. doi:10.1177/1744629513495265

Kinoshita, Y., Furukawa, T. A., Kinoshita, K., Honyashiki, M., Omori, I. M., Marshall, M., … Kingdon, D. (2013). Supported employment for adults with severe mental illness. *Cochrane Database of Systematic Reviews*, (9). doi:10.1002/14651858.CD008297.pub2

Luecking, R. G. (2011). Connecting employers with people who have intellectual disability. *Intellectual and Developmental Disabilities, 49*(4), 261–273. doi:10.1352/1934-9556-49.4.261

Lysaght, R., Cobigo, V., & Hamilton, K. (2012). Inclusion as a focus of employment-related research in intellectual disability from 2000 to 2010: A scoping review. *Disability and Rehabilitation, 34*(16), 1339–1350. doi:10.3109/09638288.2011.644023

Lysaght, R., Ouellette-Kuntz, H., & Morrison, C. (2009). Meaning and value of productivity to adults with intellectual disability. *Intellectual and Developmental Disabilities, 47*(6), 413–424. doi:10.1352/1934-9556-47.6.413

Mautz, D., Storey, K., & Certo, N. (2001). Increasing integrated workplace social interactions: The effects of job modification, natural supports, adaptive communication instruction, and job coach training. *Research and Practice for Persons with Severe Disabilities, 26*(4), 257–269. doi:10.2511/rpsd.26.4.257

McDermott, S., Edwards, R., Abello, D., & Katz, I. (2010). *Ageing and Australian disability enterprises.* Retrieved from https://www.dss.gov.au/sites/default/files/documents/05_2012/op27.pdf

McInnes, M. M., Ozturk, O. D., McDermott, S., & Mann, J. R. (2010). Does supported employment work? *Journal of Policy Analysis and Management, 29*(3), 506–525. doi:10.1002/pam.20507

Mechling, L. C., & Ortega-Hurndon, F. (2007). Computer-based video instruction to teach young adults with moderate intellectual disability to perform multiple step, job tasks in a generalized setting. *Education and Training in Developmental Disabilities, 42*(1), 24–37.

Menchetti, B. M., & Garcia, L. A. (2003). Personal and employment outcomes of person-centered career planning. *Education and Training in Developmental Disabilities, 38*(2), 145–156.

Migliore, A., Hall, A. C., Butterworth, J., & Winsor, J. (2010). What do employment specialists really do? A study on job development practices. *Research & Practice for Persons with Severe Disabilities*, *35*(1–2), 15–23. doi:10.2511/rpsd.35.1-2.15

Minarovic, T. J., & Bambara, L. M. (2007). Teaching employees with intellectual disability to manage changing work routines using varied sight-word checklists. *Research & Practice for Persons with Severe Disabilities*, *32*(1), 31–42. doi:10.2511/rpsd.32.1.31

Moore, C. L. (2001). Disparities in closure success rates for African Americans with mental retardation: An ex-post-facto research design. *Journal of Applied Rehabilitation Counselling*, *32*(2), 31–36.

Moore, C. L., Feist-Price, S., & Alston, R. J. (2002a). Competitive employment and mental retardation: Interplay among gender, race, secondary psychiatric disability, and rehabilitation services. *Journal of Rehabilitation*, *68* (1), 14–19.

Moore, C. L., Feist-Price, S., & Alston, R. J. (2002b). VR services for persons with severe/profound mental retardation: Does race matter? *Rehabilitation Counselling Bulletin*, *45* (3), 162–167. doi:10.1177/003435520204500305

Moore, C. L., Harley, D. A., & Gamble, D. (2004). Ex-post-facto analysis of competitive employment outcomes for individuals with mental retardation: National perspective. *Mental Retardation*, *42*(4), 253–262. doi:10.1352/0047-6765(2004)42<253:EAOCEO>2.0.CO;2

National Council on Intellectual Disability (NCID). (2013). *Proposal to minister shorten: Increasing the employment participation of Australians with intellectual disability via evidence based employer and jobseeker strategies.* Retrieved from https://submissions.employment.gov.au/empforms/Archive/Employment-Participation-of-People-with-Disability/Documents/National_Council_on_Intellectual_Disability.pdf

Nazarov, Z. E., Golden, T. P., & von Schrader, S. (2012). Prevocational services and supported employment wages. *Journal of Vocational Rehabilitation*, *37*(2), 119–129. doi:10.3233/JVR-2012-0605

Nord, D., Lueking, R., Mank, D., Kieman, W., & Wray, C. (2013). The state of the science of employment and economic self-self-sufficiency for people with intellectual and developmental disabilities. *Intellectual and Developmental Disabilities*, *51*(5), 376–384.

O'Brien, J., & Callahan, M. (2010). Employment support as knowledge creation. *Research & Practice for Persons with Severe Disabilities*, *35*(1–2), 31–38. doi:10.2511/rpsd.35.1-2.31

O'Brien, J., & Dempsey, I. (2004). Comparative analysis of employment services for people with disabilities in Australia, Finland, and Sweden. *Journal of Policy and Practice in Intellectual Disability*, *1*(3/4), 126–135. doi:10.1111/j.1741-1130.2004.04027.x

Parliament of Australia. (2013). *Background Paper 2 1995–1996 Commonwealth Disability Policy 1983–1995.* Retrieved from http://www.aph.gov.au/About_Parliament/Parliamentary_Departments/Parliamentary_Library/Publications_Archive/Background_Papers/bp9596/96bp06

Parmenter, T. R. (1999a). Effecting a system change in the delivery of employment services for people with disabilities: A view from Australia. *Journal of Vocational Rehabilitation*, *13*, 117–129.

Parmenter, T. R. (1999b). Implications of social policy for service delivery: The promise and the reality "Are we getting real?". *Journal of Intellectual & Developmental Disability*, *24*(4), 321–331. doi:10.1080/13668259900034081

Parsons, M. B., Reid, D. H., Green, C. W., & Browning, L. B. (2001). Reducing job coach assistance for supported workers with severe multiple disabilities: An alternative off-site/ on-site model. *Research in Developmental Disabilities*, *22*, 151–164. doi:10.1016/S0891-4222(01)00064-6

Post, M., Campbell, C., Heinz, T., Kotsonas, L., Montgomery, J., & Storey, K. (2010). Collaboration between supported employment and human resource services: Strategies for success. *Research & Practice for Persons with Severe Disabilities*, *35*(1–2), 24–30. doi:10.2511/rpsd.35.1-2.24

Sharma, R. N., Singh, S., & Kutty, A. T. T. (2006). Employment leads to independent living and self-advocacy: A comparative study of employed and unemployed persons with cognitive disabilities. *Asia Pacific Disability Rehabilitation Journal*, *17*, 50–60.

Stephens, D. L., Collins, M. D., & Dodder, R. A. (2005). A longitudinal study of employment and skill acquisition among individuals with developmental disabilities. *Research in Developmental Disabilities*, *26*(5), 469–486. doi:10.1016/j.ridd.2003.12.003

Storey, K. (2003). A review of research on natural support interventions in the workplace for people with disabilities. *International Journal of Rehabilitation Research*, *26*(2), 79–84.

Tuckerman, P. (2002). How successfully are people with a significant intellectual disability accessing employment? *Interaction: The Australian Magazine on Intellectual Disability*, *14*(4), 6–10.

Tuckerman, P., Cain, P., Long, B., & Klarkowski, J. (2012). An exploration of trends in open employment in Australia since 1986. *Journal of Vocational Rehabilitation*, *37*, 173–183. doi:10.3233/JVR-2012-0612

United Nations. (2008). *Convention on the Rights of Persons with Disabilities.* Retrieved from https://www.un.org/development/desa/disabilities/convention-on-the-rights-of-persons-with-disabilities/convention-on-the-rights-of-persons-with-disabilities-2.html

Villotti, P., Corbiere, M., Fossey, E., Fraccaroli, F., Lecomte, T., & Harvey, C. (2016). Work accommodations and natural supports for employees with severe mental illness in social businesses: An international comparison. *Community Mental Health Journal.* doi:10.1007/s10597-016-0068-5

Vornholt, K., Uitdewilligen, S., & Nijhuis, F. J. N. (2013). Factors affecting the acceptance of people with disabilities at work: A literature review. *Journal of Occupational Rehabilitation*, *23*, 463–475. doi:10.1007/s10926-013-9426-0

Wehman, P. (2012). Introduction to special issue: Supported employment: What is it? *Journal of Vocational Rehabilitation*, *37*, 139–142. doi:10.3233/JVR-2012-0607

West, M. D., Wehman, P. B., & Wehman, P. (2005). Competitive employment outcomes for persons with intellectual and developmental disabilities: The national impact of the best buddies jobs programs. *Journal of Vocational Rehabilitation*, *23*, 51–63.

Williams, J., & Mavin, S. (2012). Disability as constructed difference: A literature review and research agenda for management and organization studies. *International Journal of Management Reviews*, *14*, 159–179. doi:10.1111/j.1468-2370.2012.00329.x

Emerging trends affecting future employment opportunities for people with intellectual disability: The case of a large retail organisation

Katherine Moore, Paula McDonald and Jennifer Bartlett

ABSTRACT

Background: Despite existing literature identifying the organisational drivers and constraints of employing people with disability, little research has explored how organisations embed disability-inclusive recruitment practices to facilitate ongoing employment opportunities for people with intellectual disability (ID).

Method: An embedded case study methodology was used to explore how supervisors and co-workers within a large Australian retail organisation legitimise disability recruitment practices for people with ID and how different operating environments can influence ongoing employment opportunities.

Results: Future employment opportunities for people with ID were limited by centralised recruitment process, the availability of suitable roles, and productivity and efficiency demands of the local operating environment, despite the presence of organisational diversity strategies supporting disability employment.

Conclusions: The future employability of people with ID is influenced by technological changes to work environments and an increasing focus on efficiency. Future research should address innovative task modifications to enhance employment opportunities for people with ID.

The global problem of labour market exclusion of people with disability is a major concern across industrialised countries (OECD, 2010). Australia, where the current study was undertaken, has one of the lowest employment participation rates of people with disability in the OECD, ranking 21st out of 29 countries (OECD, 2010). Approximately 53% of people with disability of working age participate in the workforce compared to around 83% of working-age people without a disability (Australian Bureau of Statistics [ABS], 2012). People with intellectual disability (ID) in Australia tend to experience higher unemployment (34.9%) than those with moderate or mild physical disability (8.1%) or sensory and speech disability (7.6%) (ABS, 2012). Although these statistics suggest that there is generally a lack of employment opportunities for people with disability, including ID, in Australia (Lantz & Marston, 2012), they also suggest that organisations do employ people with disability. However, if every organisation in Australia, for example, was to adopt disability-inclusive recruitment practices and provide *x* number of opportunities at one point in time, this would represent only a small step toward addressing the problem of the low employment rate for people with disability, including individuals with ID. We argue that to address the problem of low employment participation rates of people with ID, organisations not only need to maintain employment for current employees with ID but also commit to facilitating ongoing employment opportunities for these individuals. Hence, the key to understanding the persistent high unemployment rate of people with ID may lie in knowledge of how organisations that currently employ people with disability, particularly individuals with ID, systemically embed disability-inclusive practices to legitimise the facilitation of ongoing disability employment opportunities.

Existing research has tended to focus on the reasons why organisations are reluctant to hire people with disability. For example, the limited and relatively dated research exploring disability practices within organisations (Ellenkamp, Brouwers, Embregts, Joosen, & van Weeghel, 2016; Ju, Roberts, & Zhang, 2013) suggests that the adoption of disability employment practices is primarily constrained by concerns regarding the additional costs to the organisation (Kaye, Jans, & Jones, 2011; Markel & Barclay, 2009). Managers have reported that the extent to which the organisation considers making reasonable adjustments to the physical workplace for people with disabilities (Gerwurtz &

Kirsh, 2009), changes to the work activities, such as job carving (Citron et al., 2008), and modified work schedules for the employee (Harlan & Robert, 1998), plays a fundamental role when deciding whether to employ a person with disability (Copeland, Chan, Bezyak, & Fraser, 2010; Vornholt, Uitdewilligen, & Nijhuis, 2013). Furthermore, as the findings of Chan et al. (2010) study revealed, the absence of disability as an identified group in the organisation's diversity strategy as well as inadequate knowledge and training about anti-discrimination legislation and reasonable accommodations have emerged as significant barriers to the recruitment of people with disability. Therefore, although a manager may believe that recruiting a person with disability offers benefits to the organisation (Graffam, Smith, Shinkfield, & Polzin, 2002; Hernandez & McDonald, 2010), in the absence of disability-inclusive recruitment practices that legitimise the disability employment within the organisations (Erickson, von Schrader, Bruyère, & VanLooy, 2014), the actual recruitment of people with disability may not eventuate.

A general lack of awareness of disability can also affect employers' future decisions concerning the recruitment of people with disability (Chan et al., 2010). However, disability is a broad term that is used to cover an array of impairments. Disabilities may be categorised according to levels of severity: mild, moderate, or severe; whether the impairment is congenital (present from birth or shortly after) or acquired; or if the impairment is visible or invisible to others (Smart, 2001). These categories not only reflect the individual's health and capacity to work but also have been found to influence recruitment decision-making processes of potential employers (Nota, Santilli, Ginevra, & Soresi, 2014). Nafukho, Roessler, and Kacirek (2010) also argue that tensions between management and employees with disability, such as conflict and mistrust, often arise within organisational settings that display a lack of awareness of the various forms of disability. These tensions subsequently lead to the failure to achieve individual and organisational performance goals and can reduce the likelihood of disability-inclusive recruitment becoming a legitimate organisational practice. In summary, the primary constraints to organisations legitimising disability employment practices to facilitate ongoing employment opportunities for people with disability are the lack of managerial support for recruiting people with disability, the lack of disability awareness training, and experience of working with people with different types of disabilities.

The literature focusing on disability employment within competitive employment also highlights activities that can assist organisations to successfully adopt disability-inclusive recruitment practices, which in turn would legitimise the facilitation of ongoing employment opportunities for people with disability. Providing specific training on disability types, including ID (Burges, Ouellette-Kuntz, & Lysaght, 2007), and collaboration with specialised disability employment services and job coaches (Ellenkamp et al., 2016) have been found to encourage organisations to be more open to employing people with disability and to reduce potential stigma (Post et al., 2010). Previous experience of working with people with disability (Gilbride, Stensrud, Vandergoot, & Golden, 2003; McManus, Feyes, & Saucier, 2011; Morgan & Alexander, 2005) and prior social contact with people with disability (Scherbaum, Scherbaum, & Popovich, 2005) have also been found to counteract the effects of negative pressures associated with stigma and increase the likelihood of considering employing a person with disability.

Although previous research has provided insights into the reasons why organisations are reluctant to adopt disability employment practices, for example, cost–benefit rationalisations (Hartnett, Stuart, Thurman, Loy, & Batiste, 2011; Unger, 2002), and individual managerial attitudes toward employees with disability (Burke et al., 2013), the extant literature has afforded relatively less attention to the organisational mechanisms that facilitate ongoing employment opportunities for people with disability, and specifically for people with ID. There is also a gap in the research around how single organisations embed disability employment practices within existing organisational structures to facilitate ongoing employment opportunities for people with ID. The current study addresses these knowledge gaps by exploring how employees within a large Australian retail organisation legitimise disability employment recruitment practices within the context of their local operating environment, and to what extent do current disability employment practices affect the facilitation of ongoing disability employment opportunities for people with ID. The following research questions were addressed: *To what extent do current disability inclusive-recruitment practices affect future employment opportunities for people with ID?* and *How does the local organisational operating environment impact on future employment opportunities for people with ID?*

Theoretical framework

As the study focuses on the organisational mechanisms that may facilitate the ongoing recruitment of people with disability, an organisational theory was used to explore how actors employed at different local workplaces of the case organisation legitimise current disability employment practices within their operating environments, and the extent to which these existing organisational practices are likely to facilitate ongoing employment opportunities for people with ID. The research used the three institutional pillar model (Scott, 2008) as the theoretical lens to explain how organisational practices become sustained over time, or institutionalised. The framework posits that organisational activities appear legitimate and become embedded within operating environments when they are supported by three institutional pillars, regulative, normative, and cultural–cognitive, of organisational activities (Scott, 2008). An organisational strategy is more likely to be sustained when it is supported by all three pillars. This model has been used to explain how organisational practices such as accounting (Järvenpää, 2009), communication management (Grandien & Johansson, 2012), and project governance (Müller, Pemsel, & Shao, 2015) have become systemically embedded within everyday practices and have been sustained over time.

The regulative institutional pillar gives prominence to explicit regulatory processes to guide and constrain behaviours, as far as rules and laws provide a convenient and pragmatic means for organisational actors to meet regulatory requirements and legitimise activities (Scott, 2008). The presence of diversity management policies and disability-inclusive recruitment practices are underpinned by the regulative institutional pillar. The normative pillar rests on conformity to a "moral basis" (Scott, 1995), and activities are legitimised in terms of whether an activity aligns with socially constructed norms and values (Scott, 2008). Social expectations that large organisations have a moral obligation to provide employment opportunities for people with disability rests on the normative institutional pillar, and organisations typically signal compliance with such expectations through publicly displaying their commitment (Meyer & Rowan, 1977).

The cultural–cognitive pillar emphasises the use of common schemas and other shared symbolic representations that guide behaviours. Our study focused on the latter at the individual level insofar as activities appear legitimate when they conform to common meanings, motives for compliance, and shared logics of action which may become visible in routines and organising schemas. Organisational practices that are legitimised by the cultural–cognitive pillar are repeated over time and become unquestionable (Scott, 1995, 2008). Focusing on the cultural–cognitive institutional pillar (Scott, 2008) allowed for a detailed exploration of the extent to which disability-inclusive recruitment practices within an organisation have become legitimised by managers and co-workers who work directly with employees with disability, and thus have become an unquestionable organisational practice that is likely to continue in the future. This theoretical lens also provided a framework for identifying departures from disability-inclusive recruitment practices in relation to people with ID compared to people with other types of disability, which may impact on the facilitation of future employment opportunities. The organisation selected was ideal to examine the research questions because firstly, it has an existing regulatory basis for disability recruitment practices, exhibited by a diversity management policy, and secondly, it has demonstrated a social responsibility to respond to the external demands of its customers and shareholders in relation to employing people with disability, through publicly advertising the disability-inclusive diversity strategy in the organisational annual reports over the previous 5 years.

Method

Case organisation and participants

The sample consisted of 28 managers and co-workers of employees with disability employed by the case organisation chosen for the research, referred to henceforth as RetailCo. The qualitative embedded case study methodology (Yin, 2014) adopted for the research provided the opportunity for multiple levels of analysis within and across different workplaces in the same organisation to explain the complexity of disability employment practices. RetailCo was chosen as the case organisation as it is one of Australia's largest retail organisations, and the retail industry is the fourth highest industry that employs people with disability in Australia (ABS, 2012). RetailCo has promoted disability-inclusive recruitment practices within their diversity policy, annual reports, and on the organisational website. According to annual report data, the case organisation employs approximately 195,000 employees across the country, with approximately 3000 employees reporting that they have a disability. Thus, disability-inclusive recruitment practices across the organisation have been supported by the *regulative institutional pillar*, by way of organisational strategies and policies, and by the *normative institutional pillar* through strategically communicating to stakeholders and public that the organisation is meeting normative expectations of employing people with disability. In contrast, the cultural–cognitive institutional pillar as the focus for analysis helps explain similarities and differences in the ways local-level employees legitimise disability-inclusive recruitment practices for people with different disabilities, and within different operating environments.

The case organisation had a nested organisational structure wherein the Parent Company oversees multiple Business Units, each comprising multiple local stores. This structure facilitated the decentralisation of management authority and responsibilities to the local level of the organisation. Exploring a nested organisational structure allowed for a comparative examination of the actual practices and logics of actions that serve to form common schemas for disability-inclusive recruitment practices in and across local workplace contexts. A stratified purposeful sampling strategy (Creswell, 2007) was used to select contrasting Business Units and local store sites where people with disability had been employed. Business Units and stores were selected based on two criteria: trading periods and whether at least one person with disability was working in the store. The first Business Unit, Supermarket, was well established and had been trading for a considerable time. The second Business Unit, Hardware, was a relatively new addition to the organisation and had been operating only for a period of approximately three years. The selection of the Supermarket and Hardware Business Units allowed for a comparison between an established and a new organisation under the same Parent Company. Three stores within each Business Unit and at least three staff members within each store participated in the research. Selecting more than one store within the two Business Units, and multiple staff members from within each store, allowed for replicating the interpretation of findings and triangulation of data to establish convergence and robustness of the findings (Yin, 2014). The stores selected into the study provided access to interviewees who had some level of experience with disability employment.

Interviews

The use of semi-structured interviews (Galletta & Cross, 2013) generated a rich description of how current disability-inclusive recruitment practices have become legitimised by local-level staff who work alongside employees with disability. Employees with disability were not the unit of analysis for this study as the guiding research questions asked how managers and co-workers of employees with disability legitimised disability recruitment practices. Examples of the broad interview questions included: *What happens when a person with disability is employed? What roles do the employees with disability (past and present) perform?*, and *How are store staff informed of the person's disability and any special requirements they may need to perform their role*? Table 1 displays the positions held by the 28 interviewees according to Business Unit and local stores, their interviewee codes, and the types of disabilities and roles held by the employees with disability in each store. Individual interviews were conducted in a private space at the store location. The interview questions primarily focussed on the nature of current disability recruitment practices, and how these practices had emerged as

Table 1. Demographics of employees with disability across the stores in each business unit.

		Interviewee identifying code	Number of employees with disability	Type of disability	Type of job role
Supermarket Business Unit	Store 1	Manager, Supermarket 1	2	Vision impaired	Inventory manager
		Floor Staff 1,Supermarket 1		Physically impaired	Customer service
		Floor Staff 2, Supermarket 1			
		Floor Staff 3, Supermarket 1			
	Store 2	Manager, Supermarket 2	2	Intellectual disability	Store presentation
		Floor Staff 1, Supermarket 2		Acquired brain injury	Store presentation
		Floor Staff 2, Supermarket 2			
		Floor Staff 3, Supermarket 2			
	Store 3	Manager, Supermarket 3	2	Intellectual disability	Cleaning
		Floor Staff 1, Supermarket 3		Intellectual disability	Cleaning
		Floor Staff 2, Supermarket 3			
		Floor Staff 3, Supermarket 3			
Hardware Business Unit	Store 1	Manager, Hardware Store 1	2	Physically impaired	Customer service
		Floor Staff 1, Hardware Store 1		Intellectual disability	Watering plants
		Floor Staff 2, Hardware Store 1			
		Floor Staff 3, Hardware Store 1			
		Floor Staff 4, Hardware Store 1			
		Floor Staff 5, Hardware Store 1			
	Store 2	Manager, Hardware Store 2	2	Learning disability	Stock replenishment
		Floor Staff 1, Hardware Store 2		Learning disability	Stock replenishment
		Floor Staff 2, Hardware Store 2			
		Floor Staff 3, Hardware Store 2			
		Floor Staff 4, Hardware Store 2			
	Store 3	Manager, Hardware Store 3	3	Physically impaired	Customer service
		Floor Staff 1, Hardware Store 3		Learning disability	Trolley collection
		Floor Staff 2, Hardware Store 3		Learning disability	Customer service
		Floor Staff 3, Hardware Store 3			
		Floor Staff 4, Hardware Store 3			

legitimate in the organisation. Information relevant to disability employment from the case organisation's website and annual reports was also accessed for triangulation purposes. The interviews averaged 50 minutes in duration and were audio recorded and transcribed verbatim.

Analysis

Data coding of the interview transcripts was theory-driven and informed by the assumptions of the cultural–cognitive institutional pillar (Scott, 2008) as they related to disability recruitment practices. Data analysis identified the common schemas and understandings, shared logic of actions, and more specifically the activities and behaviours associated with the facilitating of ongoing disability employment opportunities within each Business Unit. This process ensured consistency with the underlying assumptions of the cultural–cognitive pillar and the practices, activities, and behaviours coded, thereby enhancing construct validity of the interpretation of the findings (Yin, 2014). During the qualitative coding phase, the guiding description and the underlying assumptions of the cultural–cognitive pillar (Scott, 2008) were revisited as often as possible to ensure the process of inquiry remained within its original parameters (Yin, 2014). Axial coding (Strauss & Corbin, 1998) was then used to prioritise, integrate, synthesise, and conceptualise the codes to identify patterns and associations within the data such as common understandings and exceptions to these schemas that underpinned the legitimacy of disability employment practices in the stores across the Supermarket and Hardware Business Units and in relation to employees with ID (Fereday & Muir-Cochrane, 2006). A comparison between the findings of the two Business Units was achieved through pattern matching and explanation building (Yin, 2014). These comparisons strengthened the use of rival explanations to explain different findings at different organisational settings of the case organisation.

Results

The data analysis revealed the ways in which the interviewees had legitimised current disability-inclusive recruitment practices within their local operating environments, and also how these practices had produced the unintended consequence of reducing the possibility of future employment opportunities for people with ID. Specifically, the move to a centralised online recruitment system, coupled with dynamic demands of the local operating environment with a focus on efficiency, has negatively impacted on the number of suitable roles and the opportunity to create specialised roles for people with ID.

Organisational recruitment practices

RetailCo adopted a centralised web-based recruitment process approximately 5 years prior to the time of the study. This recruitment procedure was used within the Supermarket Business Unit whereby the store manager would inform the human resource department of the vacancy so that they would facilitate the advertisement of a position (on the online recruitment website). The human resource department would shortlist applicants according to the required skill set for the position, and the store managers would conduct the interviews and make the final hiring decision. The online recruitment process had the facility for the job applicant to nominate whether they have a disability and what type of support or workplace accommodations they may require while performing the role. In this scenario, the person with disability was recruited according to the extent to which their skill set and personal attributes aligned with the requirements of the vacant position and with consideration of workplace accommodations. Within Supermarket 1, the employees with physical and sensory impairments were recruited via this centralised process and were appointed to customer service and stock logistic roles (see Table 1), with the facilitation of minor workplace modifications to assist them to perform their duties.

Although the changes to the recruitment process had maintained accessibility for people with disability to apply for advertised jobs and receive the workplace modifications they required, the centralised online system had potentially marginalised prospective job applicants with ID. For example, some interviewees had difficulty recalling any recent recruitment of a person with ID through the online recruitment process.

> Interviewer: Apart from the employees in this store, when was the last person you have employed with an intellectual disability?
>
> Manager Supermarket 3: Well, I'd have to go back to my Victorian days. We put [name of employee] on in long life … so that's probably going back to 2000.

Indeed, prior to the introduction of the centralised online recruitment process, the store managers were often approached directly by specialised disability employment services and roles were customised to suit the abilities of the potential employee, otherwise known as job carving (Citron et al., 2008). This process was evident across the two supermarket stores, where the three employees with ID were employed in modified roles and rostered for short shifts. However, the introduction of the new centralised online recruitment process was identified by some staff members as constraining future recruitment opportunities for people with ID as there was limited opportunity to centrally advertise a modified or specially created role for the individual job applicant. As one floor staff member of Supermarket 3, where two employees with ID were employed, stated:

> ... see back then we didn't have to go through that process as much, a lot of it was done through the stores. But now we do go through that recruitment process ... so we basically don't see them. (Floor Staff 3, Supermarket 1)

It was also identified by a floor staff member in Supermarket 1 that the online recruitment process has limited the access to store managers by specialised disability employment services to negotiate suitable positions for people with ID.

> Last year I was still getting [people with ID] for work experience ... , but lately I haven't seen anyone, for the last six months. I did get a phone call from the [specialised disability employment service] that runs it and he said they had [people] ready to place, and they would ring our HR. So that was a few weeks ago, but I haven't heard back. (Floor Staff 1, Supermarket 1)

The initial recruitment of people with disability across the stores in the Hardware Business Unit, a recent addition to RetailCo, was driven by a targeted diversity recruitment strategy for the new stores. This strategy aligned with the overarching organisational diversity program and was facilitated through specialised disability employment services.

> I know here with [Hardware Business Unit] ... a big part of our on-boarding was our diversity program, and how we work with different agencies to employ people with disabilities where we can. (Manager, Hardware Store 3)

However, this emerged as a one-time only scenario for each new hardware store upon opening and it became evident, particularly within Hardware Stores 2 and 3, that the ongoing recruitment of people with disability had not become an embedded and legitimate organisational practice.

> We've never really gone, okay, well let's get [the disability agency] right back in and see who they've got or whatever. Because they've approached us from different disability agencies that we first used. They've engaged us a few times, but we just haven't had positions to put anyone in. (Floor Staff 4, Hardware Store 3)

When specifically questioned about the likelihood of more people with disability being employed in the future, the common views expressed by the Hardware Store Managers suggested that future disability recruitment practices would be administered via the centralised recruitment system. This suggests that the recruitment of new employees with disability would be based on matching the skill set of the candidate with the requirements of the vacant job, rather than negotiating with specialised disability employment services to modify existing roles to specifically suit the abilities of people with ID.

The change in the Parent Company's recruitment practices, although remaining disability inclusive, had unintentionally impacted on the likelihood of the stores within both Business Units facilitating ongoing employment opportunities for people with ID.

Local-level contextual factors

One supermarket store manager observed that technological changes to work systems had impacted on the availability of suitable jobs for individuals with ID.

> I have had experience with bringing people with Down Syndrome through as well. But unfortunately, I find that our business has moved on so far with technology and the way that the expectations of our customers. (Manager, Supermarket 1)

Therefore, available roles for people with ID may become more limited due to technological innovations aimed at increasing efficiency, thus reducing the need for manual completion of repetitive tasks, which have been typically included in roles held by employees with ID in the organisation. Concerns were also raised by the Manager of Supermarket 3 about the contextual factors of the supermarket work environment, for example, use of machinery, quality assurance, and number of employees already employed, that would limit future employment opportunities for people with ID.

> ... in this particular store, I think two is enough, because of the job functions that we've got available for them, plus you can't put them in butchers, delis where there's machinery, bakeries where there's machinery, and probably produce might be a little bit difficult for them, knowing and understanding how important quality is. (Manager, Supermarket 3)

Indeed, a floor staff member within Supermarket 3 recalled that the two employees with ID were provided with full-time support from the specialised disability employment service primarily due to workplace safety concerns.

> I think our Store Manager wanted it that way as well because just for safety for the girls and with the stores getting busier and busier and people having sort of less time I guess to dedicate to helping them there's so many things that could happen where they might be unsafe. (Floor Staff 3, Supermarket 3)

Similarly, the Manager of Supermarket 2 explained that "basically [the specialised disability employment service] come in and support [him]," which ensured that the employee with ID remained productive in his role with negligible impact on the day-to-day operations of the store. So, without the outside support of a specialised disability employment service, the future employment opportunities for people with ID would be limited due to contextual workplace factors, such as workplace safety and productivity concerns.

The current context of the Hardware Business Unit operating environment was found to be limiting the future recruitment of people with disability. As a new entrant to the "Big Box" Hardware market, the Hardware Business Unit was under pressure from their major competitor. The Business Unit was in fact operating at a loss and the focus on cost efficiencies was paramount for the Hardware Store Managers.

> ... since I started here we've been in a process of driving up our productivity, or driving down the number of hours we use in the store. So, we haven't really been in any major recruitment phases where it's actually been more about we've been dropping hours and dropping people out of our business. (Manager, Hardware Store 3)

Some floor staff have observed little evidence of the store managers in the Hardware Stores being invested in the future recruitment of people with ID in the short term, as they seemed to be disconnected from the additional time and support that employees with ID require to become productive and efficient.

> They employed them, yeah, but that's all they did. It relies on the people that deal with them day to day ... obviously the carers [who helped] them get into the workforce .... (Floor Staff 2, Hardware Store 2)

Hence, despite the initial targeted diversity recruitment strategy implemented in each new store, the facilitation of ongoing disability employment opportunities appeared to be primarily constrained by business objectives focussed on productivity concerns and cost efficiencies within the Hardware Business Unit's operating environment.

Although productivity concerns were raised across both Business Units, technology, workplace safety, and quality assurance concerns emerged as particular constraints on the future employment opportunities for people with ID in the supermarket stores.

Organisational roles

A clear distinction between individuals with ID and individuals with physical and sensory disabilities was evident in the types of roles employees held across the stores in both the Supermarket and Hardware Business Units. In Supermarket 3, the duties of the two employees with ID were primarily related to cleaning. When questioned if the roles were specifically created for the employees to suit their individual abilities or whether these roles were specified within the structure of the store, the Store Manager of Supermarket 2 expressed the job match process as a convenience for the business that at the same time created employment opportunities.

> [the role] is part of the process of the day-to-day running of the store, so it has to happen. So, it wasn't created especially for [the two employees], it was more created for we've got an opportunity here and why not utilise these guys to do it. It's normally a night fill role. As long as the role is done, like it gets completed and it's still within that timeframe. (Manager, Supermarket 2)

However, the Store Manager of Supermarket 3 stated that he did not feel comfortable with their roles being confined to only cleaning. Yet, at the same time, he recognised that repetitious roles were best suited to these employees because of their disability.

> We like to try to not just use them for just cleaning. We get them to date code, stamp things ... a lot of it is very, very repetitious ... they're very comfortable with that, they're very confident with that. If you change things, sometimes it might throw them out. (Manager, Supermarket 3)

Common schema about the type of roles that employees with ID should perform emerged in the data. Some interviewees from the supermarket business unit had worked in other stores and recalled that employees with ID they had previously worked with had primarily worked in store presentation, cleaning, and stock filling roles, rather than customer service roles.

> [other employees with ID] were employed in the long-life department ... mainly because of their disability, we didn't really put them on a register. The use of money and what not ... they used to go into probably the long life with packing and ticketing .... (Floor Staff 3, Supermarket 1)

However, one Supermarket floor staff interviewee expressed the need to consider both type of disability and the person's abilities when considering suitable roles.

> I mean it all comes down to obviously their disability and what you're working with and their strengths and their weaknesses I suppose and whether they're suitable for different roles. It's the same with people without disabilities. (Floor Staff 1, Supermarket 2)

The future recruitment of people with ID in the Supermarket Business Unit could be constrained by the complexity of tasks, the frequency with which these tasks are required to be performed, and the common understandings of the types of roles that people with ID could perform.

Only one employee with ID was employed in the Hardware stores in the sample. Her role was watering plants: a task that would usually be incorporated into a broader customer service role. As the plants require watering only once per day, this is another example of how the future recruitment of people with ID within the Hardware Business Unit may be constrained by the availability of roles deemed suitable for applicants with ID. Yet, one Hardware Store Manager also referred to the personal attributes of supervisors and floor staff as considerations when deciding whether a person with ID would be a suitable job candidate.

> Because I think you do need to match the right sort of candidate, it really needs to be the right fit for the store and for the people. I'd consider if we were putting someone on, I'd consider the department manager that I'd put them with, because some would handle it better than others. Depending on the situation, others might handle it better than others. (Manager, Hardware Store 3)

The future recruitment of people with ID in the Hardware Business Unit could be constrained by the availability of suitable roles, as in the Supermarket Business Unit, but also by personal attributes of the supervisors and co-workers, and as previously stated, the stores' focus on driving productivity and reducing hours worked by existing staff.

In summary, prior to the introduction of the centralised online recruitment process, store managers had been afforded autonomous decision-making regarding disability recruitment. Regarding people with ID, store managers could modify existing roles to suit the abilities of the job candidate, and the support offered by specialised disability employment services was assurance that the employee with ID would perform their job effectively with minimal support from other staff. The introduction of the centralised recruitment process diminished this autonomy and limited direct access to stores by specialised disability employment services, thus reducing the provision of additional on-the-job support. Furthermore, due to the roles that have been previously assigned to people with ID, common understandings of the types of tasks people with ID can perform have emerged. Yet, an unintended consequence of creating roles consisting only of less complex tasks and activities required to be completed once per day, or even less frequently, has limited future employment opportunities for people with ID.

Discussion and conclusion

The aim of the study was to explore how employees within a large Australian retail organisation legitimise disability-inclusive recruitment practices within the context of their local operating environment, and to what extent these contextual factors influence the facilitating of ongoing disability employment opportunities for people with ID. The findings revealed trends within the organisation that have limited the facilitation of future employment opportunities for people with ID. These trends did not stem from negative attributions as found in previous studies (Vornholt et al., 2013), but emerged due to technological changes to the recruitment practices, increasing efficiency demands impacting on workers' productivity, and the reduction in the ongoing available roles deemed suitable for individuals with ID. Although these findings are relatively consistent with previous research for people with disability generally (Houtenville & Kalargyrou, 2012), our study has highlighted these emerging trends within workplaces that are likely to substantially impact the future employability of individuals with ID, despite organisational efforts to legitimise disability-inclusive recruitment practices.

First, the trend towards streamlining recruitment practices by large organisations through centralised web-based platforms has become a barrier to employment for people with ID (De Lima, 2016). As the findings of the current study revealed, despite provisions for applicants to nominate if they have a disability, shortlisting decisions are more likely to be based on skill-matching to the requirements of the role rather than consideration for diversity management strategies. Despite the value of customised job search for people with ID (Griffin, Hammis, Geary, & Sullivan, 2008), centralisation of the HR-managed, online process has limited the opportunities for face-to-face negotiations between specialised disability employment services and store managers (Carlson, Smith, & Rapp, 2008; Migliore, Butterworth, Nord, Cox, & Gelb, 2012) to adjust existing roles to accommodate the abilities of individuals with ID (Citron et al., 2008; Luecking, Fabian, & Tilson, 2004), previously found to be essential for successful employment outcomes. The broader implications, according to the cultural–cognitive institutional pillar used in the analysis of this study, is that the recruitment of people with ID has become less of an *unquestionable organisational practice* (Scott, 2008) within this centralised recruitment process, due to reduced involvement by the store managers, thus disrupting existing routines and organising schemas previously drawn upon to legitimise the customisation of jobs for people with ID. Although this was an emerging theme within the current study, future research should explore this trend from a longitudinal perspective to measure actual impact on future employment opportunities for people with ID.

Second, technological innovations have facilitated more efficient work systems in organisations thus prioritising productivity over workplace diversity. Routine tasks that have been typically deemed suitable for people with ID (Lysaght, Ouellette-Kuntz, & Lin, 2012) have become replaced with automation, thus limiting the availability of future roles for these individuals. Despite technological advances being made to enhance the social inclusion of people with ID (Boot, Dinsmore, Khasnabis, & MacLachlan, 2017; Tanis et al., 2012), more attention needs to be afforded to creating innovative organisational responses to the high levels of unemployment of people with ID through developing work activities that could be completed efficiently by these employees. Indeed, the future employability of people with ID will rely on changes to the ways both organisations and the society respond to the rapidly evolving dynamics of work.

Third, and finally, as organisational diversity strategies are supported by the regulative institutional pillar, the employment of people with ID may be legitimised against the associated policies and practices (Chan et al., 2010). Yet, organisational diversity strategies are often understood in terms of efficiency and value adding to the demands of the operating environment (Kalargyrou, 2014). Hence, there is greater opportunity for managers to legitimise *not* employing people with ID compared to other diversity groups, as they may be perceived to be less efficient (Unger, 2002). Furthermore, as the findings of the current study suggest, the declining availability of suitable roles for people with ID will often exclude them from consideration for employment opportunities. Consequently, there is a high probability that people with ID are more likely to be marginalised within broader organisational diversity strategies, without specific inclusion in diversity programs. Disability, including ID, as a category within organisational diversity strategies is currently an under-researched area, and further exploration into the impact of specifically including people with ID, and more broadly, people with disability, within organisational diversity management plans is required.

The findings of the study have made a unique contribution to the literature exploring the drivers and constraints of employment opportunities for people with ID through the lens of an organisational theory to gain an understanding of how staff within an organisation that employs people with disability, legitimise the facilitation of ongoing employment opportunities for people with ID. Although the study was conducted in the Australian context, employment opportunities for people with ID remain limited across most industrialised countries and future research from different international perspectives is imperative to redress this disadvantage.

Disclosure statement

No potential conflict of interest was reported by the authors.

ORCID

Katherine Moore http://orcid.org/0000-0003-4176-9927

References

Australian Bureau of Statistics. (2012). *Disability, Australia, 2009*. Retrieved from http://www.abs.gov.au/AUSSTATS/abs@.nsf/ProductsbyTopic/C7C72D7706E9BED0CA257DE2000BDC60?OpenDocument

Boot, F. H., Dinsmore, J., Khasnabis, C., & MacLachlan, M. (2017). Intellectual disability and assistive technology: Opening the GATE wider. *Frontiers in Public Health*. Retrieved from http://go.galegroup.com.ezp01.library.qut.edu.au/ps/i.do?p=HRCA&sw=w&u=qut&v=2.1&it=r&id=GALE%7CA482283723&sid=summon&asid=b63d419ea42bb0494f593bba47d4fb76

Burges, P., Ouellette-Kuntz, H., & Lysaght, R. (2007). Public views on employment of people with intellectual disabilities. *Journal of Vocational Rehabilitation*, *26*, 29–37.

Burke, J., Bezyak, J., Fraser, R. T., Pete, J., Ditchman, N., & Chan, F. (2013). Employers' attitudes towards hiring and retaining people with disabilities: A review of the literature. *The Australian Journal of Rehabilitation Counselling*, *19*(1), 21–38. doi:10.1017/jrc.2013.2

Carlson, L., Smith, G., & Rapp, C. A. (2008). Evaluation of conceptual selling as a job development planning process. *Psychiatric Rehabilitation Journal*, *31*, 219–225. doi:10.2975/31.3.2008.219.225

Chan, F., Strauser, D., Maher, P., Lee, E., Jones, R., & Johnson, E. (2010). Demand- side factors related to employment of people with disabilities: A survey of employers in the Midwest region of the United States. *Journal of Occupational Rehabilitation*, *20*, 412–419. doi:10.1007/s10926-010-9252-6

Citron, T., Brooks-Lane, N., Crandell, D., Brady, K., Cooper, M., & Revell, G. (2008). A revolution in the employment process of individuals with disabilities: Customized employment as the catalyst for system change. *Journal of Vocational Rehabilitation*, *28*(3), 169–179.

Copeland, J., Chan, F., Bezyak, J., & Fraser, R. (2010). Assessing cognitive and affective reactions of employers toward people with disabilities in the workplace. *Journal of Occupational Rehabilitation*, *20*, 427–434. doi:10.1007/s10926-009-9207-y

Creswell, J. W. (2007). *Qualitative inquiry & research design: Choosing among five approaches* (2nd ed.). Thousand Oaks, CA: Sage.

De Lima, M. P. (2016). Online recruitment of people with disabilities: Technology in favor of diversity? *Revista De Administração Mackenzie*, *17*(2), 42–66. doi:10.1590/1678-69712016/administracao.v17n2p42-66

Ellenkamp, J. J., Brouwers, E. P., Embregts, P. J., Joosen, M. C., & van Weeghel, J. (2016). Work environment-related factors in obtaining and maintaining work in a competitive employment setting for employees with intellectual disabilities: A systematic review. *Journal of Occupational*

Rehabilitation, *26*(1), 56–69. doi:10.1007/s10926-015-9586-1

Erickson, W. A., von Schrader, S., Bruyère, S. M., & VanLooy, S. A. (2014). The employment environment: Employer perspectives, policies, and practices regarding the employment of persons with disabilities. *Rehabilitation Counseling Bulletin*, *57*(4), 195–208. doi:10.1177/0034355213509841

Fereday, J., & Muir-Cochrane, E. (2006). Demonstrating rigor using thematic analysis: A hybrid approach of inductive and deductive coding and theme development. *International Journal of Qualitative Methods*, *5*(1), 80–92. doi:10.1177/160940690600500107

Galletta, A., & Cross, W. E. (2013). *Mastering the semi-structured interview and beyond: From research design to analysis and publication*. New York: New York University Press.

Gerwurtz, R., & Kirsh, B. (2009). Disruption, disbelief and resistance: A meta-synthesis of disability in the workplace. *Work*, *34*(1), 33–44.

Gilbride, D., Stensrud, R., Vandergoot, D., & Golden, K. (2003). Identification of the characteristics of work environments and employers open to hiring and accommodating people with disabilities. *Rehabilitation Counseling Bulletin*, *46*(3), 130–137. doi:10.1177/00343552030460030101

Graffam, J., Smith, K., Shinkfield, A., & Polzin, U. (2002). Employer benefits and costs of employing a person with a disability. *Journal of Vocational Rehabilitation*, *17*(4), 251–263.

Grandien, C., & Johansson, C. (2012). Institutionalization of communication management. *Corporate Communications: An International Journal*, *17*(2), 209–227. doi:10.1108/13563281211220247

Griffin, G., Hammis, D., Geary, T., & Sullivan, M. (2008). Customized employment: Where we are, where we're headed. *Journal of Vocational Rehabilitation*, *28*, 135–139.

Harlan, S., & Robert, P. (1998). The social construction of disability in organisations. *Work and Occupations*, *25*(4), 397–435. doi:10.1177/0730888498025004002

Hartnett, H. P., Stuart, H., Thurman, H., Loy, B., & Batiste, L. C. (2011). Employers' perceptions of the benefits of workplace accommodations: Reasons to hire, retain and promote people with disabilities. *Journal of Vocational Rehabilitation*, *34*(1), 17–23.

Hernandez, B., & McDonald, K. (2010). Exploring the costs and benefits of workers with disabilities. *Journal of Rehabilitation*, *76*(3), 15–23.

Houtenville, A., & Kalargyrou, V. (2012). People with disabilities: Employers' perspectives on recruitment practices, strategies, and challenges. *Leisure and Hospitality*, *53*(1), 40–52.

Järvenpää, M. (2009). The institutional pillars of management accounting function. *Journal of Accounting & Organizational Change*, *5*(4), 444–471. doi:10.1108/18325910910994676

Ju, S., Roberts, E., & Zhang, D. (2013). Employer attitudes toward workers with disabilities: A review of research in the past decade. *Journal of Vocational Rehabilitation*, *38* (2), 113–123.

Kalargyrou, V. (2014). Gaining a competitive advantage with disability inclusion initiatives. *Journal of Human Resources in Hospitality & Tourism*, *13*(2), 120–145. doi:10.1080/15332845.2014.847300

Kaye, H. S., Jans, L. H., & Jones, E. C. (2011). Why don't employers hire and retain workers with disabilities? *Journal of Occupational Rehabilitation*, *21*(4), 526–536. doi:10.1007/s10926-011-9302-8

Lantz, S., & Marston, G. (2012). Policy, citizenship and governance: The case of disability and employment policy in Australia. *Disability & Society*, *27*(6), 853–867. doi:10.1080/09687599.2012.686881

Luecking, R. G., Fabian, E. S., & Tilson, G. P. (2004). *Working relationships: Creating career opportunities for job seekers with disabilities through employer partnerships*. Baltimore, MD: Paul H. Brookes.

Lysaght, R., Ouellette-Kuntz, H., & Lin, C. (2012). Untapped potential: Perspectives on the employment of people with intellectual disability. *Work (Reading, Mass.)*, *41*(4), 409–422.

Markel, K. S., & Barclay, L. A. (2009). Addressing the underemployment of persons with disabilities: Recommendations for expanding organisational social responsibility. *Employee Responsibilities and Rights Journal*, *21*(4), 305–318. doi:10.1007/s10672-009-9125-3

McManus, J. L., Feyes, K. J., & Saucier, D. A. (2011). Contact and knowledge as predictors of attitudes toward individuals with intellectual disabilities. *Journal of Social and Personal Relationships*, *28*(5), 579–590. doi:10.1177/0265407510385494

Meyer, J. W., & Rowan, B. (1977). Institutionalized organisations: Formal structure as myth and ceremony. *American Journal of Sociology*, *83*(2), 340–363. doi:10.1086/226550

Migliore, A., Butterworth, J., Nord, D., Cox, M., & Gelb, A. (2012). Implementation of job development practices. *Intellectual and Developmental Disabilities*, *50*(3), 207–218. doi:10.1352/1934-9556-50.3.207

Morgan, R. B., & Alexander, M. (2005). The employer's perception: Employment of individuals with developmental disabilities. *Journal of Vocational Rehabilitation*, *23*(1), 39–49.

Müller, R., Pemsel, S., & Shao, J. (2015). Organizational enablers for project governance and governmentality in project-based organizations. *International Journal of Project Management*, *33*(4), 839–851. doi:10.1016/j.ijproman.2014.07.008

Nafukho, F. M., Roessler, R. T., & Kacirek, K. (2010). Disability as a diversity factor: Implications for human resource practices. *Advances in Developing Human Resources*, *12*, 395–406. doi:10.1177/1523422310379209

Nota, L., Santilli, S., Ginevra, M. C., & Soresi, S. (2014). Employer attitudes towards the work inclusion of people with disability. *Journal of Applied Research in Intellectual Disabilities*, *27*(6), 511–520. doi:10.1111/jar.12081

OECD. (2010). Transforming disability benefits into an employment instrument. In *OECD, sickness, disability and work: Breaking the barriers: A synthesis of findings across OECD countries* (pp. 103–124). Paris: OECD Publishing. doi:10.1787/9789264088856-6-en

Post, M., Campbell, C., Heinz, T., Kotsonas, L., Montgomery, J., & Storey, K. (2010). Collaboration between supported employment and human resource services: Strategies for success. *Research & Practice for Persons with Severe Disabilities*, *35*(1/2), 24–30. doi:10.2511/rpsd.35.1-2.24

Scherbaum, C. A., Scherbaum, K. L., & Popovich, P. M. (2005). Predicting job-related expectancies and affective reactions to employees with disabilities from previous work experience. *Journal of Applied Social Psychology, 35*(5), 889–904. doi:10.1111/j.1559-1816.2005.tb02151.x

Scott, W. R. (1995). *The institutional construction of organizations: International and longitudinal studies.* Thousand Oaks, CA: Sage.

Scott, W. R. (2008). *Institutional and organisations: Ideas and interests* (3rd ed.). Thousand Oaks, CA: Sage.

Smart, J. (2001). *Disability, society, and the individual.* Austin, TX: Pro-ed.

Strauss, A. L., & Corbin, J. M. (1998). *Basics of qualitative research: Techniques and procedures for developing grounded theory.* Thousand Oaks, CA: Sage.

Tanis, E. S., Palmer, S., Wehmeyer, M., Davies, D. K., Stock, S. E., Lobb, K., & Bishop, B. (2012). Self-report computer-based survey of technology use by people with intellectual and developmental disabilities. *Intellectual and Developmental Disabilities, 50*(1), 53–68. doi:10.1352/1934-9556-50.1.53

Unger, D. (2002). Employers' attitudes toward persons with disabilities in the workforce: Myths or realities? *Focus on Autism and Other Developmental Disabilities, 17*(1), 2–10. doi:10.1177/108835760201700101

Vornholt, K., Uitdewilligen, S. & Nijhuis, F. (2013). Factors affecting the acceptance of people with disabilities at work: A literature review. *Journal of Occupational Rehabilitation Review, 23*(4). 463–475. doi:10.1007/s10926-013-9426-0

Yin, R. (2014). *Case study research: Design and methods* (5th ed.). Los Angeles, CA: Sage.

Factors that affect the perceived health of adults with intellectual disability: A Western Australian study

Errol Cocks, Allyson Thomson, Stian Thoresen, Richard Parsons and Lorna Rosenwax

ABSTRACT

Background: Adults with intellectual disability (ID) experience poorer overall health than the wider population. Identification of personal, support service and lifestyle factors affecting health status will provide opportunities to improve health outcomes.

Methods: The study was a cross-sectional survey of adults with ID. Interviews were conducted between January and July 2013. Univariate and multivariate analyses were performed using self- or proxy-reported general health as the dependent variable.

Results: "Not good" health was independently associated with increasing age, financial hardship, smoking, and living in a home of their own. Physical exercise was inversely associated with not good health.

Conclusions: Subjective health may be improved by attention to the factors identified in this study. This could include closer monitoring of the health of people with ID as they age and if they live in a home of their own. Similarly, targeted programs promoting physical activity and smoking reduction could improve general health for adults with ID.

The Western Australian Study of Health and Intellectual Disability (WASHID) was a cross-sectional survey of various aspects of health in adults with intellectual disability (ID), including social and behavioural determinants of health. A previous publication presented the demographic profiles and health status of the study participants (Cocks, Thomson, Thoresen, Parsons, & Rosenwax, 2016). Overall, adults with ID generally experience poorer objective health than members of the wider population (Australian Institute of Health and Welfare, 2014; Havercamp & Scott, 2015) and WASHID participants were no exception (Cocks et al., 2016).

In common with other studies, for example, Davis and Joyce (2011), and the Department of Health (2011), the subjective health variable is distinct from measures of psychological health and well-being. However, health and healthiness are integral to quality of life and are often specifically measured as sub-scales within quality of life scales, such as the Comprehensive Quality of Life Scale - ID (Hensel, Rose, Kroese, & Banks-Smith, 2002). Similarly well-being and psychological health are often components of various health scales, such as the Medical Outcomes Study Short Form-36 (Essink-Bot, Krabbe, Bonsel, & Aaronson, 1997). This paper is concerned with the subjective view of participant health, regardless of physical and psychological conditions.

Health is affected by a number of diverse but interconnected factors we have divided into three domains: Personal, Lifestyle, and Support service (Figure 1) that correspond to some degree with three of the four domains identified as key indicators of health (Cocks et al., 2016; Perry et al., 2010). For some factors the decision to place them within one or the other domain was somewhat arbitrary as there was little or conflicting evidence available. For example, a lack of health knowledge by the person with ID may be indicative of poor education (Personal), show incomplete "reasonable accommodation" by health professionals or lead to poor access to health promotion campaigns and health services (Support service). Improved health knowledge may lead to healthier lifestyle choices and behaviours, to increased self-satisfaction, or to more effective engagement with health services (Bazzano et al., 2009; Jobling & Cuskelly, 2006). As identified by Ouellette-Kuntz and colleagues (2005) the interconnectedness of the factors implicated in health status leads to complex pathways between them.

Personal

The Personal domain includes largely socio-demographic factors such as poverty, increasing age, limited education, social isolation, and lack of employment opportunities, all of which have been reported to adversely

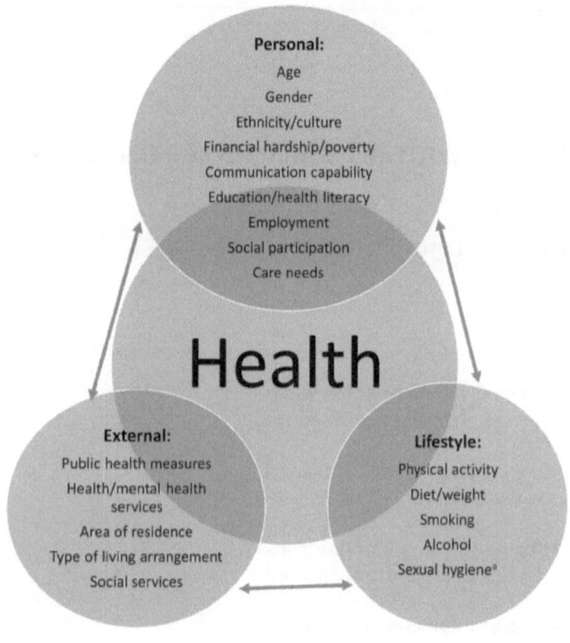

Figure 1. Personal, support service and lifestyle factors affecting general health.
[a]Not included in survey.

affect health (Commission on Social Determinants of Health, 2008; Emerson et al., 2011; Emerson & Hatton, 2008b; Marmot, 2005) (Figure 1). Financial position, education level and employment all contribute to socio-economic status that has, in turn, been linked to both self-rated health and to health-related quality of life (Delpierre et al., 2012). Poorer health has been associated with higher support needs in people with ID (Sutherland, Couch, & Iacono, 2002; van Schrojenstein Lantman-de Valk et al., 1997), although there is no clear pathway from high support need to poorer health. Health knowledge may be poor among both people with ID, especially those with high support needs, and their families and support workers (Jobling & Cuskelly, 2006; Melville et al., 2009; Swaine, Parish, Luken, Son, & Dickens, 2014) (Figure 1). Although some people with ID can understand and explain aspects of healthy behaviour (Caton et al., 2012), there is no clear evidence that such knowledge results in the person engaging in healthy behaviour.

Lifestyle

Factors such as physical activity, diet, smoking, alcohol consumption, and sexual hygiene (Heller, McCubbin, Drum, & Peterson, 2011; McGuire, Daly, & Smyth, 2007; Temple, Frey, & Stanish, 2006; Tracy & Hosken, 1997) are included in the Lifestyle domain (Figure 1). Adults with ID are reportedly less likely than the general population to observe healthy lifestyle choices, such as healthy eating and physical exercise, although people with more severe intellectual limitations rarely smoke or drink excess alcohol (Havercamp & Scott, 2015; Heller et al., 2011).

Among the identified barriers to physical activity for people with ID are individual factors (mobility, attitude to exercise), carer attitudes (risk, incapacity), access issues (transport, availability, costs), and service provider policies (Caton et al., 2012; Howie et al., 2012; Melville et al., 2009; Temple & Walkley, 2007). Many of these barriers are similar to those experienced by the general population, however carer attitudes and service provider policies are more specific to people with disability, especially ID.

Overweight and obesity are reportedly more common in people with ID than in the general population (Hsieh, Rimmer, & Heller, 2014; Rimmer & Yamaki, 2006). Various programs aim to reduce the incidence of obesity in people with and without ID (Bazzano et al., 2009; Heller et al., 2011; Marinescu et al., 2013; Marks, Sisirak, & Chang, 2013). Many of these programs have the desired outcomes but may be expensive and difficult to establish and maintain, especially in supported accommodation where staff turnover may be high (Heller, Fisher, Marks, & Hsieh, 2014).

Support service

Factors within this domain include health, social and mental health services, and residential factors (Figure 1). Social services, such as welfare, and health policies and legislation, play an important part in supporting people with disability (Hogg, Juhlberg, & Lambe, 2007; Kidd, Watts, & Saltman, 2008; Scheepers et al., 2005). Reduced access to health services and reduced quality of available services are common health inequities experienced by people with ID (Ali et al., 2013; Allerton & Emerson, 2012; Pradhan, Slade, & Spencer, 2009; Wilkinson, Dreyfus, Bowen, & Bokhour, 2013). Research has identified insufficient disability-specific training within health professional education across Australia and this can contribute to inadequate services for people with ID (Phillips, Morrison, & Davis, 2004; Tracy & McDonald, 2015).

Type of living arrangement has been reported to affect overall health, with people living in institutional care generally having poorer health when compared to people living in community settings (Hayden, Kim, & DePaepe, 2005). People with ID living in small or large congregate care in the United States of America (USA) were more likely to have a psychiatric diagnosis than people living in a family home (Davidson et al., 2003). People in supported accommodation in the UK and in small group homes in the USA were more likely to report good to very good health (Emerson & Hatton, 2008b; Janicki et al., 2002). However, evidence connecting health and type of residence is ambiguous and may require up-dating (Sutherland et al., 2002).

Public health preventive measures, such as screening tests and vaccinations, are not always provided to people with ID (Robertson, Roberts, Emerson, Turner, & Greig, 2011; Sullivan et al., 2003), although there is some indication these measures are effective in improving health for people with ID (Lennox, Ware, Bain, Taylor Gomez, & Cooper, 2011; Robertson et al., 2011). In addition, although people with ID are at higher risk of developing mental health problems, primary and secondary mental health prevention early in life is often lacking (Allen et al., 2013). There is limited evidence that people with ID are targeted or engaged in preventive population health strategies and programs in Australia (Lennox et al., 2010).

Study objectives

WASHID investigated a number of health-related factors in a sample of adults with ID. The specific objectives were:

- To identify baseline health status of adults with ID in Western Australia (WA)
- To identify factors affecting the health of adults with ID in WA
- To identify health disparities experienced by adults with ID in WA

Some of the factors that affect the subjectively reported general health of adults with ID in WA are discussed within this research paper.

Method

Study design

The WASHID was a cross-sectional survey, similar in form to those undertaken in the European Union (Walsh, Hall, & Ryan, 2008) and the UK (Emerson & Hatton, 2008a, 2008b). The survey was administered as a face-to-face interview with people with ID or their carer or family member. The interviews were conducted by trained interviewers and held at a place chosen by the participants; primarily their place of residence. People interviewed were from across both metropolitan and regional WA.

Participants

Participants comprised respondents to invitations sent to people aged 18 or over, having ID, and living in WA. Invitations were distributed by the Disability Services Commission (DSC) and a variety of service providers and nongovernment organisations. The result was thus a self-selected opportunistic sample drawn from the estimated 7,000–9,000 adults with ID in WA.

The broad reach of recruitment resulted in expressions of interest from 413 people with ID or family members of whom 328 (59% male) completed the study. The ages of participants ranged from 18–82 years with 67% being under the age of 45. The majority of participants were non-Indigenous and most were Australian-born (91%). Few participants had ever married (17%) or had children (8%) (Cocks et al., 2016).

The socio-demographic profile of WASHID participants was similar to the profiles of adults with ID represented on the DSC database that contains all Western Australians registered for services with the Commission and was the major source of study invitations (Cocks et al., 2016). However, we cannot claim the WASHID sample is representative of the target population as people with mild or borderline levels of ID may not be registered for DSC services.

Respondents were adults with ID or a family member or support person comprising proxy informant only (55%), participant only (24%), and joint informants (21%) depending on support need and communication ability. People who answered for themselves or jointly often had only intermittent support (90% and 70%, respectively), while those who had a proxy respondent where more likely to have higher support needs (29%; $p < .000$).

Measures and methods

A review of ID-specific health surveys was conducted to determine the most appropriate indicators of health (Department of Health, 2011; Krahn, Fox, Campbell, Ramon, & Jesien, 2010; McCarron et al., 2011; Perry et al., 2010; Rimmer & Hsieh, 2011; Walsh et al., 2008). With assistance from an expert reference group, comprising representatives from a number of stakeholder groups, a survey instrument was prepared to include items from the domains of socio-demographic profile, health status, health behaviours, and use of health services (Cocks et al., 2016). Copies of the survey questionnaire are available on request. Surveys were administered as an interview by trained interviewers, either face-to-face or by telephone between January and July 2013.

This paper reports on factors affecting subjectively reported general health including personal, lifestyle and support service factors (Figure 1). Poverty was measured using nine items from the Millennium Poverty and Social Exclusion Survey as described by Emerson and

Hatton (2008b); the activities of daily living using an 11-item scale adapted from Emerson and Hatton (2008a); and communication difficulties using four items from the Survey of Disability, Ageing and Carers (Australian Bureau of Statistics, 2009). Other factors were assessed using a variety of means: multiple choice items, text boxes, and the completion of tables. For example, "In the last week, how many days did you do at least ten minutes at once of hard exercise?", "In the last year, have you stayed in hospital overnight?"

Statistical analysis

Standard descriptive statistics were used to summarise the survey responses: frequencies, and percentages for categorical variables; means and standard deviations for variables measured on a continuous scale. Percentages were based on all valid responses, excluding missing data, and therefore denominators may not add up to the total number of participants.

A single item measure of subjective general health was used "How is your health in general? (*Very good*, *Good*, *Fair*, *Bad*, or *Very bad*)". This variable correlated reasonably well with a composite measure derived from total number of current health conditions, sensory impairment, mental health diagnoses, and dental problems, and was therefore chosen as the dependent variable for this set of analyses. This is consistent with studies from other regions such as the United Kingdom (UK) "Adults with Learning Difficulties in England" survey (Emerson, 2010; Emerson & Hatton, 2008a, 2008b), the USA "Longitudinal Health and Intellectual Disability Study" (Rimmer & Hsieh, 2011), and the "European Social Survey" (Alvarez-Galvez & Salvador-Carulla, 2013). The responses to this item were skewed toward the good and very good, therefore they were dichotomously categorised into the dependent variable as "*Very good/Good*" (Good) vs "*Fair/Bad/Very bad*" (Not good).

These analyses are concerned with factors associated with subjective health (rather than other measures, such as those based on medical profile). A series of univariate logistic regression models were performed, using independent variables from within the three domains described in the introduction and shown in Figure 1. Results are shown as odds ratios (ORs) with 95% confidence intervals. An OR measures how many times bigger the odds of one outcome, in this case subjective not good health, is for one value of a variable when compared with another value. For example, the person with ID as respondent compared with a support person answering on the person's behalf. An OR indicates the direction and the strength of the relationship between the two variables, similarly to an effect size (http://www.theanalysisfactor.com/effect-size-statistics-logistic-regression/).

All individual factors that were found to be significantly associated with the outcome variable from univariate analyses were then included in a multivariate logistic regression. A backwards elimination strategy was used to reduce the model to the most parsimonious. In this method, variables were dropped, one at a time, until all variables remaining in the model were significantly associated with the outcome ($p < .05$). Some variables were treated as categorical while others were continuous. When the most parsimonious model involving only main effects was obtained, all pairwise interaction terms between these main effects were introduced into the model (one at a time) and tested for statistical significance. Interaction terms not significantly associated with the outcome were dropped from the model. Statistical analyses were conducted using the SAS version 9.2 software (SAS Institute Inc, Cary, NC, USA, 2008).

Ethics

Approval for this study (HR87/2012) was provided by the Human Research Ethics Committee of Curtin University. Comprehensive information sheets were provided to all potential participants, including a plain English version. Participants were assured that their personal data would be kept private and confidential. Written informed consent was collected from all participants or their representative.

Results

Three-quarters of informants ($n = 243$: 78%) described participant health as Good with the remainder rated as Not good ($n = 70$: 22%). Fifteen people did not provide a rating and were excluded from this analysis.

Within each of the domains below, the characteristics of the study participants are first described and then the significant univariate correlations are presented in both tables and text.

Personal factors

Three-quarters (74%) of participants had some communication difficulty and 26% needed extensive assistance with activities of daily living. More than four-fifths (82%) of participants had social contact at least weekly, and 78% reported no financial hardship.

Most participants had attended senior high school (68%) or junior high school (16%), often in special education schools or centres or in mainstream schools with an aide. Half of the participants (49%) attended

Alternatives to Employment (equivalent to day activities) at least once per week. Fewer than half the participants (42%) were in paid employment, with half of these employed fewer than 16 hours per week.

The personal factors "increasing age", "being unable to afford one or more items from the poverty scale", and "needing intermittent support for activities for daily living" were all associated with Not good subjective health (Table 1). When the person with ID was the sole responder, they were significantly more likely to report Not good health than cases where a support person was involved in the response (Table 1).

Lifestyle factors

One-fifth (19%) of participants did some vigorous activity at least two days per week (highest activity) and similar numbers did no vigorous or moderate activity per week. Few participants (15%) reportedly consumed a diet meeting health guidelines for fruit and vegetables, water, soft drink, and take-away food. Most participants (79%) were not exposed to cigarette smoke and only a small proportion (6%) currently smoked themselves. About one-third (35%) currently drank alcohol.

Almost one-half of participants (45.2%) spent an average of seven hours or more per day sitting down and a majority were overweight or obese (55.9%). Eleven percent used a wheelchair at all times.

People doing little or no physical activity were more likely to report Not good health, and when compared with non-smokers, current smokers were disproportionately represented among participants reporting "Not good" health (Table 2).

Support service factors

A majority of participants (74.5%) lived in the Perth metropolitan area with the remainder in regional or remote areas. Most participants lived in a family home (53%), with the remainder living in their own home (22%) or some form of congregate living (25%).

Hospital visits were common over the previous year and most participants had a regular general practitioner (94%). Almost one-quarter of participants (23%) had seen a mental health professional, and more than half had visited a dentist (68.2%) or allied health professional (60.4%), over the previous year.

Considerably more of the people living in their own home were reported to have Not good health than people living in other arrangements, and more people reporting Not good health had seen a mental health professional (Table 3).

Many participants received the Disability Support Pension (94%), and almost two-thirds (72%) received support services funding from the Disability Services Commission WA (DSC). Most participants (97%) had a Commonwealth Health Care Card entitling them to greatly reduced medical costs while two-thirds (63%) had private health insurance.

The proportion of participants using screening and diagnostic tests was variable. Two-thirds had an annual physical examination (66%), and 59% of women over 50 had a mammogram within the past two years. In the previous five years, 53% of participants had the annual flu vaccine and 51% had a cholesterol test (Table 4). Fewer than half of the participants had a glucose tolerance test (34%) or bone density scan (11%) over the previous five years. Within the previous two years, 18% of women over 20 years old had a Pap smear (Table 4).

Multivariate regression

The incidence of poorer subjective health increased as age increased and decreased as physical activity increased. It was significantly worse for people of limited financial means. While the number of smokers in the sample was small ($n = 18$), the majority of smokers reported Not good health. This was significantly higher than the proportion of non-smokers who reported Not good health. Finally, significantly more participants who lived in their own home reported Not good health compared to participants who lived in a group home or family home (Table 5).

Discussion

Previous studies have shown that poorer subjective health is generally associated with higher future morbidity and earlier mortality (Eriksson, Unden, & Elofsson, 2001; French et al., 2012), and with the physical function and vitality subscales of the Medical Outcomes Study 36-item Short Form (Mavaddat et al., 2011). WASHID participants reporting Not good health had a tendency to report more chronic or long-term conditions and to take more medications (Cocks et al., 2016). This paper investigated the impact of various factors within the personal, lifestyle and support service domains on the subjectively rated general health of WASHID participants.

Personal factors

The most consistent factor affecting overall health, whether subjectively or objectively measured, is age. Older people, with or without ID, tend to report poorer health (Eriksson et al., 2001; McCarron et al., 2011) and

Table 1. Personal factors in relation to subjective general health among WASHID participants.

Variable	Not good health % (n/N)	*OR*	95% CI	*p*-value (Univariate)
Age[a]		1.43	1.18–1.72	.0002
Gender				
Male	23.7 (44/186)	1 (reference)		
Female	20.5 (26/127)	0.83	0.48–1.44	.5072
Indigenous				
No	22.5 (68/302)	1 (reference)		
Yes	18.2 (2/11)	0.77	0.16–3.62	.7355
Poverty/hardship score[b]				
0	18.1 (44/243)	1 (reference)		
1–2	36.1 (13/36)	2.56	1.20–5.45	.0148
3–9	38.2 (13/34)	2.80	1.30–6.02	.0083
Employed				
No	25.1 (46/183)	1 (reference)		
Yes	18.5 (24130)	0.67	0.39–1.18	.1640
Social outings				
Frequent	21.9 (34/155)	1(reference)		
Weekly	18.8 (13/69)	0.83	0.41–1.69	.5998
Monthly	16.7 (7/42)	0.71	0.29–1.74	.4572
Rare/never	34.0 (16/47)	1.84	0.90–3.75	.0948
Communication[c]				
4 (no problems)	25.8 (8/31)	1 (reference)		
3	17.3 (9/52)	0.60	0.21–1.77	.3153
2	21.1 (16/76)	0.77	0.29–2.03	.7652
1	21.8 (19/87)	0.80	0.31–2.08	.8989
0 (many problems)	26.9 (18/67)	1.06	0.40–2.78	.3479
Activities of daily living[d]				
0–2	31.4 (21/67)	1 (reference)		
3–4	23.4 (15/64)	0.67	0.31–1.46	.3123
5–9	16.8 (17/101)	0.44	0.21–0.92	.0297
10+	21.0 (17/81)	0.58	0.28–1.22	.1533
Respondent				
Participant alone	33.8 (27/80)	1 (reference)		
Support person	19.0 (31/163)	0.46	0.25–0.85	.0123
Both	17.1 (12/70)	0.41	0.19–0.88	.0227

Note. OR = odds ratio; CI = confidence interval.
[a]Age is treated as a continuous variable. The *OR* is the change in risk of poorer subjective health, the odds of poor health increases by 1.43 for every decade of age.
[b]Adapted from Emerson and Hatton (2008b). Number of items rated *always* or *most of the time.*
[c]Adapted from Australian Bureau of Statistics (2009).
[d]Adapted from Emerson and Hatton (2008a). Activities of Daily Living total score.

to have more chronic or long-term health conditions (Rimmer & Hsieh, 2011). Similarly, older WASHID participants were more likely to report Not good health than younger adults, independent of any other factor. Further investigation would be required to determine if this result is due to a cohort effect with younger adults

Table 2. Lifestyle factors in relation to subjective general health among WASHID participants.

Variable	Not good health % (n/N)	*OR*	95% CI	*p*-value (Univariate)
Physical activity[a]				
4 (highest)	13.1 (8/61)	1 (reference)		
3	17.5 (11/63)	1.40	0.52–3.76	.5031
2	23.5 (16/68)	2.04	0.80–5.17	.1338
1	26.8 (15/56)	2.42	0.94–6.27	.0678
0 (no activity)	30.8 (20/65)	2.94	1.18–7.32	.0202
Diet[b]				
Healthy	23.9 (11/46)	1 (reference)		
Moderate	22.7 (29/128)	0.93	0.42–2.06	.8621
Unhealthy	17.7 (22/124)	0.69	0.30–1.56	.3678
Smoking				
Not exposed	19.4 (48/248)	1 (reference)		
Passive	21.3 (10/47)	1.13	0.52–2.42	.7613
Smoker	66.7 (12/18)	8.33	2.98–23.33	<.0001
Alcohol use				
No	20.8 (42/202)	1 (reference)		
Yes	25.2 (28/111)	1.29	0.74–2.22	.3685

Note. OR = odds ratio; CI = confidence interval.
[a]Ordinal scale based on two items. Highest is at least twenty minutes of vigorous activity for two or more days.
[b]Ordinal scale based on four items corresponding to dietary recommendations.

Table 3. Support service factors in relation to subjective general health among WASHID participants.

Variable	Not good health % (n/N)	*OR*	95% CI	*p*-value (Univariate)
Living arrangement				
Family home	17.4 (28/161)	1 (reference)		
Own home	42.4 (28/66)	3.50	1.85–6.61	.0001
Group home[a]	14.5 (11/76)	0.80	0.38–1.72	.5723
Hospital visit				
No	19.6 (33/168)	1 (reference)		
Yes	25.5 (37/145)	1.40	0.82–2.39	.2146
Regular GP				
No	27.6 (8/29)	1 (reference)		
Yes	21.8 (62/284)	0.73	0.31–1.74	.4799
Regular specialist				
No	22.8 (41/180)	1 (reference)		
Yes	21.8 (29/133)	0.95	0.55–1.62	.8381
Mental health professional				
No	19.0 (46/242)	1 (reference)		
Yes	33.8 (24/71)	2.18	1.21–3.91	.0095
Health screening and maintenance guidelines				
No	21.6 (54/250)	1 (reference)		
Yes	25.4 (16/63)	1.24	0.65–2.35	.5185

Note. OR = odds ratio; CI = confidence interval.
[a]Includes hostels, nursing homes and aged care.

being healthier than older adults, or if it is due to a perception that growing older adversely affects health.

Financial hardship has been associated with poorer subjective health in people with ID in this and other studies (Emerson & Hatton, 2008b) and in a general population sample from France (Delpierre et al., 2012). However, more than three-quarters of all WASHID participants, and two-thirds of participants reporting Not good health, reported no financial hardship. This may indicate that the Australian welfare system provides sufficient financial support for people with ID, or that family members supply extra money for some items. People living in group homes or the family home may not know how food and utility bills are paid, and many people with higher levels of impairment do not use a telephone and visit pubs or clubs. Thus there were considerable numbers of *Not applicable* or *Not answered* responses to some hardship questions. Further investigation is needed to clarify the role of financial hardship in the subjective health ratings of adults with ID, particularly when relevant costs are included in the assessment of hardship.

Table 4. Frequencies of regular diagnostic or screening tests for WASHID participants.

Test	Frequency % (*n*)	95% CI
Annual physical examination	65.9 (193)	60.8–71.3
Mammogram (females 50–69 years; last two years)	59.1 (13)	36.9–79.2
Flu vaccine (annual)	53.4 (156)	47.6–59.6
Cholesterol test (last five years)	51.2 (129)	44.8–57.1
Prostate examination or PSA test (males 50 years old and over; last five years)	50.0 (12)	28.6–70.8
Bowel cancer test (50 years old and over; last 5 years)	48.0 (24)	34.1–61.4
Glucose tolerance (last five years)	34.1 (87)	28.2–40.0
Pap smear (females 20 years old and over; last two years)	17.8 (16)	9.4–25.8
Bone density scan (last five years)	11.2 (28)	7.6–15.7

Note. CI = confidence interval.

Table 5. Factors independently associated with Not good subjective general health among WASHID participants after multivariate analysis.

Variable	Not good health % (n/N)	*OR*	95% CI	*p*-value
Age[a]		1.47	1.12–1.74	.0026
Physical Activity[a]		0.78	0.63–0.98	.0302
Poverty/hardship score[b]				
0 (no hardship)	18.1 (44/243)	1 (reference)		
1 or more	37.1 (26/70)	2.19	1.12–4.25	.0215
Smoking status				
Non-smoker	19.7 (58/295)	1 (reference)		
Current smoker	66.7 (12/18)	4.98	1.63–15.19	.0048
Home type				
Family home	18.1 (31/171)	1 (reference)		
Own home	42.4 (28/66)	2.20	1.10–4.41	.0260
Group home	14.5 (11/76)	0.45	0.19–1.05	.0635

Note. OR = odds ratio; CI = confidence interval.
[a]Variables treated as a continuous scale. The OR is the change in risk of poorer subjective health. For age, this means the odds of Not good health increases by 1.47 for every decade of age, and for Physical activity, as the score moves up by 1 point on the scale, the odds of poor health declines (*OR* = 0.78).
[b]Adapted from Emerson and Hatton (2008b). Number of items rated *always* or *most of the time*.

Lifestyle factors

In common with most studies of people with ID (Havercamp & Scott, 2015; Peterson, Janz, & Lowe, 2008; Temple & Walkley, 2007), and indeed the general population (Australian Institute of Health and Welfare, 2014), few WASHID participants engaged in sufficient recommended physical activity. Sedentary behaviours are common in people with ID, especially females and those living in the community (Rimmer & Hsieh, 2011). As the reported amount of physical activity decreased among WASHID participants so their reports of Not good health increased; a factor that was independent of any other influence. This supports a correlation between subjective health and exercise, but the causal pathway may be in either direction. Less exercise may be a consequence of Not good health or of limitations arising from health problems. Alternatively, doing insufficient exercise may lead to a perception of being unfit and therefore result in reports of Not good health.

Although very few WASHID participants were current smokers, more smokers reported Not good health when compared to non-smokers. Earlier reports estimated higher rates of smoking for people with ID, however these studies tended to be limited to people with mild levels of ID (Carroll Chapman & Wu, 2012; Lunsky, Emery, & Benson, 2002; Tracy & Hosken, 1997). More diverse groups from the USA, the UK, and Ireland were reportedly less likely to be smokers (Havercamp & Scott, 2015; McGuire et al., 2007; Rimmer & Hsieh, 2011), although these studies did not compare subjective general health between smokers and non-smokers.

Support service factors

WASHID participants living in their own home were much more likely to have reported Not good health than those living in family homes or some form of congregate care. People with ID living in their own home generally have higher functional capabilities (Felce, Perry, & Kerr, 2011) and more control over their environments, including lifestyle factors (Nota, Ferrari, Soresi, & Wehmeyer, 2007). In the USA, people with ID living in their own home are reportedly less likely to engage in physical exercise, to have poor oral hygiene, to have poorer diets, and to smoke or drink alcohol more than people living in family, supported or group homes (Rimmer & Hsieh, 2011). These findings may reflect reduced influence from family members and carers when living alone, and therefore poorer lifestyle factors. Indeed low levels of physical exercise and smoking were both identified in this study as significantly associated with poorer subjective general health, but independently of the type of residence.

Another factor associated with Not good subjective health for WASHID participants was seeing a mental health professional within the previous year. For many people, mental health disorders are regarded as indicators of poorer health (French et al., 2012; Mavaddat et al., 2011), however, mental health and behavioural disorders may also be a result of health conditions (Davidson et al., 2003). Studies linking physical and mental ill-health have suggested that problem or challenging behaviour may be a way of expressing health problems (May & Kennedy, 2010) or have some relation to pain signalling (Peebles & Price, 2012). Further investigation of the mental health issues requiring consultation is necessary before any attribution can be made for this study group.

Overall, WASHID participants seemed to have adequate access to health care services, including mental health services. This is in contrast to the poor access to health services reported for people with chronic health problems or impairments in the UK (Allerton & Emerson, 2012), and the inequality of health services provision identified by the Health Issues Special Interest Research Group of the International Association for the Scientific Study of Intellectual Disabilities (Scheepers et al., 2005). In addition, access to health care services was not associated with the subjective health reports in WASHID.

WASHID participants generally reported rates of preventive health activities similar to the general population, with the exception of cervical cancer tests (Australian Institute of Health and Welfare, 2014; Davis & Joyce, 2011). However, data from the USA National Core Indicators Consumer Survey show that people with intellectual and developmental disability were more likely than people without disability to have an annual physical examination, but less likely to have bowel, breast, and cervical cancer screening tests (Havercamp & Scott, 2015; Ouellette-Kuntz, Cobigo, Balogh, Wilton, & Lunsky, 2015). This suggests that some, but not all, public health measures reach this vulnerable population. However, preventative health activities were not associated with subjective health in this study.

Limitations

Therefore, as noted previously, the study was not population-based and may not be representative of adults with ID. This limits the explanatory power of the study.

A lack of comparison data on health services access for the general population meant conclusions could not be drawn with regard to unmet need or dissatisfaction with services on the part of WASHID participants. This requires further investigation.

The relative lack of people reporting financial hardship may reflect the opt-in nature of the recruitment process. Opt-in approaches have been reported to cause some bias in other studies (Hunt, Shlomo, & Addington-Hall, 2013) and it may be that potential participants with financial difficulties failed to respond to the study invitation. In addition, opt-in recruitment may deter people with physical or mental health problems, high levels of life stress, or culturally and linguistically diverse backgrounds from volunteering to participate. All of these possibilities could lead to a response bias towards healthier, wealthier people who are coping well.

Among the limitations to this project was the use of a combination of self or proxy reporting for both subjective and objective data. Previous studies have reported a disjunction between some measures of health when reported by either a person with mild ID or a carer (Lunsky et al., 2002; Mileviciute & Hartley, 2015). However the twin goals of collecting subjective views of health and ensuring accuracy of objective data are difficult to attain with people with ID; particularly for people with limited communication and cognitive function (Fujiura & RRTC Expert Panel on Health Measurement, 2012).

These limitations notwithstanding, a single-item subjective health measure is commonly used in research studies. In this instance it was considered important to obtain a subjective assessment of health status from adults with ID and their support person.

Conclusions

Older age, low physical activity, financial difficulty, smoking, and living in one's own home were all independent risk factors for poorer subjective health in WASHID participants.

Health practitioners should ensure timely detection and treatment of health conditions that may become more frequent as their patients with ID become older (Heller et al., 2014; Lennox et al., 2011). Greater efforts should be made to ensure people with ID are financially supported to live a good life. Further research is needed to make sense of the complexities surrounding living arrangements and their relationship to perceived health.

Physical activity interventions, and the resources required to support physical exercise, could improve health (Bazzano et al., 2009; Heller et al., 2011; Howie et al., 2012; Peterson, Peterson, Lowe, & Nothwehr, 2009). Although the number of participants currently smoking was small, it would benefit their health if targeted programs to support quitting were available (Kerr, Lawrence, Darbyshire, Middleton, & Fitzsimmons, 2013).

Improving health literacy by using evidence-based and accessible education programs is an important factor in supporting adults with ID to take greater control of their own health by encouraging regular health checks and preventive measures (Heller et al., 2014; Hubbard, Bandini, Folta, Wansink, & Must, 2014; Jobling & Cuskelly, 2006; Marks, Sisirak, & Hsieh, 2008). The development and dissemination of Easy Read health information brochures and other resources is a vital step in improving the health literacy of children and adults with ID, especially people with lower levels of support need who may be living in the community (Hubbard et al., 2014). For adults with higher functional limitations, the support of health advocates can redress some of the health disparities identified in this study (Brolan et al., 2012).

Acknowledgements

The investigators thank representatives from Developmental Disabilities WA, National Disability Services WA, the Mental Health Commission WA, People with Disability WA, and the Disability Services Commission WA for acting on the expert reference group for this study. Assistance and advice on the development of the interview schedule was received from local, national and international experts.

Thank you to the adults with intellectual disability, their families, and advocates who gave of their time and knowledge to support this project.

Disclosure statement

No potential conflict of interest was reported by the authors.

Funding

This study was funded by the Disability Services Commission of Western Australia.

References

Ali, A., Scior, K., Ratti, V., Strydom, A., King, M., & Hassiotis, A. (2013). Discrimination and other barriers to accessing health care: Perspectives of patients with mild and moderate intellectual disability and their carers. *PLoS One*, *8*(8), 1–13. doi:10.1371/journal.pone.0070855

Allen, D., Langthorne, P., Tonge, B., Emerson, E., McGill, P., Fletcher, R., … Kennedy, C. (2013). Towards the prevention of behavioural and psychiatric disorders in people with intellectual disabilities. *Journal of Applied Research in Intellectual Disabilities*, *26*, 501–514. doi:10.1111/jar.12050

Allerton, L., & Emerson, E. (2012). British adults with chronic health conditions or impairments face significant barriers to accessing health services. *Public Health*, *126*, 920–927. doi:10.1016/j.puhe.2012.08.003

Alvarez-Galvez, J., & Salvador-Carulla, L. (2013). Perceived discrimination and self-rated health in Europe: Evidence from the European Social Survey (2010). *PLoS One*, *8*(9), 1–10. doi:10.1371/journal.pone.0074252

Australian Bureau of Statistics (ABS). (2009). *Disability, ageing and carers, Australia: Summary of findings* (4430.0). Canberra: Author.

Australian Institute of Health and Welfare (AIHW). (2014). *Australia's health 2014*. Canberra: Author.

Bazzano, A. T., Zeldin, A. S., Diab, I. R. S., Garro, N. M., Allevato, N. A., & Lehrer, D. (2009). The Healthy Lifestyle change program: A pilot of a community-based health promotion intervention for adults with developmental disabilities. *American Journal of Preventive Medicine*, *37*, S201–S208. doi:10.1016/j.amepre.2009.08.005

Brolan, C. E., Boyle, F. M., Dean, J. H., Taylor Gomez, M., Ware, R. S., & Lennox, N. G. (2012). Health advocacy: A vital step in attaining human rights for adults with intellectual disability. *Journal of Intellectual Disability Research*, *56*, 1087–1097. doi:10.1111/j.1365-2788.2012.01637.x

Carroll Chapman, S. L., & Wu, L.-T. (2012). Substance abuse among individuals with intellectual disabilities. *Research in Developmental Disabilities*, *33*, 1147–1156. doi:10.1016/j.ridd.2012.02.009

Caton, S., Chadwick, D., Chapman, M., Turnbull, S., Mitchell, D., & Stansfield, J. (2012). Healthy lifestyles for adults with intellectual disability: Knowledge, barriers, and facilitators. *Journal of Intellectual & Developmental Disability*, *37*, 248–259. doi:10.3109/13668250.2012.703645

Cocks, E., Thomson, A., Thoresen, S., Parsons, R., & Rosenwax, L. (2016). Health status and use of medications by adults with intellectual disability in Western Australia. *Journal of Intellectual & Developmental Disability*, *41*, 87–96. doi:10.3109/13668250.2015.1125456

Commission on Social Determinants of Health. (2008). *Closing the gap in a generation: Health equity through action on the social determinants of health. Final report of the Commission on Social Determinants of Health*. Geneva: United Nations.

Davidson, P. W., Janicki, M. P., Ladrigan, P., Houser, K., Henderson, C. M., & Cain, N. N. (2003). Associations between behavior disorders and health status among older adults with intellectual disability. *Aging & Mental Health, 7*, 424–430. doi:10.1080/13607860310001594673

Davis, P., & Joyce, S. (2011). *Health and wellbeing of adults in Western Australia 2010, overview and trends*. Perth: Department of Health.

Delpierre, C., Kelly-Irving, M., Munch-Petersen, M., Lauwers-Cances, V., Datta, G. D., Lepage, B., & Lang, T. (2012). SRH and HrQOL: Does social position impact differently on their link with health status? *BMC Public Health, 12*(19), 1–12. doi:10.1186/1471-2458-12-19

Department of Health. (2011). *Victorian population health survey of people with an intellectual disability 2009*. Melbourne: Author.

Emerson, E. (2010). Self-reported exposure to disablism is associated with poorer self-reported health and well-being among adults with intellectual disabilities in England: A cross-sectional survey. *Public Health, 124*, 682–689. doi:10.1016/j.puhe.2010.08.020

Emerson, E., & Hatton, C. (2008a). Self-reported well-being of women and men with intellectual disabilities in England. *American Journal on Mental Retardation, 113*, 143–155. doi:10.1352/0895-8017(2008)113[143:SWOWAM]2.0.CO;2

Emerson, E., & Hatton, C. (2008b). Socioeconomic disadvantage, social participation and networks and the self-rated health of English men and women with mild and moderate intellectual disabilities: Cross sectional survey. *The European Journal of Public Health, 18*, 31–37. doi:10.1093/eurpub/ckm041

Emerson, E., Madden, R., Graham, H., Llewellyn, G., Hatton, C., & Robertson, J. (2011). The health of disabled people and the social determinants of health. *Public Health, 125*, 145–147. doi:10.1016/j.puhe.2010.11.003

Eriksson, I., Unden, A. L., & Elofsson, S. (2001). Self-rated health. Comparisons between three different measures. Results from a population study. *International Journal of Epidemiology, 30*, 326–333.

Essink-Bot, M.-L., Krabbe, P. F. M., Bonsel, G. J., & Aaronson, N. K. (1997). An empirical comparison of four generic health status measures: The Nottingham Health Profile, the Medical Outcomes Study 36-item short-form health survey, the COOP/WONCA charts, and The EuroQol instrument. *Medical Care, 35*, 522–537.

Felce, D., Perry, J., & Kerr, M. (2011). A comparison of activity levels among adults with intellectual disabilities living in family homes and out-of-family placements. *Journal of Applied Research in Intellectual Disabilities, 24*, 421–426. doi:10.1111/j.1468-3148.2010.00620.x

French, D. J., Browning, C., Kendig, H., Luszcz, M. A., Saito, Y., Sargent-Cox, K., & Anstey, K. J. (2012). A simple measure with complex determinants: Investigation of the correlates of self-rated health in older men and women from three continents. *BMC Public Health, 12*(649), 1–12. doi:10.1186/12-649

Fujiura, G. T., & RRTC Expert Panel on Health Measurement. (2012). Self-reported health of people with intellectual disability. *Intellectual and Developmental Disabilities, 50*, 352–369. doi:10.1352/1934-9556-50.4.352

Havercamp, S. M., & Scott, H. M. (2015). National health surveillance of adults with disabilities, adults with intellectual and developmental disabilities, and adults with no disabilities. *Disability and Health Journal, 8*, 165–172. doi:10.1016/j.dhjo.2014.11.002

Hayden, M. F., Kim, S. H., & DePaepe, P. (2005). Health status, utilization patterns, and outcomes of persons with intellectual disabilities: Review of the literature. *Mental Retardation, 43*, 175–195.

Heller, T., Fisher, D., Marks, B., & Hsieh, K. (2014). Interventions to promote health: Crossing networks of intellectual and developmental disabilities and aging. *Disability and Health Journal, 7*, S24–S32. doi:10.1016/j.dhjo.2013.06.001

Heller, T., McCubbin, J. A., Drum, C., & Peterson, J. (2011). Physical acitivity and nutrition health promotion interventions: What is working for people with intellectual disabilities? *Intellectual and Developmental Disabilities, 49*, 26–36. doi:10.1352/1934-9556-49.1.26

Hensel, E., Rose, J., Kroese, B. S., & Banks-Smith, J. (2002). Subjective judgements of quality of life: A comparison study between people with intellectual disability and those without disability. *Journal of Intellectual Disability Research, 46*, 95–107.

Hogg, J., Juhlberg, K., & Lambe, L. (2007). Policy, service pathways and mortality: A 10-year longitudinal study of people with profound intellectual and multiple disabilities. *Journal of Intellectual Disability Research, 51*, 366–376. doi:10.1111/j.1365-2788.2006.00884.x

Howie, E. K., Barnes, T. L., McDermott, S., Mann, J. R., Clarkson, J., & Meriwether, R. A. (2012). Availability of physical activity resources in the environment for adults with intellectual disabilities. *Disability and Health Journal, 5*, 41–48. doi:10.1016/j.dhjo.2011.09.004

Hsieh, K., Rimmer, J. H., & Heller, T. (2014). Obesity and associated factors in adults with intellectual disability. *Journal of Intellectual Disability Research, 58*, 851–863. doi:10.1111/jir.12100

Hubbard, K. L., Bandini, L. G., Folta, S. C., Wansink, B., & Must, A. (2014). The adaptation of a school-based health promotion programme for youth with intellectual and developmental disabilities: A community-engaged research process. *Journal of Applied Research in Intellectual Disabilities, 27*, 576–590. doi:10.1111/jar.12104

Hunt, K., Shlomo, N., & Addington-Hall, J. (2013). Participant recruitment in sensitive surveys: A comparative trial of 'opt in' versus 'opt out' approaches. *BMC Medical Research Methodology, 13*(3), 1–8. doi:10.1186/1471-2288-13-3

Janicki, M. P., Davidson, P. W., Henderson, C. M., McCallion, P., Taets, J. D., Force, L. T., … Ladrigan, P. M. (2002). Health characteristics and health services utilization in older adults with intellectual disability living in community residences. *Journal of Intellectual Disability Research, 46*, 287–298.

Jobling, A., & Cuskelly, M. (2006). Young people with Down syndrome: A preliminary investigation of health knowledge and associated behaviours. *Journal of Intellectual & Developmental Disability, 31*, 210–218. doi:10.1080/13668250600999186

Kerr, S., Lawrence, M., Darbyshire, C., Middleton, A. R., & Fitzsimmons, L. (2013). Tobacco and alcohol-related interventions for people with mild/moderate intellectual disabilities: A systematic review of the literature. *Journal of Intellectual Disability Research*, *57*, 393–408. doi:10.1111/j.1365-2788.2012.01543.x

Kidd, M. R., Watts, I. T., & Saltman, D. C. (2008). Primary health care reform: Equity is the key. *Medical Journal of Australia*, *189*, 221–222.

Krahn, G. L., Fox, M. H., Campbell, V. A., Ramon, I., & Jesien, G. (2010). Developing a health surveillance system for people with intellectual disabilities in the United States. *Journal of Policy and Practice in Intellectual Disabilities*, *7*, 155–166.

Lennox, N., Bain, C., Rey-Conde, T., Taylor, M., Boyle, F. M., Purdie, D. M., & Ware, R. S. (2010). Cluster randomized-controlled trial of interventions to improve health for adults with intellectual disability who live in private dwellings. *Journal of Applied Research in Intellectual Disabilities*, *23*, 303–311. doi:10.1111/j.1468-3148.2009.00533.x

Lennox, N., Ware, R., Bain, C., Taylor Gomez, M., & Cooper, S. A. (2011). Effects of health screening for adults with intellectual disability: A pooled analysis. *British Journal of General Practice*, *61*, 193–196. doi:10.3399/bjgp11X561186

Lunsky, Y., Emery, C. F., & Benson, B. A. (2002). Staff and self-reports of health behaviours, somatic complaints, and medications among adults with mild intellectual disability. *Journal of Intellectual & Developmental Disability*, *27*, 125–135. doi:10.1080/13668250220135079-4

Marinescu, L. G. M. N., Sharify, D., Krieger, J. M. D. M. P. H., Saelens, B. E. P., Calleja, J., & Aden, A. (2013). Be Active Together: Supporting physical activity in public housing communities through women-only programs. *Progress in Community Health Partnerships: Research, Education, and Action*, *7*, 57–66. doi:10.1353/cpr.2013.0003

Marks, B., Sisirak, J., & Chang, Y.-C. (2013). Efficacy of the *HealthMatters Program* train-the-trainer model. *Journal of Applied Research in Intellectual Disabilities*, *26*, 319–334. doi:10.1111/jar.12045

Marks, B., Sisirak, J., & Hsieh, K. (2008). Health services, health promotion, and health literacy: Report from the State of the Science in Aging with Developmental Disabilities Conference. *Disability and Health Journal*, *1*, 136–142. doi:10.1016/j.dhjo.2008.04.003

Marmot, M. (2005). Social determinants of health inequalities. *The Lancet*, *365*, 1099–1104.

Mavaddat, N., Kinmonth, A. L., Sanderson, S., Surtees, P., Bingham, S., & Khaw, K. T. (2011). What determines Self-Rated Health (SRH)? A cross-sectional study of SF-36 health domains in the EPIC-Norfolk cohort. *Journal of Epidemiology and Community Health*, *65*, 800–806. doi:10.1136/jech.2009.090845

May, M. E., & Kennedy, C. H. (2010). Health and problem behavior among people with intellectual disabilities. *Behavior Analysis in Practice*, *3*(2), 4–12.

McCarron, M., Swinburne, J., Burke, E., McGlinchey, E., Mulryan, N., Andrews, V., … McCallion, P. (2011). *Growing older with an intellectual disability in Ireland 2011: First results from the intellectual disability supplement of the Irish longitudinal study on ageing*. Dublin: Trinity College Dublin.

McGuire, B. E., Daly, P., & Smyth, F. (2007). Lifestyle and health behaviours of adults with an intellectual disability. *Journal of Intellectual Disability Research*, *51*, 497–510. doi:10.1111/j.1365-2788.2006.00915.x

Melville, C. A., Hamilton, S., Miller, S., Boyle, S., Robinson, N., Pert, C., & Hankey, C. R. (2009). Carer knowledge and perceptions of healthy lifestyles for adults with intellectual disabilities. *Journal of Applied Research in Intellectual Disabilities*, *22*, 298–306. doi:10.1111/j.1468-3148.2008.00462.x

Mileviciute, I., & Hartley, S. L. (2015). Self-reported versus informant-reported depressive symptoms in adults with mild intellectual disability. *Journal of Intellectual Disability Research*, *59*, 158–169. doi:10.1111/jir.12075

Nota, L., Ferrari, L., Soresi, S., & Wehmeyer, M. (2007). Self-determination, social abilities and the quality of life of people with intellectual disability. *Journal of Intellectual Disability Research*, *51*, 850–865. doi:10.1111/j.1365-2788.2006.00939.x

Ouellette-Kuntz, H., Cobigo, V., Balogh, R., Wilton, A., & Lunsky, Y. (2015). The uptake of secondary prevention by adults with intellectual and developmental disabilities. *Journal of Applied Research in Intellectual Disabilities*, *28*, 43–54. doi:10.1111/jar.12133

Ouellette-Kuntz, H., Garcin, N., Lewis, M. E., Minnes, P., Martin, C., & Holden, J. J. (2005). Addressing health disparities through promoting equity for individuals with intellectual disability. *Canadian Journal of Public Health*, *96*, S8–S22.

Peebles, K. A., & Price, T. J. (2012). Self-injurious behaviour in intellectual disability syndromes: Evidence for aberrant pain signalling as a contributing factor. *Journal of Intellectual Disability Research*, *56*, 441–452. doi:10.1111/j.1365-2788.2011.01484.x

Perry, J., Linehan, C., Kerr, M., Salvador-Carulla, L., Zeilinger, E., Weber, G., … Tossebro, J. (2010). The P15 - A multinational assessment battery for collecting data on health indicators relevant to adults with intellectual disabilities. *Journal of Intellectual Disability Research*, *54*, 981–991. doi:10.1111/j.1365-2788.2010.01322.x

Peterson, J. J., Janz, K. F., & Lowe, J. B. (2008). Physical activity among adults with intellectual disabilities living in community settings. *Preventive Medicine*, *47*, 101–106. doi:10.1016/j.ypmed.2008.01.007

Peterson, J. J., Peterson, N. A., Lowe, J. B., & Nothwehr, K. F. (2009). Promoting leisure physical activity participation among adults with intellectual disabilities: Validation of self-efficacy and social support scales. *Journal of Applied Research in Intellectual Disabilities*, *22*, 487–497. doi:10.1111/j.1468-3148.2009.00500.x

Phillips, A., Morrison, J., & Davis, R. W. (2004). General practitioners' educational needs in intellectual disability health. *Journal of Intellectual Disability Research*, *48*, 142–149.

Pradhan, A., Slade, G. D., & Spencer, A. J. (2009). Access to dental care among adults with physical and intellectual disabilities: Residence factors. *Australian Dental Journal*, *54*, 204–211.

Rimmer, J. H., & Yamaki, K. (2006). Obesity and intellectual disability. *Mental Retardation and Developmental Disabilities Research Reviews*, *12*, 22–27.

Rimmer, J., & Hsieh, K. (2011, May). *Longitudinal health and intellectual disability study (LHIDS) on obesity and health risk behaviors*. Paper presented at the State of the Science Conference: Lifespan health and function of adults with intellectual and developmental disabilities: Translating research into practice, Bethesda, Maryland.

Robertson, J., Roberts, H., Emerson, E., Turner, S., & Greig, R. (2011). The impact of health checks for people with intellectual disabilities: A systematic review of evidence. *Journal of Intellectual Disability Research, 55*, 1009–1019. doi:10.1111/j.1365-2788.2011.01436.x

Scheepers, M., Kerr, M., O'Hara, D., Bainbridge, D., Cooper, S. A., Davis, R., … Wehmeyer, M. (2005). Reducing health disparity in people with intellectual disabilities: A report from health issues special interest research group of the International Association for the Scientifc Study of Intellectual Disabilities. *Journal of Policy and Practice in Intellectual Disabilities, 2*, 249–255.

van Schrojenstein Lantman-de Valk, H. M., van den Akker, M., Maaskant, M. A., Haveman, M. J., Urlings, H. F., Kessels, A. G., & Crebolder, H. F. (1997). Prevalence and incidence of health problems in people with intellectual disability. *Journal of Intellectual Disability Research, 41*, 42–51.

Sullivan, S. G., Glasson, E. J., Hussain, R., Petterson, B. A., Slack-Smith, L. M., Montgomery, P. D., & Bittles, A. H. (2003). Breast cancer and the uptake of mammography screening services by women with intellectual disabilities. *Preventive Medicine, 37*, 507–512.

Sutherland, G., Couch, M. A., & Iacono, T. (2002). Health issues for adults with developmental disability. *Research in Developmental Disabilities, 23*, 422–445.

Swaine, J. G., Parish, S. L., Luken, K., Son, E., & Dickens, P. (2014). Test of an intervention to improve knowledge of women with intellectual disabilities about cervical and breast cancer screening. *Journal of Intellectual Disability Research, 58*, 651–663. doi:10.1111/jir.12062

Temple, V. A., Frey, G. C., & Stanish, H. I. (2006). Physical activity of adults with mental retardation: Review and research needs. *American Journal of Health Promotion, 21*, 2–12.

Temple, V. A., & Walkley, J. W. (2007). Perspectives of constraining and enabling factors for health-promoting physical activity by adults with intellectual disability. *Journal of Intellectual & Developmental Disability, 32*, 28–38. doi:10.1080/13668250701194034

Tracy, J., & Hosken, R. (1997). The importance of smoking education and preventative health strategies for people with intellectual disability. *Journal of Intellectual Disability Research, 41*, 416–421. doi:10.1111/j.1365-2788.1997.tb00729.x

Tracy, J., & McDonald, R. (2015). Health and disability: Partnerships in health care. *Journal of Applied Research in Intellectual Disabilities, 28*, 22–32. doi:10.1111/jar.12135

Walsh, P. N., Hall, L., & Ryan, D. (2008). *Health indicators for people with intellectual disability: Using an indicator set.* Dublin, Ireland: European Commission.

Wilkinson, J., Dreyfus, D., Bowen, D., & Bokhour, B. (2013). Patient and provider views on the use of medical services by women with intellectual disabilities. *Journal of Intellectual Disability Research, 57*, 1058–1067. doi:10.1111/j.1365-2788.2012.01606.x

Complexity of medication regimens of people with intellectual and developmental disabilities*

Steven R. Erickson†, Drita Nicaj† and Sasha Barron†

ABSTRACT

Background: People with intellectual and developmental disabilities (IDD) may be at risk for medication-related problems due to complex medication regimens. The objective of this study was to determine the medication regimen complexity of adults with IDD.

Methods: This retrospective study compared the Medication Regimen Complexity Index (MRCI) scores and number of medications of patients with IDD to a group without IDD (GenMed group), as well as a subanalysis between type of IDD.

Results: The MRCI score of the IDD group ($29.0 + 8.1$, $n = 200$) was significantly higher than that of the GenMed group (16.7 ± 12.0, $n = 200$), $p < .001$. IDD patients had significantly more medications (11.2 ± 6.5) compared with the GenMed group (7.4 ± 5.1), $p < .001$. There were no significant differences between the number of medications prescribed or the MRCI scores between types of IDD.

Conclusion: Clinicians must be aware that patients who have IDD have more complex medication regimens and higher potential for medication-related problems.

The complexity of medication regimens may have negative implications for patients. Greater complexity may hinder a person's ability to self-manage their medication; may create greater burden on a caregiver who assists an individual with medication management; and may be associated with medication nonadherence and medication-related adverse events, including hospitalisations (Ferreira, Galato, & Melo, 2015; Leendertse, Egberts, Stoker, & van den Bemt, 2008; Willson, Greer, & Weeks, 2014; Wimmer et al., 2014). The complexity of medication regimens is dependent on factors such as the total number of medications in the regimen, the number of times per day medications are taken, the route of administration, and special instructions such as taking medication on an empty stomach.

People with intellectual or developmental disabilities (IDD) are at risk for having complex medication regimens in part due to having multiple illnesses with associated polypharmacy and having medical conditions that necessitate medication therapy that is taken more frequently than once daily or that is administered by routes other than by mouth (Doan, Lennox, Taylor-Gomez, & Ware, 2013; McDermott, Moran, Platt, & Dasari, 2006; Scheepers et al., 2005). In a population health survey conducted in 2013 of people who have IDD living in Victoria, Australia, medication use ranged from 88.3% of people between the ages of 18 and 39 years, to over 94.7% for people over age 60 years (Haider, 2015). The prevalence of polypharmacy, with five or more medications, ranged from 30.4% to 45.5% of people who have IDD, increasing with age.

The complexity of the regimen, coupled with a patient's cognitive and physical abilities, as well as the level of involvement of their support network are key points that may be associated with the safe and effective use of medications by people with IDD. The purpose of this study was to determine the extent of polypharmacy and the level of complexity of medication regimens of adults with IDD and to compare these outcomes to adults without IDD, all of whom are patients of the same university health system adult general internal medicine clinic practices. The Medication Regimen Complexity Index (MRCI), used in the present study, is a validated instrument used to assess the complexity of medication regimens (George, Phun, Bailey, Kong, & Stewart, 2004; Libby et al., 2013). An index score is derived from three subscales related to characteristics of medication regimens. The subscales include the frequency of doses taken per day, the route of administration, and special instructions for using the

*The article was presented as a poster at the American Association for Intellectual and Developmental Disabilities Annual Meeting in Atlanta, Georgia, June 2016.
†All authors have contributed to, seen, and approved of the manuscript and agree to the order of authors as listed on the title page.

medication. Information about the complexity of medication regimens taken by people with IDD may be of interest to clinicians who provide care for people with IDD, to support agencies that provide medication training for support staff, and to policy-makers who may need information regarding the needs of people for whom they provide supports. Information from this study may also be of interest to medication safety programs in health systems, demonstrating that patients with IDD may be an unrecognised group at risk for adverse medication events due in part to the complexity of their medication regimens.

Methods

Study design and subjects

This was a cross-sectional study design. Subjects were patients of the adult general internal medicine clinic practices of the University of Michigan Medical Center (Ann Arbor, Michigan, United States). Working with the health system's data warehouse, a total of 751 patients were identified as receiving care from the clinics in 2012 who met the inclusion criteria of (a) being 18 years of age or older; (b) having an ICD-9-CM diagnosis of mental retardation (IDD) code of 317, 318.0, 318.1, 318.2, or 319 or developmental delay, or having a diagnosis associated with IDD, such as autism spectrum disorder, Down syndrome, Williams syndrome, Fragile X syndrome, cerebral palsy, or foetal alcohol syndrome; and (c) treatment by a general internal medicine clinician within the year. A random sample of 200 patients was chosen from this group to create the IDD group. A comparison group of 200 patients without IDD was constructed by obtaining a random sample of the adult (age 18 years and older) patients seen by clinicians in the same time period and in the same clinics as patients in the IDD group. This group was referred to as the "GenMed" group. The study was approved by the Institutional Review Board (IRB).

Data collection

Researchers obtained data by reviewing the electronic medical record of each patient. Data collection efforts focused on the calendar year of 2012. The medications documented for the study were those in the medical record on the day of the last primary care visit in 2012. No data were used from inpatient hospitalisations.

Data

Patient demographic information included age and gender. IDD-related conditions were documented for the IDD group and included Down syndrome, cerebral palsy, autism spectrum disorder, developmental delay, or "other". The developmental delay group included patients with diagnoses documented as developmental delay, mental retardation, or developmental disability. The "other" group included conditions such as Williams syndrome, foetal alcohol syndrome, Prader–Willi syndrome, and Fragile X syndrome, as examples.

Characterisation of the burden of illness for patients was accomplished by determining the overall number of diagnoses for chronic diseases documented for each patient, the Elixhauser Comorbidity Index (Elixhauser, Steiner, Harris, & Coffey, 1998), and the Health-Related Quality of Life Comorbidity Index (HRQL-CI) (Ou, Lin, Erickson, & Balkrishnan, 2016). Both the Elixhauser and HRQL-CI indices are composed of lists of diagnoses associated with mortality, healthcare utilisation, and for the HRQL-CI, functioning and sense of well-being. Although some conditions overlap between the two comorbidity indices, the combination of the two for this study allowed for standardisation of comorbid conditions using validated instruments. The individual medical diagnoses that comprise each index were used to describe and compare the medical conditions reported for subjects in the study.

Medication information was obtained from review of all active prescription and nonprescription medication orders listed on patients' electronic profiles on the last clinic visit in 2012. Information documented about each medication included the name of medication, the strength, the frequency that the medication was taken per day, the route of administration, and any special instructions on how to take or use the medication. Medications were then categorised into common therapeutic groups.

This information was then used to calculate the MRCI score (George et al., 2004; Libby et al., 2013). The MRCI score for each patient was derived by assigning pre-specified points based on three attributes: route of administration, dosing frequency, and special instructions. The MRCI worksheet can be found in the appendix. The "route of administration" score ranged from 1 for tablets and capsules to 5 for nebulised medication. Points were assigned based only on the first occurrence of a dosage form. The "dosing frequency" score ranged from 0.5 for "once daily as needed" to 12.5 for "every 2 hours", with values assigned to every medication in the drug regimen. Finally, the "special instructions" section was scored similarly to the "dosing frequency" section, by assigning an appropriate score to each drug regimen with a special instruction. "Special instruction" scores ranged from 1 for "break or crush tablet" to 2 for "alternating doses". The overall MRCI score for each patient is the sum of the "route of administration", "dosing frequency", and "special instructions" section scores.

Analysis

Subject characteristics are presented as means with standard deviations for continuous variables and as frequencies with per cent for categorical variables. Comparisons between the IDD and the GenMed groups were made using Student's *t*-test or Chi-squared test. Age, gender, medication categories, and comorbidity indices were compared between groups. Further analysis to determine the strength of association between the MRCI and group assignment (IDD patient group versus GenMed group), controlling for age, gender, and Elixhauser Comorbidity Index was conducted using multivariable linear regression. The Elixhauser comorbidity index was the comorbidity measure used for analysis because it produced the greatest difference between the two groups in bivariate analysis.

A subgroup analysis of only the IDD group was conducted to determine if there were differences in the total number of prescribed medications or the MRCI score based on the IDD condition. Comparisons were made using one-way ANOVA with the Scheffe test for between-group differences. A "*p*"-value of $\leq .05$ was considered to be a statistically significant difference. Analysis was conducted using IBM SPSS Statistics version 23.

Results

The age and gender of the patients from the IDD group were significantly different from the GenMed group, with the IDD group having a greater proportion of males and younger mean age. There were no differences between the two groups in terms of total number of chronic illness diagnoses, Elixhauser Comorbidity Index score, or HRQL-CI score (refer to Table 1 for results). As for the specific diagnoses, significantly more patients in the IDD group had hypothyroidism, electrolyte variations, psychoses, bipolar disease, anxiety disorder, paralysis, weight loss, seizures, topical fungal infections, and behavioural challenges. Significantly more patients in the GenMed group had hypertension and hypertension with complications, depression, chronic kidney disease, substance abuse, coronary artery disease, osteoarthritis, and headache. Refer to Table 2 for a comparison between the two groups.

There was a significantly greater proportion of patients in the IDD group compared with the GenMed group who were prescribed at least one medication from each of the following categories: analgesics, vitamins and supplements, antihistamines and nasal steroids, topical antifungals, eye or ear drops, muscle relaxants, skin and mouth care, seizure, psychotropics, and gastrointestinal. Refer to Table 3 for a comparison of medication categories between the two groups. There were a significantly greater

Table 1. Comparison of characteristics of patients with IDD and the general medicine patients without IDD.

	IDD sample $N = 200$ Mean (standard deviation) or frequency (per cent)	General medicine sample $N = 200$ Mean (standard deviation) or frequency (per cent)	*p*-Value	Effect size Cohn's *d*; 95% CI; Effect size interpretation
Age – years	49.4 ± 12.0	58.4 (16.7)	<.001	0.62; −0.82 to −0.42; medium
Gender – female	92 (46.0)	118 (59)	.009	0.29; 0.07 to 0.51; small
Number of diagnoses for chronic illnesses	8.75 (3.97)	8.34 (4.52)	.336	0.1; −0.1 to 0.29; small
Elixhauser Comorbidity Index Score	2.6 (1.8)	2.9 (2.0)	.16	−0.14; −0.33 to 0.06; small
HRQL-CI Score	6.5 (5.1)	7.0 (5.1)	.28	0.11; −0.088 to 0.30; Small
MRCI score	29.0 (18.1)	16.7 (12.0)	<.001	0.80; 0.60 to 1.01; Large
Dosage form – weight score	6.6 (5.0)	4.3 (3.6)	<.001	0.53; 0.33 to 0.73; medium
Dosage frequency – weight score	17.7 (11.4)	10.3 (7.8)	<.001	0.76; 0.55 to 0.96; medium
Special instructions – weight score	5.1 (3.6)	3.7 (2.7)	<.001	0.44; 0.24 to 0.64; small
MRCI score – range	2 to 91	1 to 66	–	
Number of medications	11.2 (6.5)	7.4 (5.1)	<.001	0.65; 0.45 to 0.85; medium
Number of subjects with 5 or more medications (polypharmacy)	173 (86.5)	138 (69.0)	<.001	0.58; 0.30 to 0.86; medium
Number of subjects with 10 or more medications (super polypharmacy)	110 (55.0)	56 (28.0)	<.001	0.62; 0.39 to 0.85; medium

Table 2. List of diagnoses of the Elixhauser Comorbidity Index and HRQL-CI (combined) and comparison between IDD and general medicine groups.

Medical diagnosis	IDD *N* (%)	GenMed *N* (%)	*p*-Value
Solid tumour	9 (4.5)	17 (8.5)	.11
Cancer with metastases	6 (1.5)	6 (1.5)	.99
Lymphoma	0	0	
Hypertension without complications	62 (31.0)	91 (45.5)	.003
Hypertension with complications	0	4 (2.0)	.04
Pulmonary disease	41 (20.5)	47 (23.5)	.47
Diabetes without complications	29 (14.5)	30 (15.0)	.89
Diabetes with complications	6 (3.0)	13 (6.5)	.10
Depression	40 (20.0)	62 (31.0)	.012
Arrhythmia	18 (9.0)	25 (6.3)	.26
Rheumatoid conditions	7 (3.5)	14 (7.0)	.12
Heart failure	7 (3.5)	10 (5.0)	.46
Peripheral vascular disease	2 (1.0)	7 (3.5)	.09
Chronic kidney disease	11 (5.5)	23 (11.5)	.03
Hypothyroid	43 (21.5)	27 (13.5)	.04
Anaemia	32 (16.0)	25 (12.5)	.32
Anaemia secondary to blood loss	2 (1.0)	2 (1.0)	.999
Fluid/electrolyte abnormalities	21 (10.5)	5 (1.3)	.001
Other neurological disease/stroke	19 (9.5)	18 (9.0)	.86
Psychoses	27 (13.5)	5 (2.5)	<.001
Cardiac valvular	9 (4.5)	16 (4.0)	.15
Coagulopathy	13 (6.5)	9 (4.5)	.38
Paralysis	5 (2.5)	0	.02
Peptic ulcer disease	6 (3.0)	9 (4.5)	.43
Obesity	63 (31.5)	68 (34.0)	.59
Liver disease	25 (12.5)	16 (8.0)	.14
Alcohol abuse	3 (1.5)	9 (4.5)	.08
Drug abuse	0	10 (2.5)	.001
Pulmonary circulation disorder	3 (1.5)	4 (2.0)	.70
Unintended weight loss	12 (6.0)	2 (1.0)	.007
HIV/AIDS	0	0	
Coronary artery disease	5 (2.5)	22 (11.0)	.001
Asthma	32 (16.0)	41 (20.5)	.24
Osteoarthritis	32 (16.0)	60 (30.0)	.001
Headache	19 (9.5)	40 (20.0)	.003
Spinal column disorder	2 (1.0)	0	.16
Seizure	75 (37.5)	4 (2.0)	<.001
Gastroesophageal reflux disease	81 (40.5)	74 (37.0)	.47
Mental illness (anxiety/depression/psychosis	77 (38.5)	38 (19.0)	<.001
Visual condition	61 (30.5)	51 (25.5)	.27
Fungal infection skin/toenails	55 (27.5)	15 (7.5)	<.001
Behavioural	22 (11.0)	0	<.001

proportion of patients in the GenMed group compared with the IDD group who were prescribed at least one medication from each of the following categories: gout, antiviral, cardiovascular, and hormones. The greatest difference in proportion of patients on a medication class between group exists for gastrointestinal medication (74.5% IDD versus 43.0% GenMed, $p < .001$), seizure medication (42.5% IDD versus 12.5% GenMed, $p < .001$), psychotropics (67.5% IDD versus 41.0% GenMed, $p < .001$), topical antifungals (38.5% IDD versus 14.5% GenMed, $p < .001$), skin and mouth care (23.5% IDD versus 3.0% GenMed, $p < .001$), vitamins and supplements (72% IDD versus 55.5% GenMed, $p = .001$), muscle relaxants (15.5% IDD versus 5% GenMed, $p = .001$), and antihistamine and nasal steroids (37% IDD versus 27% GenMed, $p = .03$).

The IDD group had a significantly higher mean MRCI score (29.0 ± 18.1 versus 16.7 ± 12.0, $p < .001$) compared with the GenMed group. The overall range in scores was greater for the IDD group, with the highest MRCI score being 91, while the highest score for the GenMed group was 66. Differences in all three components of the MRCI were also significantly different, with the IDD group having higher scores for "dosage form", "dosing frequency", and "special instructions". The largest difference between the two groups was for "dosing frequency".

The total number of medications in a patient's regimen was significantly greater in the IDD group compared with the GenMed group, almost twofold in scope. The percentage of patients in the IDD group prescribed five or more medications was 86.5%, significantly greater than the 69.0% of the GenMed group ($p < .001$). The IDD group had the highest proportion of patients prescribed 10 or more medications (55%) compared to the GenMed group (28%), $p < .001$.

Table 3. Frequency and per cent of patients on at least one medication in each medication class.

Drug category	IDD	GenMed	*p*-Value
Analgesic	112 (56)	82 (41)	.03
Vitamin or supplement	144 (72)	111 (55.5)	.001
Antihistamine or nasal steroid	74 (37)	54 (27)	.03
Topical antifungal	77 (38.5)	29 (14.5)	<.001
Glaucoma	8 (4.0)	12 (3.0)	.36
Gout	3 (1.5)	11 (5.5)	.03
Antiviral	7 (3.5)	17 (8.5)	.04
Eye or ear drop	22 (11.0)	9 (4.5)	.02
Topical steroid	49 (24.5)	37 (18.5)	.14
Systemic immune modulators	5 (2.5)	17 (4.3)	.008
Bladder or prostate	36 (18.0)	32 (16.0)	.59
Muscle relaxant	31 (15.5)	10 (5.0)	.001
Central nervous system	23 (11.5)	26 (13.0)	.65
Skin or mouth care	47 (23.5)	6 (3.0)	<.001
Osteoporosis	13 (6.5)	6 (3.0)	.1
Cardiovascular	104 (52.0)	126 (63.0)	.03
Seizure	85 (42.5)	25 (12.5)	<.001
Electrolytes	72 (36.0)	56 (28.0)	.09
Psychotropics	135 (67.5)	82 (41.0)	<.001
Diabetes	28 (14.0)	31 (15.5)	.67
Gastrointestinal	149 (74.5)	86 (43.0)	<.001
Hormone	8 (4.0)	29 (7.3)	<.001
Thyroid	39 (19.5)	27 (13.5)	.11
Pulmonary	42 (21.0)	49 (24.5)	.4

The multivariable linear regression model, with the MRCI score as the dependent variable and with the independent variables being group assignment (IDD versus non-IDD), age, gender, and the Elixhauser Comorbidity Index, had an R^2 of 0.28 (adjusted $R^2 =$ 0.23). All three predictor variables were statistically significant, with group assignment having the highest standardised coefficient Beta = −0.432 ($p < .001$), followed by the Elixhauser Comorbidity Index score with a standardised coefficient Beta = 0.25 ($p < .001$), and age with a standardised coefficient Beta = 0.114 ($p = .02$). Higher medication regimen complexity was associated with being in the IDD group, having a higher Elixhauser Comorbidity Scale score (greater burden of illness), and older age.

Of the IDD group, the largest proportion of subjects had a diagnosis of cerebral palsy (41%), followed by developmental delay (36.5%), Down syndrome (9%), "other" (7%), and autism spectrum disorder (6.5%) (refer to Table 4). There were no significant differences between the number of medications prescribed or the MRCI scores between these groups.

Discussion

It is recognised that people with IDD experience problems associated with medications due to many causes. Polypharmacy, poor communication between clinicians and patients, reliance on caregivers with varying levels of competence in administering and monitoring medication therapy, and excessive use of psychotropic medication to manage behaviour are but a few of the risk factors (Erickson, Salgado, & Tan, 2016; Haider, 2015; Krahn, Hammond, & Turner, 2006; Straetmans, van Schrojenstein Lantman-de Valk, Schellevis, & Dinant, 2007). The value of the present study is that for the first time, using a validated, standardised measure of medication regimen complexity, it was demonstrated that the medication regimens of people with IDD are almost twice as complex as the regimens of people prescribed medications but who do not have IDD. Importantly, the differences in regimens are not only due to a higher number of medications prescribed for people with IDD, but also in the frequency of dose administration per day, prescribing of medications that are given by routes of administration other than by mouth, and prescribing of medications that require the patient to adhere to special instructions for administration, such as taking medication during certain times of the day or avoiding taking medications with food or other drugs. Differences in the attributes of medication regimen complexity are based on the medical conditions and associated treatments for patients who have IDD versus then general population. Although the overall measures of comorbidity were similar between the two groups, the distribution of the types of medical conditions and associated therapies were different. Medication therapies that were more common in patients with IDD included those that are taken more frequently per day (seizure medications, for example) and have routes of administration other than by mouth (more medications applied to the eye, ear, and skin, for example).

Table 4. Medication data for categories of patients with IDD.

IDD-related condition/ diagnosis	MRCI score Mean (standard deviation)	Number of medications Mean (standard deviation)
Cerebral palsy (*n* = 82)	31.7 (20.2)	11.9 (7.2)
Developmental delay (*n* = 73)	28.5 (17.9)	11.3 (6.4)
Down syndrome (*n* = 18)	21.9 (11.9)	8.7 (4.4)
Other (*n* = 14)	28.3 (16.5)	12.3 (6.0)
Autism spectrum disorder (*n* = 3)	24.8 (10.0)	8.7 (4.2)

Note. One-way ANOVA; Scheffe's test – no statistically significant differences between group mean scores (*p*-values ranged from 0.99 to 0.36).

The MRCI scores of the IDD group were similar to those found in other studies of older patients that are associated with medication-related adverse events. Studies that used the MRCI have demonstrated that the level of medication regimen complexity is associated with medication nonadherence, adverse medication-related outcomes such as hospitalisations due to medication-related problems, and is able to predict ability to self-medicate. In a population-based study conducted in Brazil, the MRCI score was significantly correlated with the number of potential medication-related problems identified by clinicians (Ferreira et al., 2015). The investigators categorised patients into one of six groups based on the MRCI score. Subjects with an MRCI score of greater than or equal to 25.4 had the lowest self-reported medication adherence (44.4% adherent) and had the greatest association with having potential drug-related problem (100%) identified. The MRCI score for the patients in the IDD group for the present study was 29, which, based on the study by Ferreira et al., would place these patients at highest risk for nonadherence and potential drug-related problems. A study of patients aged 65 years and older who had an MRCI score calculated at the time of hospital discharge found that the score was significantly associated with adherence to prescribed medication, with higher MRCI scores associated with greater nonadherence (Mansur, Weiss, & Beloosesky, 2012).

Willson et al. assessed the association between rehospitalisation for a medication-related problem and MRCI scores (2014). This study determined that the MRCI score calculated at the time of discharge was associated with a greater likelihood of being readmitted within 30 days of discharge. An MRCI score of 8 or greater was predictive of the medication-related readmission. However, those who were readmitted within 30 days tended to have higher MRCI scores, with a mean discharge MRCI score of over 34. The overall mean for people with IDD in the current study was 29, meaning that there were patients in the IDD group with MRCI scores in the range of the patients in the Willson paper associated with higher readmission rates. Although assessment of medication adherence, presence of medication-related problems, and hospitalisation were not measured in the present study, the MRCI scores for people with IDD found in the present study were generally in the range of poorer adherence and greater risk of hospitalisation found in other studies.

There are a number of limitations with this study. It did not explore the relationship between the MRCI scores and outcomes such as medication adherence, medication-related problems, and medication-related hospitalisations, nor did it conduct an in-depth exploration of the patient, illness, and treatment factors that were associated with the MRCI score. Future studies are warranted to determine the potential impact of the more complex medication regimens on these important outcomes for people who have IDD. Another limitation is that this study used patients from a single academic medical centre. The prescribing decisions made by clinicians in this centre may be different from that of other practices in the community or other health systems. The patients with IDD who are cared for by primary care clinics in this academic medical centre may also differ from those who are cared for in community-based clinical practices in that they may have a higher burden of illness which led them to seek care at this tertiary referral medical centre. Future research could investigate whether attributes of the prescribers and the health systems in which they work are associated with differences in medication prescribing patterns that may lead to complex medication regimens.

Regular review of medications by either the prescriber or by an independent healthcare provider familiar with the medication regimens prescribed for people with IDD may prove useful in improving prescribing and reducing the complexities of drug regimens (Beange, Lennox, & Parmenter, 1999). Pharmacists' review of medication regimens has led to a reduction in medication regimen complexity for older patients (Elliott, O'Callaghan, Paul, & George, 2013). As for patients who have IDD, there is limited research into ways to improve prescribing for them. A narrative review of pharmacists' interventions found only eight papers associated with research to assess activities to improve prescribing and use of medications by people with IDD (O'Dwyer, Mestrovic, & Henman, 2015). The authors conclude that more work is needed to demonstrate the value of interventions to ensure safe use of medications by people with IDD.

The complex regimens may present a burden to care-providers who assist with medication management. Use of medications with once daily dosing frequencies, such as sustained release products, will reduce the complexity of medication regimens and the time taken to administer medicines by caregivers. Another potential prescribing solution to reduce complexity would be to use medication products that contain more than one drug when multi-drug therapy is required. For example, inhaled controller medications for the treatment of asthma that contain both a long-acting beta-agonist with a corticosteroid is an example of a combined product that would reduce the need to use multiple inhalers.

Conclusion

Adult patients with IDD, cared for in primary care settings throughout an academic medical centre, have complex medication regimens. Previous research has demonstrated an association between adverse medication-related outcomes and complex medication regimens. Clinicians who prescribe for patients with IDD must be aware that their patients may be at risk for adverse medication events due to the complexity of their therapies.

Disclosure statement

No potential conflict of interest was reported by the authors.

References

Beange, H., Lennox, N., & Parmenter, T. R. (1999). Health targets for people with an intellectual disability. *Journal of Intellectual & Developmental Disability, 24*, 283–297. doi:10.1080/13668259900034051

Doan, T. N., Lennox, N. G., Taylor-Gomez, M., & Ware, R. S. (2013). Medication use among Australian adults with intellectual disability in primary healthcare settings: A cross-sectional study. *Journal of Intellectual and Developmental Disability, 38*, 177–181. doi:10.3109/13668250.2013.778968

Elixhauser, A., Steiner, C., Harris, D. R., & Coffey, R. M. (1998). Comorbidity measures for use with administrative data. *Medical Care, 36*, 8–27.

Elliott, R. A., O'Callaghan, C., Paul, E., & George, J. (2013). Impact of an intervention to reduce medication regimen complexity for older hospital inpatients. *International Journal of Clinical Pharmacy, 35*, 217–224. doi:10.1007/s11096-012-9730-3

Erickson, S. R., Salgado, T. M., & Tan, X. (2016). Issues in the medication management process in people who have intellectual and developmental disabilities: A qualitative study of the caregivers' perspective. *Intellectual and Developmental Disabilities, 54*, 412–426.

Ferreira, J. M., Galato, D., & Melo, A. C. (2015). Medication regimen complexity in adults and the elderly in a primary healthcare setting: Determination of high and low complexities. *Pharmacy Practice, 13*, 659–659. doi:10.18549/PharmPract.2015.04.659

George, J., Phun, Y.-T., Bailey, M. J., Kong, D. C. M., & Stewart, K. (2004). Development and validation of the Medication Regimen Complexity Index. *Annals of Pharmacotherapy, 38*, 1369–1376. doi:10.1345/aph.1D479

Haider, S. I. (2015). *Victorian population health survey of people with an intellectual disability 2013*. Melbourne: State Government of Victoria, Health Intelligence Unit, Systems Intelligence and Analytics, Department of Health & Human Services.

Krahn, G. L., Hammond, L., & Turner, A. (2006). A cascade of disparities: Health and health care access for people with intellectual disabilities. *Mental Retardation and Developmental Disability Research Reviews, 12*, 70–82. doi:10.1002/mrdd.20098

Leendertse, A. J., Egberts, C. G., Stoker, L. J., van den Bemt, P. M. L. A., for the HARM Study Group. (2008). Frequency of and risk factors for preventable medication-related hospital admissions in the Netherlands. *Archives of Internal Medicine, 168*, 1890–1896.

Libby, A. M., Fish, D. N., Hosokawa, P. W., Linnebur, S. A., Metz, K. R., Nair, K. V., ... Hirsch, J. D. (2013). Patient-level medication regimen complexity across populations with chronic disease. *Clinical Therapeutics, 35*, 385–398.e1. doi:10.1016/j.clinthera.2013.02.019

Mansur, N., Weiss, A., & Beloosesky, Y. (2012). Looking beyond polypharmacy: Quantification of medication regimen complexity in the elderly. *The American Journal of Geriatric Pharmacotherapy, 10*, 223–229. doi:10.1016/j.amjopharm.2012.06.002

McDermott, S., Moran, R., Platt, T., & Dasari, S. (2006). Variation in health conditions among groups of adults with disabilities in primary care. *Journal of Community Health, 31*, 147–159. doi:10.1007/s10900-005-9008-y

O'Dwyer, M., Mestrovic, A., & Henman, M. 2015. Pharmacists' medicines-related interventions for people with intellectual disabilities: A narrative review. *International Journal of Clinical Pharmacy, 37*, 566–578. doi:10.1007/s11096-015-0113-4

Ou, H. T., Lin, C. Y., Erickson, S. R., & Balkrishnan, R. (2016). Refined comorbidity index based on dimensionality of comorbidity for use in studies of health-related quality of life. *Quality of Life Research, 25*, 2543–2557. doi:10.1007/s11136-016-1306-6

Scheepers, M., Kerr, M., O'Hara, D., Bainbridge, D., Cooper, S.-A., Davis, R., ... Wehmeyer, M. (2005). Reducing health disparity in people with intellectual disabilities: A report from the health issues special interest research group of the international association of intellectual disability. *Journal of Policy and Practice in Intellectual Disabilities, 2*, 249–255. doi:10.1111/j.1741-1130.2005.00037.x

Stilley, C. S., Bender, C. M., Dunbar-Jacob, J., Sereika, S., & Ryan, C. M. (2010). The impact of cognitive function on medication management: Three studies. *Health Psychology, 29*, 50–55. doi:10.1037/a0016940

Straetmans, J. M., van Schrojenstein Lantman-de Valk, H. M., Schellevis, F. G., & Dinant, G. J. (2007). Health problems of people with intellectual disabilities: The impact for general practice. *The British Journal of General Practice, 57*, 64–66.

Willson, M. N., Greer, C. L., & Weeks, D. L. (2014). Medication regimen complexity and hospital readmission for an adverse drug event. *Annals of Pharmacotherapy, 48*, 26–32. doi:10.1177/1060028013510898

Wimmer, B. C., Dent, E., Bell, J. S., Wiese, M. D., Chapman, I., Johnell, K., & Visvanathan, R. (2014). Medication regiment complexity and unplanned hospital readmissions in older people. *Annals of Pharmacotherapy, 48*, 1120–1128. doi:10.1177/1060028014537469

Appendix. Scoring the Medication Regimen Complexity Index

Patient ID______________________

Total number of medications (including PRNs) ________________________

Instructions:

1. MRCI applies only to prescribed medications. All entries are to be made only based on information on the label or drug chart (at the time of dispensing, discharge, or visit). No assumptions are to be made based on clinical judgment.
2. There are three sections in the scale. Complete each section before proceeding to the next. At the end, add the scores for the three sections to give the MRCI.
3. If the same mediation (same brand and same dosage form) is present more than once in different strengths in a regimen (e.g., marevan 5mg, 3mg and 1 md mud), it is still considered as one medication.
4. In cases where the dosage is optional, choose the dosing instruction with the smallest dose/frequency. (e.g., Ventolin MDI 1 to 2 puffs, 2 to 3 times daily will get weightings for "metered dose inhalers", "variable dose" and "twice daily"; but not for multiple units at one time.
5. In certain cases the dosing frequency needs to be calculated (e.g., Ranitidine 1 in the morning and 1 at night is twice daily).
6. It is possible that with certain "use as directed" instructions, the regimen will not get a score under dosing frequency (e.g., prednisone 5mg as directed)
7. If there is more than one dosing frequency direction, they should be scored for all the dosing frequency directions (e.g., Ventolin MDI 2 puffs BID and PRN, will get scores for "metered dose inhalers", "multiple units at one time", "twice daily", as well as "prn".
8. Instances where two or more medications are mutually exclusive, they need to be scored twice or more as PRN with the recommended dosing frequency (e.g., Ventolin MDI or Ventolin nebulizer twice daily will get scores for both "metered dose inhalers" and "nebulizer" under dosage forms, but needs to be score d two times for "twice daily prn").
9. In cases where there is no matching option, choose the closest option (e.g., six times daily could be considered as "q4h").

Section A

Circle the weighting corresponding to each dosage form (once only) present in the regimen.

Dosage Form	Dosage Form	Weighting
Oral	Capsule/tablet	1
	Gargles/mouthwashes	2
	Gums/lozenges	2
	Liquids	2
	Powders/granules	2
	Sublingual sprays/tabs	2
Topical	Cream/gels/ointments	2
	Dressing	3
	Paints/solutions	2
	Pastes	3
	Patches	2
	Spray	1
Ear,Eye, Nose	Ear drops/creams/ointments	3
	Eye drops	3
	Eye gels/ointments	3
	Nasal drops/cream/ointment	3
	Nasal spray	2
Inhalation	Accuhalers	3
	Aerolizers	3
	Metered dose inhaler	4
	Nebulizer	5
	Oxygen/concentrator	3
	Turbohalers	3
	Other inhalers (diskus)	3
Others	Dialysate	5
	Enemas	2
	Injections – prefilled	3
	Injections – ampules/vials	4
	Pessaries	3
	Patient controlled analgesia	2
	Suppositories	2
	Vaginal creams	2

Section A Total ____________

Section B

For each medication in the regimen, check a box corresponding to the dosing frequency. Then, add the number of checks in each category and multiply by the assigned weighting. In cases where there is no exact option, choose the best option.

Dosing Frequency	Medications	Total	Weighting	Weighting x number of medications
Once daily			1	
Once daily prn			0.5	
Twice daily			2	
Twice daily prn			1	
Three times daily			3	
Three times daily prn			1.5	
Four times daily			4	
Four times daily prn			2	
Q 12 hr			2.5	
Q 12 hr prn			1.5	
Q 8 hr			3.5	
Q 8 hr prn			2	
Q 6 hr			4.5	
Q 6 hr prn			2.5	
Q 4 hr			6.5	
Q 4 hr prn			3.5	
Q 2 hr			12.5	
Q 2 hr prn			6.5	
Prn			0.5	
On alternate days or less frequently			2	

Section B Total ________

Section C

Check a box corresponding to the additional directions, if present in the regimen. Then, add the number of checks in each category and multiply by the assigned weight.

Additional Instructions	Medications															Total	Weighting	Weighting x number of medications
Break or crush tablet																	1	
Dissolve tablet/powder																	1	
Multiple units at one time (e.g. 2 tabs, 2 puffs)																	1	
Variable dose (e.g. 1 to 2 caps, 2 to 3 puffs)																	1	
Take/use at specified times (e.g. morning, evening, 8 AM)																	1	
Relation to food																	1	
(e.g., pc, ac, with food)																		
Take with specific fluid																	1	
Take/use as directed																	2	
Tapering/increasing dose																	2	
Alternating dose (e.g. one morning and 2 at night, one or 2 on alternate days)																	2	

Section C Total______

Add the total for sections A, B, and C together.

Medication Regimen Complexity Index Score ________________________

Does intellectual disability research consider the potential impact of geographic location?

Stuart Wark

ABSTRACT

Background: Residing in a rural location is associated with socioeconomic disadvantage and reduced access to essential services such as housing, education, transport and healthcare. However, it is not clear whether researchers consistently consider geographic impact for people with intellectual disability.

Method: All research articles since January 2000 in the *Journal of Intellectual & Developmental Disability* were reviewed to determine the geographic location of the study participants.

Results: In approximately 50% of the 428 studies reviewed it was not possible to accurately determine participants' geographic location, or in some cases even the country in which the research was conducted. Only 6% of papers either focused on rural participants, or compared rural participants against metropolitan peers.

Conclusions: Little attention has been paid to geographic location in the sampled intellectual disability literature. This failure to consider geographic disadvantage potentially limits the applicability of such research findings to a significant proportion of the community.

The Population Division of the Department of Economic and Social Affairs of the United Nations estimated that around 46% of the world's population lived outside metropolitan areas, with much of this rural populace situated in developing countries (United Nations [UN], 2014). However, while developed countries such as Australia are considered to be highly urbanised, with around 70% of the population residing in metropolitan locations (Baxter, Hayes, & Gray, 2011), it is still estimated that over 6.8 million people live in inner regional, outer regional, remote or very remote areas (Australian Bureau of Statistics [ABS], 2016). To provide a context to this figure, 6.8 million people significantly exceeds the estimated population of Australia's largest metropolis of Sydney at just over 5 million (ABS, 2016). A total of around 60 million people, or approximately 20% of the United States of America (USA) population, lives in areas defined as rural (United States Census Bureau, 2016). This is proportionally similar to the United Kingdom (UK) which reports 9.3 million (17%) rural residents (Gov.UK, 2016a). While there is no universally accepted definition of what constitutes a rural setting versus a metropolitan one (United Nations Statistical Division, 2016), these statistics underline the reality that in both developed and developing countries around the world there is a substantial proportion of people living outside of metropolitan locations.

The existing research base indicates that people living in rural and remote areas are often at a significant disadvantage to their metropolitan peers. Smith, Humphreys, and Wilson (2008) found that rurality in a number of developed countries, including Australia, USA, UK, New Zealand and Canada, may increase the impact of socioeconomic disadvantage, service access, employment opportunities and poor transportation. Rural residents can expect to face higher levels of unemployment, reduced access to essential services and support including housing, education, transport and healthcare, and have an overall lower socioeconomic status (Alston & Kent, 2004; Australian Institute of Health and Welfare, 2003; Francis, 2005; Stutz, 2015; Winterton & Warburton, 2011).

Persons with an intellectual disability are similarly also at increased risk of experiencing disadvantages in areas such as healthcare, service access and socioeconomic status (Emerson & Hatton, 2008; Krahn, Walker, & Correa-De-Araujo, 2015; Ouellette-Kuntz, 2005). Studies have shown that this impact is potentially further magnified if the individual also lives in a rural location (Eley, Boyes, Young, & Hegney, 2009; Wark & Bleechmore, 2015; Wark et al., 2015). In spite of the known background that geographic location is a significant factor in people with intellectual disability gaining appropriate assistance (e.g., Ashman, Hulme, & Suttie, 1990; Gallego et al., 2016; Wark, Hussain, & Edwards, 2013a; Weise, Pollack, Britt, & Trollor, 2016), a scoping search of the intellectual disability literature revealed minimal other research that focused on potential disparities between rural and metropolitan residents. If models of healthcare and associated government policy are to be derived from evidence-based research (e.g., Australian Government Productivity Commission, 2009), this failure to consider rural residents may result in a poor alignment of services against actual need. The goal of this paper was to review how consistently the geographic location of participants is specifically considered in intellectual disability research. No similar geographically focused reviews of the literature for people with intellectual disability have been identified.

Methods

Definition of rurality

Defining rurality across multiple countries is not a straightforward task. As noted by the United Nations Statistics Division (2016, online):

> the distinction between urban and rural population is not amenable to a single definition applicable to all countries. For this reason, each country should decide which areas are to be classified as urban and which as rural, in accordance with their own circumstances.

In order to define rurality for this article, a review of various major geographic classification definitions (e.g., ABS, 2014; European Commission, 2016; Gov.UK, 2016b; Statistics Canada, 2015; United Nations Statistical Division, 2016; United States Census Bureau, 2015) was undertaken to see if any consensus could be established as a starting point for determining rurality. However, it was immediately apparent that definitions of what constitutes a rural or metropolitan location varied considerably around the world. Different jurisdictions used disparate singular or mixes of factors, including population estimates, population density, proximity to other cities, infrastructure and access to services, among many others, in making a determination of geographic location.

For the purpose of the current investigation, a divide between rural and metropolitan was required. The United Nations has developed a twelve-stage classification system for population clusters around the world, which includes "fishing hamlet" through to "cities" (United Nations Statistical Division, 2016, online), and this global structure was used as a starting point for arriving at a definition. Each of the 12 categories is based on a population range for a distinct location, and vary from individuals not living in a defined population cluster, such as on a farm, through to areas with populations exceeding 500,000 people. However, this model does not clearly delineate between rural and metropolitan, and it was further noted by the United Nations that "This comprehensive classification would usually be too detailed for the tabulation of survey results .... For survey results, therefore, consideration may be given to a much more condensed classification" (United Nations Statistical Division, 2016, online).

An attempt was made to map the Australian, Canadian, European Commission, UK and USA definitions against the United Nations model in order to condense its categories into a rural versus metropolitan divide. When examining just the total population figures in isolation, the Australian system nominated metropolitan populations as featuring over 250,000 people, the Canadian model cited 100,000 people, the European Commission noted figures of 200,000 and 500,000 for differing regional centres, the USA Census Bureau used a figure of greater than 50,000, while the UK Government defined rural with a cut-off mark of less than 10,000 people (ABS, 2014; Gov.UK, 2016b; Statistics Canada, 2015; United Nations Statistical Division, 2016; United States Census Bureau, 2015). This reflects a vast population range, from less than 10,000 people through to potentially half a million people, and does not lend itself to an exact figure. Basic analysis revealed that the mean and median score for these five systems were 100,000 or greater, with a majority of the models (Australia, Canada and European Commission) using a figure of 100,000 or more people to define metropolitan locations. This data was found to align with the second highest category (100,000–499,000 people) in the United Nations system.

Therefore, it was decided for the purposes of this analysis that a location was classified as being non-metropolitan if it had a population below 100,000 people. This was determined prior to commencement and following careful consideration of the various different classification systems. It is acknowledged that this figure of 100,000 is arbitrary, but this was unavoidable due to the numerous different and sometimes contradictory definitions across various countries. It is also recognised that this simplistic definition fails to take into account the differences between very remote communities and a regional city with a population of 99,000 people (e.g., Wark, Ryan, Parmenter, & Hussain, 2016) and other important factors, such as the impact of a rural location's geographic proximity to a major city, however that level of analysis was beyond the scope of this paper.

Review process

The *Journal of Intellectual & Developmental Disability* was chosen as the target journal. This journal has been in continuous publication since 1970, commencing as the *Australia and New Zealand Journal of Developmental Disabilities*. It was deliberately selected as the target journal due to its scope of international multidisciplinary intellectual disability research that would include countries with a range of rural and metropolitan locations.

A commencement date for the review was determined as 1 January 2000. This date was chosen to both ensure a suitable dataset that was estimated prior to commencement to exceed 300 articles, and also for simple chronological logic. The author examined all original research or brief report journal articles from Issue 25, Volume 1 in 2000 through to Issue 42, Volume 3 (September) in 2016. This represented a total of 410 articles. An additional 18 "Latest Articles" (early on-line) were also examined as of 9 September 2016 to provide a comprehensive review from the year 2000 onwards.

The definition of whether a location was rural or metropolitan was based upon the nominated population cap of 100, 000, unless the article specifically made this distinction itself. If the article did not nominate the population for the participants' location, an online search was conducted to establish this figure whenever possible. The geographic location for each paper was determined by the participant focus of the research. In the majority of cases, it was expected that this would be persons with intellectual disability. However, the review was deliberately not limited to research solely with or on people with intellectual disability, and also included all papers reporting on issues surrounding intellectual disability. For example, research articles reporting on experiences or needs of carers or other supporters (parents of children with special needs, disability support staff and so on) were also included to ensure all relevant data were examined. Editorials, invited commentaries, rejoinders, literature reviews, meta-analyses, purely theoretical frameworks or models, reviews of policy documents, book reviews, opinions and perspectives were not included.

Table 1. Breakdown of geographic location of research papers.

Article Categories	Number	Percentage
Solely Rural Participants	11	3%
Solely Metropolitan Participants	103	24%
Rural and Metropolitan (combined results)	85	20%
Rural and Metropolitan (comparative results)	14	3%
Not Specified / Unable to Determine	215	50%
Total research articles	428	100%

The author was responsible for data extraction. The Abstract, Methods and Results section of each paper was read initially to attempt to determine the geographic location of the study's participants. If this could not be established through these three sections, the entire paper was reviewed to see if additional information could definitively identify participant locations. All papers were classified as:

- solely rural participants,
- solely metropolitan participants,
- both metropolitan and rural participants, or
- not specified / unable to determine.

Example of research that were defined as being "not specified / unable to determine" would feature vague descriptors such as "a location in Central Louisiana" or "services in Southern Ontario". Unspecified city locations were not automatically assumed to be metropolitan, as they could be smaller rural cities with populations under 100,000. If the paper reported the site as a city without a specific name, precise location or approximate population, it was classed as unspecified.

Research was considered to be both metropolitan and rural if the methodology reported recruitment procedures that covered entire regions (e.g., questionnaires sent to all education regions in the state of Ohio). However, imprecise regions (e.g., located in South-East England) was considered unspecified. The studies that had both metropolitan and rural participants were divided into two categories:

- combined data in which the metropolitan and rural data were merged and not considered separately, or
- comparative data which commented directly on rural versus metropolitan findings.

All data was recorded into a spreadsheet. A cross-checking process was implemented for all research within one calendar year. A colleague independently chose a year (2005) and followed the methodology described above. These results were then compared to the main spreadsheet for 2005; the same total number of research articles were identified and they were all classified into the same categories.

Results

A total of 428 papers meeting the eligibility criteria were reviewed. These papers reported on data from a wide range of countries with varying geographic densities. They included, among others, studies based in Europe (e.g., the UK, Ireland, France, Germany, Italy, Austria,

Finland, Netherlands, Spain, Sweden), Asia (e.g., Nepal, Singapore, China, Japan, Taiwan, Hong Kong, Malaysia, the Philippines), the middle-east (e.g., United Arab Emirates, Turkey, Jordan, Israel), USA, Canada, New Zealand, Australia and South Africa. Table 1 provides a summary of the 428 papers and how each study's participants were categorised geographically.

Solely rural participants

Eleven papers in the *Journal of Intellectual & Developmental Disability* since 2000 were found to focus solely on rurally based participants. In general, these papers reported on research designed from conceptualisation to specifically examine intellectual disability issues in rural locations. The introduction sections of these articles normally included at least one paragraph outlining the reason why a rural location was purposively chosen (e.g., Lincoln et al., 2014).

Solely metropolitan participants

Approximately a quarter of the reviewed articles reported solely on metropolitan participants (e.g., Chien, Branjerdporn, Rodger, & Copley, 2016). In contrast to the solely rural papers, there was often limited geographic context provided for the sample other than noting the location. Within the metropolitan-focused research articles there were rarely any reasons given for choosing the metropolitan location, with justifications for sample selection instead concentrating on other demographic factors.

Rural and metropolitan (combined results)

Twenty percent of all reviewed papers did include participants from across different geographic areas in congregate data analyses (e.g., Toms, Totsika, Hastings, & Healy, 2015). These papers were often large-scale questionnaires and surveys that reported on specific comparative factors, but did not specifically consider geographic location as an area of interest. It is possible that there are other papers based upon the same datasets that did report on geographic differences, but this analysis was not included in these articles.

Rural and metropolitan (comparative results)

There were very few papers (3%) that directly compared outcomes of rural versus metropolitan participants. As with the solely rural papers, generally these articles specifically outlined the rationale for including both rural and metropolitan samples, and why such comparisons were important (e.g., Iacono, Davis, Humphreys, & Chandler, 2003).

Not specified / unable to determine

The largest category in this research was "Not Specified / Unable to Determine". It was not possible to accurately determine the geographic location of participants in approximately half of all the reviewed articles. In these papers, there was not enough information to allow the reader to identify where the study took place. In a number of cases, it was not possible to even confidently determine the country in which the research was undertaken after reading the entire paper. In these situations the demographic descriptors of the participants often referred to generic residential locations, such as a group home, without providing any additional information to allow even an approximate location to be established. While a general setting could sometimes be guessed by examining the location of the Institution that provided ethical approval for the study, this method could not be considered definitive, and particularly not for projects with collaborating authors across multiple areas.

A small number of papers did accurately identify a precise geographic location, but were still classified as unspecified. There were two main situations in which this occurred. Firstly, when participants were drawn from attendees, such as at a clinic at a large metropolitan hospital, it was sometimes impossible to determine a home location for participants. Rural residents will often have to access specialist care in major cities as it is not otherwise available, but this detail was not captured within most studies. Secondly, papers reporting on forensic cases were very difficult to classify, as the participants may have been originally from a rural area, but were incarcerated in a metropolitan location (or vice versa). However, hospital or forensic studies that focused on the experiences of permanent staff were classified where possible according to location, as it was deemed reasonable to assume that the majority of such staff were resident to that local area.

It is also worth noting that a very small number of papers did report on comparisons between rural and metropolitan residents, but the focus was not actually on geographic differences. An example of this situation included comparisons between rural students without intellectual disability against metropolitan students with intellectual disability. Another example was rurally based individuals in a community setting who were compared to metropolitan-based individuals in a forensic unit, but where the variable of interest was the residential-type and not its geographic location.

Discussion

It is known that geographic location plays a significant role in access to support services for people with intellectual disability (e.g., Dew et al., 2013; Dew et al., 2012; Veitch et al., 2012; Wark, Hussain, & Edwards, 2013b, 2014), but the current paper indicates that little research actively considered rurality as a factor. Of the 428 research papers reviewed from January 2000 to September 2016, only 3% focused solely on rural participants in comparison to the 24% of articles that reported on purely metropolitan-based participants. This imbalance is considerably wider than the gross world-wide estimated rural population of 46% (UN, 2014) or specific nation's rural population data would indicate (e.g., ABS, 2014; Gov.UK, 2016a; United States Census Bureau, 2016). Half the papers did not contain enough information to allow the reader to ascertain an accurate geographic classification for the participants. Around 20% of the papers did include rural participants in their research, however, this data was aggregated with no reported findings comparing participants based on geographic locality. Only 14 of the 428 papers specifically reported on the comparative impact of a rural versus metropolitan geographic location within their analysis of the results.

The high proportion of papers in which it was not possible to determine a precise location was not expected. After reflection and discussion with colleagues familiar with rural research (one of whom was responsible for the cross-checking process outlined in the Methodology section), it is not believed that this result is solely a consequence of the geographic definition used in this paper, and any other definition may have encountered the same problem. The examined studies often nominated a generic location without contextualising it geographically. It was normal for papers to include descriptions of the location that were vague and ambiguous. Phrases such as "conducted in group homes situated in the state of… ", or "a classroom within a mainstream school" were commonplace and then provided no further information about location. Some papers would report in considerable detail on the residential type and demographics (e.g., the number of residents, their ages, gender and disability types within a small group home setting), but then not nominate the actual geographic location. Even if the definition of rurality was changed, this lack of detail would still result in most of these articles remaining unclassifiable.

It could be inferred in many of the unclassified articles that the research was undertaken in a metropolitan setting. Examples of this scenario include where the study protocols refer to weekly testing done in a metropolitan-based university laboratory or office. In such research, it is highly unlikely that the participants would travel from rural areas on a consistent basis. Unfortunately, this assumption cannot be confirmed and all such papers were therefore included in the unspecified category. Nonetheless, it is probable that the real discrepancy between the rural and metropolitan research is even greater than reported, with many of the unspecified papers being metropolitan-based.

It is worth acknowledging that geographic location is irrelevant in some research, and that reporting on precise geographic locations may breech ethical considerations regarding confidentiality. However, neither of these reasons would seem to explain the large disparities evident in the reported numbers. One contributing factor to these results may be related to the locations of universities. In Australia and many other developed countries, the majority of universities, and by extension the majority of researchers, are located in metropolitan locations (e.g., Complete University Guide, 2016; Universities Australia, 2016). Therefore, it makes sense that most researchers will focus on samples that are convenient or easily accessible to them. However, this approach may result in the observed skewed literature base.

A possible reason why there are more aggregated data studies than comparative data studies may be relate to the minimum number of participants required in each category for statistical validity. In rural areas where there is considerable geographic spread it may be difficult to obtain a sufficient number of people with intellectual disability to form valid comparison groups (Pierce & Scherra, 2012). Therefore, this would result in the greater number of combined analyses in which rural participants are included but not discriminated from metropolitan peers.

However, there were numerous examples whereby the research simply failed to consider whether geographic location had an impact. There were a number of qualitative studies (e.g., personal interview or focus groups) did include both rural and metropolitan participants, but while they would note a pseudonym, age and gender against cited quotations from participants, they did not similarly identify their geographic location. This failure removed important context from the participant's response, and limits understanding of what factors may have led to the outcomes being reported.

The 428 papers reported on a wide variety of issues, such as access to services, training, choice making, ageing, involvement in planning, parenting, quality of life and so on, but by failing to consider geographic location, the validity of some of the conclusions must be questioned. Reporting that participants with intellectual disability had little choice regarding service provision, when they may have come from a geographic location in which there were literally no alternatives, doesn't recognise the true situation. Similarly, there is little value in noting the extent of staff baseline training without also identifying that not all staff can access training readily in their local vicinity. Without taking into context the potential disadvantage or advantages that location may have on the participant, reported results within all intellectual disability research must be considered carefully.

Limitations

This brief report has a number of limitations. It examined all research papers from the year 2000 onwards, and this date range was selected prior to commencement primarily to ensure a sample of at least 300 articles. A larger sample of papers may result in different findings. However, the major limitation pertains to the simplistic definition of metropolitan versus rural. While it was based upon existing classifications, the discrepancies between models meant that rurality was arbitrarily determined by the author and a different definition would possibly result in different findings. This issue applies to both the nominated population figure of >100,000 people and also the failure to account for other important factors, such as locational proximity to capital cities and services. A future approach to this question could involve separating all research on the basis of the home country, where identified, and then using that country's definition of rurality for each nominated location. However, such an approach was beyond the scope of this brief report.

Recommendations

There are two key recommendations arising from this research; one pertaining to researchers and another to journal editors and reviewers. For researchers, it is suggested that careful consideration of geographic location is always required prior to commencing any project. If it is thought that this issue may impact on the results, the research then needs to be specifically designed to include metropolitan and non-metropolitan participants for comparative purposes. While there are a majority of universities in metropolitan areas around the world, a proactive approach to collaboration with rurally located universities could successfully address some of the identified issues.

A recommendation for journal editors is to specify in the "Instructions for Authors" section that all new manuscripts must provide adequate information to identify the geographic location of the study participants. Assessors could then be reminded to ensure every article has this prerequisite data during the review process. This minimum required information should clearly outline the participants' location, be it a single setting such as in a city or multiple sites across countries. Specific details should also include approximate populations of both the location and the wider regional jurisdiction. If the study is located solely outside of a city environment, the proximity to the nearest large regional centre or metropolitan area should also be noted. Whenever possible, data obtained from settings such as hospitals and forensic units should also identify the normal home location of participants.

Conclusion

The findings of this brief report indicate that little attention has been paid to the impact of geographic location within intellectual disability research since the year 2000 in the *Journal of Intellectual & Developmental Disability*. This is problematic, as government policy and health systems are nominally derived from evidence-based research. If the research quantum misses a significant proportion of the community, their requirements will not be considered in the development of programs of support and unmet needs will remain unrecognised. Future comparative studies that specifically examine differences for intellectual disability issues based on geographic location are important, but easy measures such as ensuring the inclusion of sufficient details in the methodology to allow the reader to accurately identify the location of the research are also necessary to provide context to all research findings.

Disclosure statement

No potential conflict of interest was reported by the author.

ORCID

Stuart Wark http://orcid.org/0000-0002-5366-1860

References

Alston, M., & Kent, J. (2004). *Social impacts of drought: A report to NSW agriculture*. Wagga Wagga: Centre for Rural Social Research, Charles Sturt University.

Ashman, A., Hulme, P., & Suttie, J. (1990). The life circumstances of aged people with intellectual disability. *Australia and New Zealand Journal of Developmental Disabilities*, *16*, 335–347. doi:10.1080/07263869000034151

Australian Bureau of Statistics (ABS). (2014). *Australian standard geographical classification*. Retrieved from http://www.abs.gov.au/websitedbs/d3310114.nsf/home/australian+standard+geographical+classification+(asgc)

Australian Bureau of Statistics (ABS). (2016). *Regional population growth, Australia, 2013–2014*. Retrieved from http://www.abs.gov.au/AUSSTATS/abs@.nsf/DetailsPage/3218.02013-14?OpenDocument

Australian Government Productivity Commission. (2009). *Strengthening evidence-based policy in the Australian federation*. Retrieved from http://www.pc.gov.au/research/supporting/strengthening-evidence/roundtable-proceedings-volume1.pdf

Australian Institute of Health and Welfare. (2003). *Rural, regional and remote health: A study of mortality*. Canberra: Author.

Baxter, J., Hayes, A., & Gray, M. (2011). *Families in regional, rural and remote Australia*. Canberra: Australian Government, Australian Institute of Family Studies.

Chien, C.-W., Branjerdporn, G., Rodger, S., & Copley, J. (2016). Exploring environmental restrictions on everyday life participation of children with developmental disability. *Journal of Intellectual & Developmental Disability*. Advance online publication. doi:10.3109/13668250.2016.1194969

Complete University Guide. (2016). *University profiles*. Retrieved from http://www.thecompleteuniversityguide.co.uk/universities/

Dew, A., Bulkeley, K., Veitch, C., Bundy, A., Lincoln, M., Brentnall, J., … Griffiths, S. (2013). Carer and service providers' experiences of individual funding models for children with a disability in rural and remote areas. *Health & Social Care in the Community*, *21*, 432–441. doi:10.1111/hsc.12032

Dew, A., Veitch, C., Lincoln, M., Brentnall, J., Bulkeley, K., Gallego, G., … Griffiths, S. (2012). The need for new models for delivery of therapy intervention to people with a disability in rural and remote areas of Australia. *Journal of Intellectual & Developmental Disability*, *37*, 50–53. doi:10.3109/13668250.2011.644269

Eley, D., Boyes, J., Young, L., & Hegney, D. (2009). Adults with intellectual disability in regional Australia: Incidence of disability and provision of accommodation support to their ageing carers. *The Australian Journal of Rural Health*, *17*, 161–166. doi:10.1111/j.1440-1584.2009.01062.x

Emerson, E., & Hatton, C. (2008). Socioeconomic disadvantage, social participation and networks and the self-rated health of English men and women with mild and moderate intellectual disabilities: Cross sectional survey. *European Journal of Public Health*, *18*, 31–37. doi:https://doi.org/10.1093/eurpub/ckm041

European Commission. (2016). *Urban-rural typology*. Retrieved from http://ec.europa.eu/eurostat/web/rural-development/methodology

Francis, K. (2005). Health and health practice in rural Australia: Where are we, where to from here? *On-line Journal of Rural Nursing and Health Care*, *5*, 28–36. doi: http://rnojournal.binghamton.edu/index.php/RNO/article/viewFile/188/163

Gallego, G., Dew, A., Lincoln, M., Bundy, A., Chedid, R. J., Bulkeley, K., … Veitch, C. (2016). Access to therapy services for people with disability in rural Australia: A carers' perspective. *Health & Social Care in the Community*. Advance online publication. doi:10.1111/hsc.12399

Gov.UK. (2016a). *Official statistics. Rural population and migration statistics*. Retrieved from https://www.gov.uk/government/publications/rural-population-and-migration/rural-population-201415

Gov. UK. (2016b). *Urban rural classification*. Retrieved from https://www.gov.uk/government/collections/rural-urban-classification

Iacono, T., Davis, R., Humphreys, J., & Chandler, N. (2003). GP and support people's concerns and priorities for meeting the health care needs of individuals with developmental disabilities: A metropolitan and non-metropolitan comparison. *Journal of Intellectual & Developmental Disability*, *28*, 353–368. doi:10.1080/13668250310001616399

Krahn, G. L., Walker, D. K., & Correa-De-Araujo, R. (2015). Persons with disabilities as an unrecognized health disparity population. *American Journal of Public Health*, *105*(Suppl. 2), S198–S206. doi:10.2105/AJPH.2014.302182

Lincoln, M., Gallego, G., Dew, A., Bulkeley, K., Veitch, C., Bundy, A., … Griffiths, S. (2014). Recruitment and retention of allied health professionals in the disability sector in rural and remote New South Wales, Australia. *Journal of Intellectual & Developmental Disability*, *39*, 86–97. doi:10.3109/13668250.2013.861393

Ouellette-Kuntz, H. (2005). Understanding health disparities and inequities faced by individuals with intellectual disabilities. *Journal of Applied Research in Intellectual Disabilities*, *18*, 113–121. doi:10.1111/j.1468-3148.2005.00240.x

Pierce, C., & Scherra, E. (2012). *The challenges of data collection in rural dwelling samples*. Retrieved from http://rnojournal.binghamton.edu/index.php/RNO/article/download/197/172

Smith, K., Humphreys, J. & Wilson, M. (2008). Addressing the health disadvantage of rural populations: How does epidemiological evidence inform rural health policies and research? *Australian Journal of Rural Health*, *16*, 56–66. doi:10.1111/j.1440-1584.2008.00953.x

Statistics Canada. (2015). *Rural areas*. Retrieved from https://www12.statcan.gc.ca/census-recensement/2011/ref/dict/geo042-eng.cfm

Stutz, F. (2015). Tackling rural disadvantage. *Independent Education*, *45*, 18–19.

Toms, G., Totsika, V., Hastings, R., & Healy, H. (2015). Access to services by children with intellectual disability and mental health problems: Population-based evidence from the UK. *Journal of Intellectual & Developmental Disability*, *40*, 239–247. doi:10.3109/13668250.2015.1045460

United Nations (UN). (2014). *World's population increasingly urban with more than half living in urban areas*. Retrieved from https://esa.un.org/unpd/wup/

United Nations Statistical Division. (2016). *Population density and urbanization*. Retrieved from http://unstats.un.org/unsd/Demographic/sconcerns/densurb/densurbmethods.htm

United States Census Bureau. (2015). *Urban and rural classification*. Retrieved from https://www.census.gov/geo/reference/urban-rural.html

United States Census Bureau. (2016). *How many people reside in urban or rural areas for the 2010 Census? What percentage of the U.S. population is urban or rural?* Retrieved from https://ask.census.gov/faq.php?id=5000&faqId=5971

Universities Australia. (2016). *Australian university profiles*. Retrieved from https://www.universitiesaustralia.edu.au/australias-universities/university-profiles#.WA1UYHqRag4

Veitch, C., Dew, A., Bulkeley, K., Lincoln, M., Bundy, A., Gallego, G., & Griffiths, S. (2012). Issues affecting therapist workforce and service delivery in the disability sector in rural and remote New South Wales, Australia: Perspectives of policy-makers, managers and senior therapists. *Rural and Remote Health*, *12*, 1–12.

Wark, S., & Bleechmore, K. (2015). Twenty-five years of community living: Changes in support staff perceptions. *Disability, CBR & Inclusive Development*, *26*, 5–24. doi:10.5463/dcid.v26i1.413

Wark, S., Canon-Vanry, M., Ryan, P., Hussain, R., Knox, M., Edwards, M., … Leggatt-Cook, C. (2015). Ageing-related experiences of adults with learning disability resident in rural areas: One Australian perspective. *British Journal of Learning Disabilities*, *43*, 293–301. doi:10.1111/bld.12145

Wark, S., Hussain, R., & Edwards, H. (2013a). Rural and remote area service provision for people aging with intellectual disability. *Journal of Policy and Practice in Intellectual Disabilities*, *10*, 62–70. doi:10.1111/jppi.12017

Wark, S., Hussain, R., & Edwards, H. (2013b). *Ageing with an intellectual disability: Support issues in rural localities*. Paper presented at the Proceedings of the 12th National Rural Health Conference, Adelaide. Retrieved from http://nrha.org.au/12nrhc/wp-content/uploads/2013/06/Wark-Stuart_ppr.pdf

Wark, S., Hussain, R., & Edwards, H. (2014). Impediments to community-based care for people ageing with intellectual disability in rural New South Wales. *Health & Social Care in the Community*, *22*, 623–633. doi:10.1111/hsc.12130

Wark, S., Ryan, P., Parmenter, T., & Hussain, R. (2016). Supporting end-of-life care across geographic diversity: What works and what needs to change? *Journal of Intellectual Disability Research*, *60*, 760. doi:10.1111/jir.12305

Weise, J., Pollack, A. J., Britt, H., & Trollor, J. N. (2016). Who provides primary health care for people with an intellectual disability: General practitioner and general practice characteristics from the BEACH dataset. *Journal of Intellectual & Developmental Disability*. Advance online publication. doi:10.3109/13668250.2016.1250252

Winterton, R., & Warburton, J. (2011). Does place matter? Reviewing the experience of disadvantage for older people in rural Australia. *Rural Society*, *20*, 187–197. doi:10.5172/rsj.20.2.187

Dialogue between workers and family members is related to their attitudes towards self-determination of individuals with intellectual disability

Vicente Martínez-Tur, Yolanda Estreder, Carolina Moliner, Esther Gracia, Luminiţa Pătraş and Ana Zornoza

ABSTRACT

Background: This study focused on attitudes of workers and family members towards self-determination of individuals with intellectual disability. First, we compare their self-determination attitudes. Second, we test the link from mutual communication (workers and family members perceive that the other party openly dialogues about self-determination) to individual attitudes. Finally, we examine the relationship between mutual communication and affinity in attitudes.

Method: We conducted a survey study with 111 organisations (914 workers and 845 family members).

Results: Workers have more positive attitudes than family members. In addition, high mutual communication was associated with individual positive attitudes towards self-determination and shared attitudes between workers and family members.

Conclusions: When both workers and family members perceive that the other party is accessible and willing to engage in open dialogue about self-determination issues, their attitudes converge.

In the context of intellectual disability, self-determination has been defined as "volitional actions that enable one to act as the primary causal agent in one's life and to maintain or improve one's quality of life" (Wehmeyer, 2005, p. 117). Self-determination is a critical factor because of its positive association with the quality of life of individuals with intellectual disability. Enabling individuals with intellectual disability to act as primary agents in their lives has positive effects on academic performance and transitions (Seong, Wehmeyer, Palmer, & Little, 2015), employability (Field & Hoffman, 2007), and independent living in general (Palmer & Wehmeyer, 2003), among others. The United Nations (2015) recently described the problems affecting people with intellectual disability (PID). Although progress has been made, self-determination and the social inclusion of PID still remain a challenge in Western societies. In fact, even individuals with intellectual disability who are not institutionalised and have a job experience abjection and isolation (Hall, 2004, p. 303). The promotion of self-determination and independence should be accompanied by adequate policies that avoid the risk of serious harm and death experienced by PID due to traffic accidents as pedestrians, drowning, falls, fire, criminal victimisation, and abuse (eg, Fyson & Kitson, 2007; Shavelle, Strauss, & Day, 2005). The policies to be implemented are aimed at minimising risks (eg, Heslop et al., 2014) and increasing the benefits derived from self-determination.

To foster self-determination, cooperation between workers in institutions and family members is needed (Carter et al., 2013). Coordinated efforts are required for the effective design and implementation of plans to improve self-determination. However, research has found a significant gap between workers and family members. In general, parents are less involved in promoting self-determination than workers (Zhang, Katsiyannis, & Zhang, 2002; Zhang, Wehmeyer, & Chen, 2005). Powers et al. (1996) pointed out that parents could feel uncertain about both the expected level of self-determination and useful strategies to improve it. These scholars also suggest that parents have concerns about the risks of self-determination. All these factors create an environment where family members feel unsure about the support of self-determination (Curryer, Stancliffe, & Dew, 2015).

One relevant factor explaining this discrepancy between workers and family members is lack of mutual communication about self-determination. Institutions and services for vulnerable people have become increasingly professionalised in modern societies (Carey, Braunack-Mayer, & Barraket, 2009), which has had positive effects because scientific criteria are thought to improve the quality of life of the service's users. However, professionals' knowledge is mainly related to the functioning of the organisation, interaction with direct uses, and decision-making, whereas communication with citizens (eg, family members of individuals with intellectual disability) may suffer (Alexander, Nank, & Stivers, 1999). Nevertheless, it is possible to open up channels for dialogue about critical objectives. The present study focuses on mutual communication about self-determination between workers and family members in organisations for individuals with intellectual disability. In a real dialogue or mutual communication, the different parties (workers and family members) play the roles of senders and receivers of information simultaneously. By contrast, unilateral communication has limitations because the receiver does not contribute to the debate and proposals. Therefore, and based on the mutuality concept (Ko, 2014; Martínez-Tur et al., 2016), optimal mutual communication between actors requires two conditions: (a) a high level of open communication and (b) a high level of agreement that this communication exists. In other words, each part of the relationship should perceive that the other part dialogues openly about self-determination.

Dialogue about self-determination is valuable in itself, but it also has additional benefits based on exposure effects. Mutual communication should stimulate positive attitudes towards self-determination, and attitudes are relevant because they guide human behaviour (Bohner & Dickel, 2011). For decades, research has strongly supported the mere-exposure effect for a wide range of objects and situations (Bornstein, 1989; Jones, Young, & Claypool, 2011; Young, Jones, & Claypool, 2016; Zajonc, 1968). It has been well established that repeated exposure to stimuli engenders positive attitudes towards the object in question. Scholars have proposed different co-acting mechanisms to explain this relationship between mere exposure and attitudes. It has been argued that repeated exposure avoids the threat (Bornstein, 1989) and arousal (Zajonc, 1968) typically associated with novel stimuli. In addition, repeated exposure facilitates fluent processing (Bornstein & Dagostino, 1994), which can be felt positively. The current research study extends the well-established direct link from repeated exposure and attitudes to open dialogue between workers and family members about self-determination of individuals with intellectual disability. Open dialogue about self-determination is a way to expose workers and family members to self-determination as a strategy to improve the quality of life of individuals with intellectual disability. This dialogue can lead to viewing self-determination of individuals with intellectual disability as a familiar and valuable objective. Therefore, mutual dialogue is related to positive attitudes towards self-determination. Based on these arguments, we propose the following hypothesis for empirical testing:

Hypothesis 1. Mutual dialogue between workers and family members about self-determination will be positively related to their attitudes towards self-determination of individuals with intellectual disability.

In addition, we aim to explore whether workers vs. family members differ in the importance of mutual communication. As mentioned above, parents tend to be less involved in fostering self-determination in their relatives with intellectual disability than workers are (Zhang et al., 2002, 2005). Compared to workers, family members also feel more uncertainty about both the degree to which self-determination should be encouraged and the strategies that can be used to improve it (Curryer et al., 2015; Powers et al., 1996). With this in mind, it is reasonable to expect that family members will be especially sensitive to mutual dialogue with workers. This dialogue can be associated with a reduction in uncertainty, facilitating a greater positive change in parents than in workers. Therefore, we propose the following hypothesis:

Hypothesis 2. The magnitude of the positive relationship between mutual dialogue and attitudes towards self-determination will be greater for family members than for workers.

Another benefit of mutual communication is that it stimulates shared attitudes between workers and family members about self-determination of individuals with intellectual disability. Open dialogue forces workers and family members to be exposed to each other. This exposure reflects fluency (ease with which information is identified and/or processed) and increases perceptions of similarity among the actors in a social context (see Claypool, Housley, Bernstein, & Mackie, 2012). Bornstein, Leone, and Galley (1987, Experiment 3) found that individuals who were previously exposed to another participant significantly increased their agreement with his/her opinion. Moreland and Beach (1992) observed that participants evaluated their classmates more similarly to themselves as the number of classes increased. Claypool et al. (2012) also found that repeated exposure led participants in the experiments to categorise targets as members of the in-group. Extending these arguments to the aforementioned interaction between workers and family members, it is reasonable to expect that when one party perceives that the other party is accessible and openly discusses self-determination, their perspectives will become closer, and attitudinal discrepancies will probably be reduced:

> *Hypothesis 3.* Mutual dialogue between workers and family members about self-determination will be positively related to affinity in their attitudes toward self-determination of individuals with intellectual disability.

In summary, the present research study answers three main questions: (a) Is there a positive relationship between mutual communication about self-determination (between workers and family members) and individual positive attitudes towards self-determination? (b) Are parents more sensitive to mutual dialogue than workers? and (c) Is mutual communication about self-determination (between workers and family members) associated with shared attitudes towards self-determination? In addition, we replicate previous research studies indicating that workers are more engaged in promoting self-determination in individuals with intellectual disability than family members (Zhang et al., 2002, 2005). Therefore, a fourth question for this study is: Do workers have more positive attitudes towards self-determination than family members?

Method

Participants and procedure

The Ethics Committee at the University of the corresponding author approved the procedure and conduct of the current survey study. A total of 111 small organisations for individuals with intellectual disability participated in the study voluntarily. All of them were affiliated with "Plena Inclusión," a Non-Governmental Organization located in Spain and dedicated to the improvement of quality of life of individuals with intellectual disability. These organisations delivered educational, therapeutic, and social-leisure services. Most of their employees were social workers, psychologists, occupational therapists, physiotherapists, and primary healthcare workers. In each centre, workers and families were randomly selected to participate in the research study. To be surveyed, the worker had to have contact with PID as part of his/her job. Following the criteria of Liden, Erdogan, Wayne, and Sparrowe (2006), organisations had to achieve the participation of at least 60% of the members under the supervision of the manager of the organisations. In addition, usable surveys from at least three families per centre had to be obtained. These strategies allowed us to be more confident that the centres were sufficiently represented and that the data could be aggregated. From each participating family, the member was selected with the most frequent and direct relationship with the organisation in question. The research team trained one worker per organisation to implement the data collection. This sampling plan resulted in the participation of 914 workers (response rate = 95%) and 845 family members (response rate = 96%). Their participation was voluntary and confidential, and they had the opportunity to drop out of the study at any time. On average, job tenure of workers was about 8 years. Workers' average age was 37.64 ($SD = 9.30$), and 75.5% of them were women. Regarding family members, on average, they had used the services of the organisations for about 11 years, 67% were women, and their average age was 57.56 ($SD = 11.60$).

Measures

Both workers and family members completed a questionnaire with well-established measures from the literature. We previously conducted a pilot study to ensure that the items could be easily understood. In addition, some experts who belonged to "Plena Inclusión" – the NGO that participated in the study – analysed the items in order to adapt the wording to the specific characteristics of the context, in collaboration with the research team. Measures are included in the Appendix.

Workers' measures

First, we included a measure of *open communication about self-determination* (OCS) based on the 3-item scale about Communication Openness from the Mutual Trusting Behaviours scale (Smith & Barclay, 1997). We adapted the wording of the three items from the original scale to the context of persons with intellectual disability, focusing on the degree to which workers perceive that family members are willing to openly discuss self-determination. Workers were explicitly told to focus their attention on the family members in the centre where they worked. Reliability scores are: alpha coefficient (.64) and composite reliability value (.74). Higher scores indicated family members' greater willingness to openly talk about self-determination, as reported by workers.

Second, to measure workers' *attitudes towards self-determination,* we considered the six items that refer to aspects of self-determination of individuals with intellectual disability included in the scale used by Verdugo, Gómez, and Árias (2007) and Martínez-Tur, Moliner, Peñarroja, Gracia, and Peiró (2015). For each of the six aspects, we created an attitude measure where workers were forced to choose their position/attitude on a scale between two bipolar adjectives: *very bad* (−3) to *very good* (+3). Reliability scores are: alpha coefficient (.90) and composite reliability value (.91). Higher scores were indicative of workers' more positive attitudes toward self-determination of individuals with intellectual disability.

Family members' measures

Regarding family members, we used the same measures as those considered for workers, but we adapted them to the role of parents and other caregivers. Therefore, open communication focused on the degree to which family members perceive that workers are willing to dialogue openly about self-determination (alpha coefficient = .62 and composite reliability value = .71). Family members were explicitly told to focus their attention on the workers in the centre they attended. We also measured family members' attitudes towards self-determination (alpha coefficient = .83 and composite reliability value = .85).

In general, reliability of workers' and family members' measures was satisfactory. The composite reliability values were above .70 (see Raykov, 2001). Alpha coefficients corresponding to Communication Openness were slightly below .70, but this is acceptable taking into account that this measure had three items. Alpha coefficients are sensitive to the number of items, and they tend to increase when the number of items increases, so that values greater than .60 can be considered adequate for scales with three items (see Dekovic, Janssens, & Gerris, 1991; Hair, Black, Babin, Anderson, & Tatham, 2006).

Aggregation issues

To compute mutual communication about self-determination at the organisational level, we followed the procedure to assess mutuality used by Smith and Barclay (1997) and Martínez-Tur et al. (2016). First, we aggregated the measure of OCS at the organisational level for both workers and family members. Because of workers' tenure at their workplace (8 years on average) and the family members' long-term relationship with the centres (11 years on average), it is reasonable to expect that shared perceptions about open communication would emerge within each of the two groups. They are subjected to similar events, structures, and processes, and, over time, they are also involved in social interactions where they share experiences and interpretations. This helps to create agreement in the way people interpret reality (see Kozlowski & Klein, 2000). Workers, on the one hand, can develop shared perceptions about the degree to which family members openly discuss self-determination. Family members, on the other hand, can also share perceptions about the extent to which the workers in the organisation in question are accessible for an open dialogue about self-determination.

Our measure of OCS is congruent with aggregation at the centre level. In fact, we used the recommended referent shift consensus model (Bashshur, Rupp, & Christopher, 2004). According to this model, the wording of our items focused on workers or family members as a whole, and not on the individual's specific experience (see the section about measures above). Statistical analyses also supported aggregation at the organisational level for both workers and family members in this first step of the aggregation. We computed the recommended Average Deviation Index from the Mean ($AD_{M(J)}$) as an indicator of within-group interrater agreement (Burke, Finkelstein, & Dusig, 1999). Dunlap, Burke, and Smith-Crowe (2003) developed a procedure to establish the cut-off for measures depending on the number of items. Scores below the cut-off indicate that agreement exists and the data can be aggregated. In the present research study, the average scores for workers (0.90) and family members (0.79) were below the cut-off of 1.17 for a 7-point rating scale (see Dunlap et al., 2003). These scores indicated the existence of within-group agreement about open communication for both workers and family members. We also calculated one-way analyses of variance to test whether there was between-organisations discrimination (see Chan, 1998). Results indicated significant between-centres discrimination for both workers ($F = 2.70_{(110,\ 778)}$, $p < .001$) and family members ($F = 2.04_{(110,\ 707)}$, $p < .001$). Taken together, our findings showed that each organisation could be considered as a meaningful entity. Thus, we used mean ratings to obtain indicators of OCS at the organisation level for both workers and family members.

Once we had two aggregated scores per centre (one for workers and one for family members), we implemented the second step in the computation of mutual communication about self-determination. To do so, we calculated the square root of the product (SRP) of workers' perceptions and family members' perceptions corresponding to OCS. Therefore, we computed one indicator of mutual communication per centre. That is:

$$\text{SRP} = [(\text{Workers' OCS perceptions}) \times (\text{Family members' OCS perceptions})]^{1/2}.$$

Smith and Barclay (1997, p. 8) recommended this strategy because it has three main advantages over other mutuality aggregation methods: (a) it respects the original metrics, facilitating interpretation; (b) there are fewer inflated correlations due to the size of the groups; and (c) it includes both level and agreement. The latter is especially relevant for the current research study, making it possible to capture mutual communication between workers and family members by considering both the level of communication and the level of agreement. In a real dialogue, both parties (workers and family members) agree that the other is highly willing to openly dialogue about self-determination. Accordingly, SRP reflects both level and agreement. Therefore, SRP is based on a combination of *direct consensus* and *dispersion* models (Chan, 1998; Dawson, González-Roma, Davis, & West, 2008). Direct consensus models assume agreement and focus on the level of construct, whereas dispersion models accept disagreement and focus on the degree to which variability exists. The SRP index is a combination of these two models because both the overall level of open communication and the variability in the communication perceived by the groups (workers and family members) are considered simultaneously. Agreement is not required in the computation of SRP because this index also reflects the extent to which open communication varies in the relation between workers and family members. In fact, disagreement has an effect on the final mutual communication, reducing the final score. For instance, disagreement between workers and family members, such as [3, 1], scores lower on mutual communication [$\sqrt{3 \times 1} = 1.73$] than agreement, such as [2, 2], [$\sqrt{2 \times 2} = 2$], even when the level in these two examples is identical: $(3 + 1)/2 = 2$; $(2 + 2)/2 = 2$.

Results

Preliminary results

Family members perceive that workers are quite willing to dialogue openly about self-determination ($M = 5.96$, $SD = 1.07$). By contrast, the workers' perception of the degree to which family members openly discuss self-determination is lower ($M = 4.42$; $SD = 1.08$). We compared these two scores, confirming a significant difference ($t_{(1705)} = 29.72$, $p < .01$). Accordingly, family members more strongly believed that workers were open to dialogue about self-determination than workers believed that families were open to this type of dialogue. Following the strategy by Brower, Lester, Korsgaard, and Dineen (2009), we also created four groups of centres based on whether workers' and family members' ratings were above or below the median on open communication. Only 30% of the centres presented high mutual communication from the perspectives of both workers and family members (high–high open communication), whereas 20% of them presented low mutual communication (low-low open communication). Regarding mixed ratings, 30% of the centres presented high open communication according to worker's perceptions, but low according to family members' perceptions, whereas 20% presented the opposite pattern. Creating a real dialogue about self-determination with high mutual communication between workers and family members does not seem easy in participating organisations. Finally, we also linked the severity of the disability to attitudes towards self-determination. It is reasonable to expect that, because of the risks of self-determination for people with high disability severity (Powers et al., 1996), positive attitudes towards self-determination would be negatively related to severity. A total of 748 family members reported the level of severity of their relatives with intellectual disability. The disability is officially described in percentages in Spain. The greater the percentage recognised, the greater the severity of the disability. Although small, the correlation between severity and attitudes towards self-determination was negative (−.07) and significant ($p < .05$). We also contacted the managers of participating centres to ask for the percentage of individuals with intellectual disability in the centre with a high level of severity of their disability. This percentage was assigned to the workers of the centre in question. We obtained this information from 81 of the participating centres. Again, the correlation was small, but negative (−.08) and significant ($p < .05$). Therefore, high severity was associated with lower positive attitudes towards self-determination.

Do workers have more positive attitudes towards self-determination than family members?

To replicate previous research findings (Zhang et al., 2002, 2005), we conducted a t test comparing professionals and family members on attitudes towards self-determination. Significant differences were observed between them ($t_{(1566)} = -9.76$, $p < .01$). More specifically, family members reported lower positive attitudes towards self-determination ($M = 2.05$, $SD = 0.89$) than professionals did ($M = 2.43$, $SD = 0.71$). The lesser commitment to self-determination, on the part of family members, is confirmed again. Nevertheless, and taking our measure (from −3 to +3) into account, family members' attitudes were also very positive.

Is there a positive relationship between mutual communication about self-determination and positive attitudes towards self-determination?

A Hierarchical Linear Model was performed to test the cross-level relationship between mutual communication at the organisational level (Level 2) – operationalised as SRP – and workers' and family members' attitudes at the individual level (Level 1). To do so, we used LISREL

8.80 (Jöreskog & Sörbom, 2006). Prior to testing this link, a necessary precondition is that there must be significant within- and between-organisation variance in self-determination attitudes (Hofmann, 1997). We assessed this requirement by estimating the null model, where the dependent variable (ie, self-determination attitudes) was specified as the outcome variable, and no individual-level or organisation-level predictors were included in the model. The results indicated that this requirement was satisfied ($\tau_{00} = 0.05$, df = 3, $\chi^2 = 4157.63$, $p < .01$). Moreover, these variance components were used to calculate the ICC(1), reflecting the percentage of variance between groups. The ICC(1) value was 0.0746 ($p < .01$), indicating that 7.46% of the variance in self-determination attitudes lies between centres. Therefore, this variance was significant and provided a basis for examining individual- and organisational-level predictors.

In order to reduce possible problems with multicollinearity (Kreft, de Leeuw, & Aiken, 1995), mutual communication (SRP) was grand-mean centred (Enders & Tofighi, 2007). Additionally, the size of the centre (number of workers) and group membership (workers vs. family members) were controlled. The size of the centre was disaggregated, assigning a score to each worker and family member individually that corresponds to the size of the centre where they work (worker) or attend (family member). For group membership, we created a dummy variable (family members = 0; workers = 1). Therefore, both the size of the centre and group membership were operationalised at Level 1. Focusing now on the hypothesised cross-level relationship (H1), the results confirmed that mutual communication (SRP) (Level 2) was significantly and positively (0.30, $p > .01$) related to self-determination attitudes of workers and family members at the individual level (Level 1) (see Table 1), explaining an additional 10.22% of the variance beyond the control variables. However, H2 was not confirmed (see Table 1). The positive relationship between mutual communication and attitudes did not depend on group membership (worker vs. family member).

Is mutual communication about self-determination associated with shared attitudes towards self-determination?

We conducted a linear regression analysis to examine the relationship between mutual communication about self-determination – operationalised as SRP – and agreement on attitudes. For the operationalisation of agreement on attitudes towards self-determination, we considered two indicators. First, we computed the $AD_{M(J)}$ as an indicator of within-organisation interrater agreement (Burke et al.,1999). Therefore, we calculated one indicator per centre. Lower scores were indicative of more agreement within the organisation between workers and family members. By contrast, higher scores on $AD_{M(J)}$ were indicative of more disagreement within the organisation. We controlled for the size of the centre (number of workers). Results confirmed a negative relationship ($\beta = -0.32$, $p < .01$) between mutual communication and disagreement on attitudes (Table 2). As expected (H3), high mutual communication in organisations (SRP) is associated with agreement between workers and family members on their attitudes towards self-determination.

Second, we also used the absolute difference between the attitude scores reported by workers and family members at the organisational level. Accordingly, "0" was assigned to organisations where there is complete agreement between workers and family members on their attitudes towards the self-determination of individuals with intellectual disability, whereas higher scores were indicative of more disagreement within the centre. Again, results supported H3. We found a negative relationship ($\beta = -0.18$, $p < .01$) between mutual communication (SRP) and disagreement, controlling for the size of the centre (Table 3).

Discussion

Results of the current research study lead to three main conclusions. First, we confirmed that workers have

Table 1. Multilevel analysis with self-determination attitudes as dependent variable.

	Model 1			Model 2			Model 3		
	Parameter	SE	Z	Parameter	SE	z	Parameter	SE	z
Level 1									
(Intercept)	2.06	0.10	20.76**	2.03	0.10	21.31**	2.03	0.10	21.34**
Control variables									
Size of the centre	−0.01	0.01	−0.16	0.01	0.01	0.16	0.01	0.01	0.17
Group membership (GM)	0.38	0.04	10.25**	0.38	0.04	10.22**	0.38	0.04	10.23**
Level 2									
Mutual communication (SRP)				0.22	0.07	3.39**	0.30	0.8	3.67**
Interaction GM*SRP							−0.13	0.09	−1.54
Explained variance (%)		6.45			16.67			16.67	

Note: Parameter = non-standardised coefficient.
**$p < .01$.

Table 2. Linear regression analysis predicting agreement in attitudes ($AD_{M(J)}$).

Steps	Agreement in attitudes ($AD_{M(J)}$) β
Step 1	
Size of the centre	0.11
ΔR^2	0.01
Step 2	
Mutual communication (SRP)	−0.32**
ΔR^2	0.10**

**$p < .01$.

more positive attitudes towards self-determination of individuals with intellectual disability than family members do, replicating previous research studies. Second, high mutual communication about self-determination at the organisational level is associated with workers' and family members' high positive individual attitudes towards self-determination. Finally, high mutual communication about self-determination at the organisational level is associated with high affinity of workers and family members in their self-determination attitudes. These findings have theoretical and practical implications that we discuss in the following paragraphs.

Workers' and family members attitudes' towards self-determination of individuals with intellectual disability are relevant because attitudes guide human behaviours (Bohner & Dickel, 2011). Therefore, it is necessary to stimulate positive attitudes in order to engage relevant actors (ie, workers and family members) in actions and plans that improve self-determination. Our findings show the existence of a positive link from mutual communication between workers and family members to positive attitudes. According to the well-established mere-exposure effect (Bornstein, 1989; Jones et al., 2011; Young et al., 2016; Zajonc, 1968), a real dialogue – where both actors perceive that the other party is willing to openly dialogue about self-determination – forces workers and family members to focus the attention on self-determination to improve the quality of life of individuals with intellectual disability. This exposure to self-determination issues is positively related to individual attitudes.

Table 3. Linear regression analysis predicting agreement in attitudes (absolute difference).

Steps	Agreement in attitudes (absolute difference) β
Step 1	
Size of the centre	−0.19*
ΔR^2	0.04*
Step 2	
Mutual communication (SRP)	−0.18*
ΔR^2	0.03*

*$p < .05$.
**$p < .01$.

In addition to individual attitudes, lack of attitudinal convergence between workers and family members is another challenge for research and practice. In consonance with previous research efforts (Zhang et al., 2002, 2005), our results indicate that workers have more positive attitudes towards self-determination of individuals with intellectual disability than family members do, although the attitudes of family members are also quite positive. If coordinated efforts are required for effective plans to improve self-determination (see Carter et al., 2013), attitudinal gaps can be a difficult obstacle to overcome. Again, mutual communication can play a role. Based on research that has shown that exposure to another person increases agreement with that person (Bornstein et al., 1987; Claypool et al., 2012; Moreland & Beach, 1992), we confirmed that the existence of real dialogue (mutual communication) is positively related to attitudinal agreement at the organisational level. When both workers and family members perceive that the other party is accessible and willing to engage in open dialogue about self-determination issues, their attitudes converge, and it is easier to consider all of them as a cohesive group in their views about self-determination.

With regard to practical implications, managers, workers, and family members (eg, representatives of families) of organisations for individuals with intellectual disability should be aware that opening up a real dialogue is positively related to attitudes towards self-determination and achieving consensual views. This is especially relevant if we consider our descriptive and comparative findings. Achieving high mutual communication – from the perspectives of both workers and family members simultaneously – is not easy (only 30% of centres had high and high medians). In addition, there were not only significant differences in attitudes, but also in the way workers and family members perceive each other in open communication: family members more strongly believed that workers were open to dialogue about self-determination than workers believed that families were open to this type of dialogue. In sum, our results reflect a relevant distance between the two actors that is associated with lack of mutual communication.

As is true for all studies, the current one has some relevant limitations that could be inputs for future efforts. Our research study has a cross-sectional nature. Therefore, causal linkages cannot be established. Although the expected relationships are based on well-established approaches (mere-exposure effects), longitudinal and experimental designs will allow the observation of solid connections between mutual communication and attitudes towards self-determination. In addition, this type of investigation could be combined with the implementation of actions for the improvement of mutual communication. The current study measured open communication and attitudes, but the potential effects of interventions are not tested. For example, future investigations can examine the role of mixed teams (composed of workers and family members) in the development of self-determination of individuals with intellectual disability. These teams could be monitored over time to investigate changes in attitudes and steps in creating consensual views. Another area for future research is related to the measurement of mere exposure. The present research study focuses on perceived exposure to open communication (see Appendix). However, other measurement alternatives are possible. A frequency scale can assess the degree to which workers and family members interact over time. Self-determination stimuli can also be manipulated in an experimental design to test the impact of exposure on attitudes. Confirming our findings by using other measures and design strategies could be a way to check generalisability. Additionally, organisational policies and practices (eg, service quality) could be investigated as obstacles/facilitators of open communication and exposure to self-determination among family members. According to our results (negative correlations between severity of disability and attitudes towards self-determination), the implementation of policies and practices is especially challenging when the severity of the disability is high. Therefore, future studies could concentrate on individuals with high severity in order to test the effect of different types of practices designed to improve self-determination attitudes and behaviours. Future research efforts could also examine the relationship between type of occupation of staff members (psychologist, social worker, etc.) and attitudes towards self-determination. For instance, some occupations may be more sensitive to self-determination, whereas others may focus more on protection from possible accidents and abuses associated with the independence of individuals with intellectual disability.

In spite of these limitations, the current research study contributes to the understanding of self-determination discrepancies between workers and family members in at least two ways. First, we confirmed the significant distance between workers and family members, not only in their attitudes towards self-determination of individuals with intellectual disability, but also in the way each party perceives the other in open communication. Second, mutual communication is related to both attitudes and consensual views about self-determination. Opening up communication channels and creating opportunities for real dialogue (where each party perceives that the other is willing to dialogue about self-determination openly) are valuable in themselves, but they are also linked to the existence of a cohesive group at the centre level, with positive attitudes towards self-determination.

Acknowledgements

The authors want to thank "PLENA INCLUSIÓN" and associated centres that participated in the studies.

Disclosure statement

No potential conflict of interest was reported by the authors.

Funding

The authors are grateful for the financial support of the Spanish Agency of Economy and Competitiveness [grant number PSI2013-48509-P], Spanish Research Agency (AEI) [grant number PSI2016-78158-R], and FEDER.

ORCID

Esther Gracia http://orcid.org/0000-0002-1354-4061

References

Alexander, J., Nank, R., & Stivers, C. (1999). Implications of welfare reform: Do nonprofit survival strategies threaten civil society? *Nonprofit and Voluntary Sector Quarterly*, *28*, 452–475. doi:10.1177/0899764099284005

Bashshur, M., Rupp, D. E., & Christopher, J. (2004, August 6–11). *Theoretically-based strategies for defining and measuring justice climate: Implications for multilevel research in organizational justice*. Paper presented at the 64th annual meeting of the Academy of Management, New Orleans, LA.

Bohner, G., & Dickel, N. (2011). Attitudes and attitude change. *Annual Review of Psychology*, *62*, 391–417. doi:10.1146/annurev.psych.121208.131609

Bornstein, R. F. (1989). Exposure and affect: Overview and meta-analysis of research, 1968–1987. *Psychological Bulletin*, *106*, 265–289. doi:10.1037/0033-2909.106.2.265

Bornstein, R. F., & Dagostino, P. R. (1994). The attribution and discounting of perceptual fluency – preliminary tests of a perceptual fluency attributional model of the mere exposure effect. *Social Cognition*, *12*, 103–128. doi:10.1521/soco.1994.12.2.103

Bornstein, R. F., Leone, D. R., & Galley, D. J. (1987). The generalizability of subliminal mere exposure effects: Influence of stimuli perceived without awareness on social behavior. *Journal of Personality and Social Psychology*, *53*, 1070–1079. doi:10.1037/0022-3514.53.6.1070

Brower, H., Lester, S., Korsgaard, M., & Dineen, B. (2009). A closer look at trust between managers and subordinates: Understanding the effects of both trusting and being trusted on subordinate outcomes. *Journal of Management*, *35*, 327–347. doi:10.1177/0149206307312511

Burke, M. J., Finkelstein, L. M., & Dusig, M. S. (1999). On average deviation indices for estimating interrater agreement.

Organizational Research Methods, *2*, 49–68. doi:10.1177/109442819921004

Carey, G., Braunack-Mayer, A., & Barraket, J. (2009). Spaces of care in the third sector: Understanding the effects of professionalization. *Health: An Interdisciplinary Journal for the Social Study of Health, Illness and Medicine*, *13*, 629–646. doi:10.1177/1363459308341866

Carter, E. W., Lane, K. L., Cooney, M., Weir, K., Moss, C. K., & Machalicek, W. (2013). Parent assessments of self-determination importance and performance for students with autism or intellectual disability. *American Journal on Intellectual and Developmental Disabilities*, *118*, 16–31. doi:10.1352/1944-7558-118.1.16

Chan, D. (1998). Functional relations among constructs in the same content domain at different levels of analysis: A typology of composition models. *Journal of Applied Psychology*, *83*, 234–246. doi:10.1037/0021-9010.83.2.234

Claypool, H. M., Housley, M. K., Bernstein, M. J., & Mackie, D. M. (2012). Easing in: Fluent processing brings others into the ingroup. *Group Processes & Intergroup Relations*, *15*, 441–455. doi:10.1177/1368430212439115

Curryer, B., Stancliffe, R. J., & Dew, A. (2015). Self-determination: Adults with intellectual disability and their family. *Journal of Intellectual and Developmental Disability*, *40*, 394–399. doi:10.3109/13668250.2015.1029883

Dawson, J. F., González-Roma, V., Davis, A., & West, M. A. (2008). Organizational climate and climate strength in UK hospitals. *European Journal of Work and Organizational Psychology*, *17*(1), 89–111. doi:10.1080/13594320601046664

Dekovic, M., Janssens, J. M. A. M., & Gerris, J. R. M. (1991). Factor structure and construct validity of the Block Child Rearing Practices Report (CRPR). *Psychological Assessment*, *3*, 182–187. doi:10.1037/1040-3590.3.2.182

Dunlap, W. P., Burke, M. J., & Smith-Crowe, K. (2003). Accurate tests of statistical significance for r(WG) and average deviation interrater agreement indexes. *Journal of Applied Psychology*, *88*(2), 356–362. doi:10.1037/0021-9010.88.2.356

Enders, C. K., & Tofighi, D. (2007). Centering predictor variables in cross-sectional multilevel models: A new look at an old issue. *Psychological Methods*, *12*, 121–138. doi:10.1037/1082-989X.12.2.121

Field, S., & Hoffman, A. (2007). Self-determination in secondary transition assessment. *Assessment for Effective Intervention*, *32*, 181–190. doi:10.1177/15345084073200306O1

Fyson, R., & Kitson, D. (2007). Independence or protection – does it have to be a choice? Reflections on the abuse people with learning disabilities in Cornwall. *Critical Social Policy*, *27*, 426–436. doi:10.1177/0261018307078850

Hair, J., Black, B., Babin, B., Anderson, R., & Tatham, R. (2006). *Multivariate data analysis* (6th ed.). Upper Saddle River, NJ: Prentice-Hall.

Hall, E. (2004). Social geographies of learning disability: Narratives of exclusion and inclusion. *Area*, *36*, 298–306. doi:10.1111/j.0004-0894.2004.00227.x

Heslop, P., Blair, P. S., Fleming, P., Hoghton, M., Marriott, A., & Russ, L. (2014). The confidential inquiry into premature deaths of people with intellectual disabilities in the UK: A population-based study. *The Lancet*, *383*, 889–895. doi:10.1016/ S0140-6736(13)62026-7

Hofmann, D. A. (1997). An overview of the logic and rationale of hierarchical linear models. *Journal of Management*, *23*(6), 723–744. doi:10.1016/S0149-2063(97)90026-X

Jones, I. F., Young, S. G., & Claypool, H. M. (2011). Approaching the familiar: On the ability of mere exposure to direct approach and avoidance behavior. *Motivation and Emotion*, *35*, 383–392. doi:10.1007/s11031-011-9228-7

Jöreskog, K. G., & Sörbom, D. (2006). *LISREL 8.80 [computer software]*. Chicago, IL: Scientific Software International.

Ko, D. G. (2014). The mediating role of knowledge transfer and the effects of client-consultant mutual trust on the performance of enterprise implementation projects. *Information & Management*, *51*, 541–550. doi:10.1016/j.im.2014.04.001

Kozlowski, S. W. J., & Klein, K. J. (2000). A multilevel approach to theory and research in organizations: Contextual, temporal, and emergent processes. In K. J. Klein & S. W. J. Kozlowski (Eds.), *Multilevel theory, research, and methods in organizations* (pp. 467–511). San Francisco, CA: Jossey-Bass.

Kreft, I. G. G., de Leeuw, J., & Aiken, L. S. (1995). The effect of different forms of centering in hierarchical linear models. *Multivariate Behavioral Research*, *30*, 1–21. doi:10.1207/s15327906mbr3001_1

Liden, R. C., Erdogan, B., Wayne, S. J., & Sparrowe, R. T. (2006). Leader–member exchange, differentiation, and task interdependence: Implications for individual and group performance. *Journal of Organizational Behavior*, *27*, 723–746. doi:10.1002/job.409

Martínez-Tur, V., Gracia, E., Moliner, C., Molina, A., Kuster, I., Vila, N., & Ramos, J. (2016). The moderating role of performance in the link from interactional justice climate to mutual trust between managers and team members. *Psychological Reports*, *118*, 870–888. doi:10.1177/0033294116647689

Martínez-Tur, V., Moliner, C., Peñarroja, V., Gracia, E., & Peiró, J. M. (2015). From service quality in organisations to self-determination at home. *Journal of Intellectual Disability Research*, *59*, 882–890. doi:10.1111/jir.12190

Moreland, R. L., & Beach, S. R. (1992). Exposure effects in the classroom – the development of affinity among students. *Journal of Experimental Social Psychology*, *28*, 255–276. doi:10.1016/0022-1031(92)90055-O

Palmer, S. B., & Wehmeyer, M. L. (2003). Promoting self-determination in early elementary school: Teaching self-regulated problem-solving and goal-setting skills. *Remedial and Special Education*, *24*, 115–126. doi:10.1177/07419325030240020601

Powers, L. E., Wilson, R., Matuszewski, J., Phillips, A., Rein, C., Schumacher, D., & Gensert, J. (1996). Facilitating adolescent self-determination: What does it take? In D. J. Sands & M. L. Wehmeyer (Eds.), *Self-determination across the life span: Independence and choice for people with disabilities* (pp. 257–284). Baltimore, MD: Brookes.

Raykov, T. (2001). Bias of Cronbach's coefficient alpha for fixed congeneric measures with correlated errors. *Applied Psychological Measurement*, *25*, 69–76. doi:10.1177/01466216010251005

Seong, Y., Wehmeyer, M. L., Palmer, S. B., & Little, T. D. (2015). Effects of the self-directed individualized education program on self-determination and transition of adolescents with disabilities. *Career Development and Transition for Exceptional Individuals*, *38*, 132–141. doi:10.1177/2165143414544359

Shavelle, R., Strauss, D., & Day, S. (2005). Deinstitutionalization in California: Mortality of persons with developmental disabilities after transfer into community care, 1997–1999. *Journal of Data Science*, *3*, 371–380.

Smith, J. B., & Barclay, D. W. (1997). The effects of organizational differences and trust on the effectiveness of selling partner relationships. *Journal of Marketing*, *61*, 3–21. doi:10.2307/1252186

United Nations. (2015). *Convention on the rights of person with disabilities*. New York, NY: Author.

Verdugo, M. A., Gómez, L. E., & Árias, B. (2007). La Escala INTEGRAL de calidad de vida: desarrollo y estudio preliminar de sus propiedades psicométricas. *Siglo Cero: Revista Española sobre Discapacidad Intelectual*, *38*, 37–56.

Wehmeyer, M. L. (2005). Self-determination and individuals with severe disabilities: Re-examining meanings and misinterpretations. *Research and Practice for Persons with Severe Disabilities*, *30*, 113–120. doi:10.2511/rpsd.30.3.113

Young, S. G., Jones, I. F., & Claypool, H. M. (2016). Stimulus threat and exposure context modulate the effect of mere exposure on approach behaviors. *Frontiers in Psychology*, *7*, 265. doi:10.3389/fpsyg.2016.01881

Zajonc, R. B. (1968). Attitudinal effects of mere exposure. *Journal of Personality and Social Psychology*, *9*, 1–27. doi:10.1037/h0025848

Zhang, D., Katsiyannis, A., & Zhang, J. (2002). Teacher and parent practice on fostering self-determination of secondary students with disabilities. *Career Development for Exceptional Individuals*, *25*, 157–169. doi:10.1177/088572880202500205

Zhang, D., Wehmeyer, M. L., & Chen, L. (2005). Parent and teacher engagement in fostering the self-determination of students with disabilities: A comparison between the United States and the Republic of China. *Remedial and Special Education*, *26*, 55–64. doi:10.1177/07419325050260010701

Appendix

Open communication about self-determination. Informant: Workers

The workers in this centre may talk to family members about the self-determination of people with intellectual disability (decide for themselves and have the chance to choose the things they want). Rate this COMMUNICATION and show your level of agreement with the following statements:

Strongly disagree	Disagree	Disagree somewhat	Neither agree nor disagree	Agree somewhat	Agree	Strongly agree
1	2	3	4	5	6	7

1-*If workers have a problem with family members about issues related to the development of self-determination in people with disabilities, family members are receptive and can discuss the problem in confidence.*

2-*The family members provide the information the workers need to know about the development of self-determination in the people with intellectual disability.*

3-*Sometimes the family members hide from the workers at this centre what they know about the difficulties and opportunities found in the development of self-determination in the people with intellectual disability (R).*

Open communication about self-determination. Informant: Family members

The family members in this centre may talk to the workers about the self-determination of people with intellectual disability (decide for themselves and have the chance to choose the things they want). Rate this COMMUNICATION and show your level of agreement with the following:

Strongly disagree	Disagree	Disagree somewhat	Neither agree nor disagree	Agree somewhat	Agree	Strongly agree
1	2	3	4	5	6	7

1-*If family members have a problem with workers about issues related to the development of self-determination in people with disabilities, workers are receptive and can discuss the problem in confidence.*

2-*The workers provide the information the family members need to know about the development of self-determination in the people with intellectual disability.*

3-*Sometimes the workers hide from the family members at this centre what they know about the difficulties and opportunities found in the development of self-determination in the people with intellectual disability (R).*

Open communication about self-determination. Informant: Family members

Please, indicate to what degree you think it is GOOD (positive, useful, appropriate, advisable) or BAD (negative, useless, inappropriate, unadvisable) that:

Very bad	Pretty bad	Somewhat bad	Not good or bad	Somewhat good	Pretty good	Very good
−3	−2	−1	0	+1	+2	+3

1-*Individuals with intellectual disability are free to invite friends home.*

2-*People with intellectual disability move independently around their community.*

3-*People with intellectual disability choose their own activities and places where they spend their free time.*

4-*People with intellectual disability decide for themselves how to spend their money.*

5-*People with intellectual disability express their own interests and goals and make plans to achieve them.*

6-*People with intellectual disability organize and decorate their personal surroundings according to their own tastes.*

Index